THE

FOUNDER

PRESENT EDITORS
Betty Radice and Robert Baldick

Theophrastus
THE CHARACTERS

Menander
PLAYS AND FRAGMENTS

TRANSLATED BY
PHILIP VELLACOTT

SECOND EDITION

PENGUIN BOOKS

Penguin Books Ltd, Harmondsworth, Middlesex, England
Penguin Books Inc., 7110 Ambassador Road, Baltimore, Maryland 21207, U.S.A.
Penguin Books Australia Ltd, Ringwood, Victoria, Australia

—

First published 1967, except for *The Bad-Tempered Man* (first
published by Oxford University Press 1960)
Second edition 1973

—

—

Made and printed in Great Britain by
Hazell Watson & Viney Ltd
Aylesbury, Bucks
Set in Monotype Bembo

The terms for performance of these
translations may be obtained from the League of Dramatists,
84 Drayton Gardens, London SW10, to whom all
applications for permission should be made

CONTENTS

PREFACE TO THE SECOND EDITION

ABOUT 800 lines from two plays of Menander, *The Shield* and *The Samian Woman*, (referred to in a footnote on page 175 of the first edition) were eventually published in 1969 (P. Bodmer xxv–xxvi; critical edition, *Menandri ASPIS et SAMIA*, ed. C. Austin, Walter de Gruyter & Co., Berlin); and this new edition includes them. There is little evidence for assigning a date to *The Samian Woman*; but its highly-developed structure and characterization suggest that it is a mature work; and we now have about four-fifths of it. Of *The Shield*, which is a less complex piece, we have nearly as much as we formerly had of *The Samian Woman*.

It is a pleasure to record my great indebtedness to Professor E. W. Handley for the most generous help of every kind which I have received from him while studying this new material.

INTRODUCTION

THEOPHRASTUS lived from 371 to 287 B.C., and Menander from 343 to 291. Thus when Theophrastus was a young man the last struggle for Greek independence was still at its height, and the greatness of Athens was still living in the leadership of Demosthenes; but Menander passed his whole life as a citizen of a subject State. By 338 Philip of Macedon had brought the whole of Greece under his authority. His son Alexander the Great died in 323 in Babylon. During Alexander's long absence in the East, Antipater, one of his generals, was his regent in Macedon and Greece; on Alexander's death Antipater became king. When he died in 319 a military struggle took place between his son Cassander and Polyperchon, who was Antipater's nominee for the succession (see Character 8). This disturbed political background seems to be taken for granted as a normal condition of life by the people we meet both in the *Characters* and in Menander's plays. The men and women depicted by these two writers seem to have devoted themselves entirely, so long as actual fighting kept at a reasonable distance, to the business of the moment – to their shopping, their gossiping, their borrowing and lending, eating and drinking, dressing and money-making, going to law, marrying, loving and quarrelling. The *Characters* and the plays give us innumerable glimpses of this vivid and varied life as it was lived by the great-grandchildren of the men who, in the age of Euripides and Aristophanes, fought the desperate battles of the Peloponnesian War. Menander's contemporaries were perhaps, as individuals, not of inferior quality; but there was no longer the cause of freedom or the glory of Athens to turn them into heroes. On their tragic stage they revived the heroic dramas of the fifth century; in Comedy they were concerned with emotions of the home and the street, with slaves and sweethearts, with dreams of wealth and fantasies of romance.

9

The author of the *Characters* was, it is said, one Tyrtamos, a native of Lesbos. Tyrtamos came to Athens to be a pupil of Aristotle; on Aristotle's death he succeeded him as head of the Lyceum, his school of philosophy in Athens; and it was Aristotle who gave him the name Theophrastus, which means 'divine speaker'. There are many passages in later writers both Greek and Latin, and particularly in Cicero, testifying to the style and eloquence which earned him this name. He was, like his master, a prolific writer on many subjects; two major works on botany survive, and some shorter pieces on various scientific topics. These are books for the specialist; the *Characters*, on the other hand, provides entertainment for the general reader, yet, curiously enough, shows little or nothing of the literary elegance for which the author was famous. The interest of these short pieces lies in their author's observation and selection of material. The Greek is sometimes obscure or inelegant, the vocabulary colloquial, the style unvaried and abrupt. Their terseness suggests notes for lectures, and they can hardly have been written for separate publication as a literary work. Though they have begotten in modern European literature a whole *genre* of 'character-writing' (famous imitators include La Bruyère, John Earle, and Ben Jonson), they stand in the ancient world as a unique book, and one whose purpose is not at first apparent.

There exists a Preface which is certainly not by Theophrastus; it is printed here at the end of the *Characters*. The writer of this Preface says that the work is the fruit of his study of human character 'both good and bad'. All the surviving Characters clearly come under the heading 'bad'; so it seems probable that the writer of this Preface had before him not only our *Characters* but a set of 'good' ones as well. He goes on, with naïve banality, to say that he has written these pieces for the moral instruction of the younger generation. This certainly does not ring true. The *Characters* have very little in them that could be called moral or ethical principle. They describe deviations from accepted standards of behaviour, some vicious, others comic; but they make no attempt to trace them to their causes. We may dismiss the suggestion that they formed a part of any serious work on ethics.

One reasonable view is that they were written as an illustrative appendix to a work on the writing of Comedy. The wide gulf that divides Menander's comedy from that of Aristophanes makes it probable that many minds were exercised during that half-century over the nature of comedy, and that many experiments must have led to nothing, before the new and living form emerged. Menander is traditionally referred to as a pupil of Theophrastus; certainly he learnt 'divine speech', from whatever source. Both authors record with the same zest many features of everyday life in fourth-century Greece – for example, the incorrigible habit of borrowing everything, from clothing to kitchen-utensils. At the same time the connection of the *Characters* with Aristophanes is equally close; perhaps even closer, since Aristophanes, being a creator of fantasy, can exaggerate, where Menander, committed to a degree of realism, must preserve balance. Theophrastus' descriptions are thorough-going and relentless, providing in each case the full data for a type; whereas Menander, the creator of individuals, would select, modify, present contradictions, and all with a gentle human appreciation which was no part of the purpose of Theophrastus.

Each Character begins with a definition of the abstract quality described, and proceeds to a detailed portrait of the person, his habits and his conversation. In eight of them (nos. 1, 2, 3, 6, 8, 10, 28, 29) the MSS attach an ending which is certainly a later addition. Most of these endings are feeble or pointless, and I have omitted from the translation all except that of no. 8, which is the longest, and will serve as an example. The authenticity of the opening definitions is also in doubt. They may well have been put in (as Ussher[1] suggests) by some one who thought he was dealing with a work on ethics.

1. R. G. Ussher, *The Characters of Theophrastus*, 1960, where the General Introduction discusses various views of the origin and nature of the work.

In a work on comedy they seem out of place; and some of them are largely irrelevant to the descriptions which follow.

For the rest, the Characters can speak for themselves. This at least we owe to the writer of the spurious Preface, that we know that one half of the work – the 'good' Characters – is missing; so we need not put down Theophrastus as the jaundiced observer he might otherwise seem to be. The types of men he describes (he has not included any women) should be compared with characters in Aristophanes, whose quality is to do nothing by halves; but the world they move in belongs to Theophrastus' own time, and is the same world which we find presented, with a wealth of variety and colour, in the plays and fragments of Menander.

*

Until the beginning of the twentieth century Menander was known to the modern world only as the Greek author whom Plautus and Terence adapted or imitated, and who through them set a pattern for European playwrights eighteen centuries later; a name to conjure with in the ancient world, where he was considered unique – 'Menander cut down to half-size' was Julius Caesar's phrase for Terence, and it was probably intended as a judicious compliment. When, some sixty years ago, a papyrus was discovered in Egypt containing large portions of *Epitrepontes* (*The Arbitration*), *Periceiromene* (*The Unkindest Cut*), and *Samia* (*The Samian Woman*), it was at once recognized that Menander's reputation was well earned. These fragments from the work of his maturity showed all that had been expected in character-drawing, interest of situation, handling of plot, and sparkle of wit. *Dyskolos* (*The Bad-Tempered Man*) was discovered in 1955, and is the only complete play we have. It was produced in 317 B.C., when Menander was twenty-five, and was awarded a prize; but it is not a play of the same calibre as the later ones now known to us. The moralizing which in later fragments flows with grace and truth, here fumbles and prates; and there is a notable lack both of subtlety and of tenderness. By the time Menander was forty he had learnt what he wanted to say and how to say it; but an author's early work has a special interest, and in the case of *Dyskolos* this is enhanced by its completeness.

'Imagine that this place is Phyle in Attica.' So *Dyskolos* begins. There must have been some in that first Athenian audience who responded to this innocent invitation with a flash of memory which would have been bitter if it had been more recent. As it was eighty-seven years old it could be dismissed before Pan began to describe the sour-tempered old farmer who was to be the butt of the entertainment; but for a moment the name Phyle might well arouse sad reflections on the very character of that entertainment, so different from the bold, libertine tradition which it had replaced three generations earlier. Those who, like Callippides and his family in the play, sometimes went picnicking at Phyle would very likely sit to enjoy their lunch in the shade of fine stone walls which must still have shown traces of their military use. In 403 B.C., the year after the final defeat of Athens by Sparta and the destruction of the Long Walls, during the dismal period of the first Spartan puppet government, the oligarchical Thirty – in that solstice of despair a group of stout-hearted democrats under Thrasybulos had held out for six months in a little fortress at Phyle in Attica, in the hilly country fifteen miles to the north of the city; they had repulsed two military expeditions, and had left their stronghold only after gaining by negotiation a fair measure of that democratic principle for which they had fought.

They were men who had known Aristophanes and the breath of freedom. By their resolute courage they were able to preserve some of the civic and political values of undefeated Athens. But Athenian Comedy, as Aristophanes had created it, died with the peace; and now, after three generations,[1] a new product was taking shape, a new and important species in the world of the theatre. We know it as the 'New Comedy'. It belonged to the afternoon of Athens as unmistakably as Aristophanes belonged to the midday, yet was destined to do what Aristophanes could not do – to take its place beside the great tragedians in guiding the development of drama, not only for four or five centuries in the ancient Mediterranean world, but for a similar period in what we call modern Europe. This was due principally to the genius of Menander; and we should remember this, and not allow the obvious comparison with his great predecessor to obscure his very different qualities.

The heart of an Aristophanes comedy was its Chorus. The fifth-century Chorus symbolized the Athenian citizen's knowledge that there was nothing he dared not think; that what he thought, he was ready to say not merely in private but in the hearing of all his fellow-citizens; and that he was no less prepared to hear what his fellow-citizen had to say, whether he liked it or not. In the Parabasis the poet voiced his own mind, and many other people's, on current topics of manners, personalities, politics and literature, without fear of reprisal either from the State or from his neighbours. The story of the play, however amusing in itself, was constructed primarily as a vehicle for satire; and the satire was crystallized in the Chorus. In Menander's day that trenchant liberty was as remote a memory as the once gallant fame of Phyle. His plays have no Chorus in the old sense. Their scenes are divided by interludes indicated in the MSS merely by the word *Chorou*, a

1. During this period of about sixty-five years after the end of the Peloponnesian War, the Old Comedy, with its Chorus of twenty-four, was too expensive, and its outspoken political criticism too dangerous. In its place there flourished what is referred to as the 'Middle Comedy'. It consisted largely of burlesque and parody, taking for its material not politicians and institutions, but the familiar heroes of mythology and the common types of everyday life. These plays were produced in great numbers; the Athenian Antiphanes alone is said to have written two hundred and sixty. Numerous titles and fragments are found in ancient records, but no complete play or scene.

performance 'of the Chorus'; and this performance seems to have been left to the imagination, interests, or resources of the producer.

If the Chorus was the heart of a comedy by Aristophanes, its flesh was the story – in the whole fantastic range of that rare imagination. In those plays the audience are led by the hand in two lines from Hellas to Hades, from Athens to Cloud-Cuckoo-Land, from a law-court to Socrates' 'thinking-shop'. From the outset the 'ordinary citizen' finds himself inescapably on the stage and deeply involved, holding urgent conversation with generals, politicians, wasps, birds, sausage-sellers, landladies, frogs, clouds, gods, poets, and slaves, all of immediate relevance in a unified world of intelligent nonsense. Since then more than one world had come and gone; and Alexander the Great was dead. Menander's Phyle contains only what Menander's audience saw when they went there hunting or picnicking – cottages, a spring, a shrine, and country people looking askance at trippers from the town. Imagination gives place to observation, fantasy to realism. The predicament of humble obstinate humanity in the organized State, protesting against wars and taxes and regulations and the power of money, is replaced by the predicament of the ordinary husband, son or lover, who in a world complicated by multifarious division into hostile camps – rich and poor, slave and free, old and young, native and foreign, and above all male and female – struggles through mischance and bewilderment to be in some degree faithful both to himself and to his neighbour; in other words, to achieve on the domestic level that same ideal of *dike* which the men and women of Tragedy sought on the heroic level.

Before we look further into this larger subject, it is worth while – since our one complete play is so recent a discovery, and a number of notable fragments have come to light since – to say something about the progress from the discovered papyrus to the stage performance. The manuscript of *Dyskolos* is in closely written lines with no division between words, and little punctuation. A change of speaker is indicated by a short stroke below the first letter of the line in which the change occurs, and generally, but not always, by a double point at the end of a speech; in some places the stroke is found above instead of below the line. The names of speakers are given only here and there, apparently with the intention of showing where a character enters the dialogue; but there are many evident mistakes. There are no stage-directions of any kind, except a single word (on page 85) meaning 'plays the flute'. The process of discovering the entrance and exit of a character, of deciding who is on stage at a given moment, may be intricately involved with the establishment of the text. Each leaf of the papyrus is damaged in one or more places, and defective lines have to be completed, if this seems possible; while in undamaged lines there are fairly frequent corruptions, and opinions differ as to the correct restoration. The discarding of one hypothesis may lead to endless revision of other passages. This part of the work is the province of the textual specialist, involves prolonged and arduous research, and can move only gradually towards completion as different scholars contribute their answers to the numerous problems which arise.

One example of these will be enough: the problem of the half-dozen nameless characters. The most important of these is Cnemon's daughter, who appears among the dramatis personae but is given no name. She is allotted a few lines in Scene 1 and again in Scene 4. The name Myrrhine (a common name in Menander) does not appear anywhere in full, but on page 91, where the papyrus is torn, Cnemon addresses '... rhine and Gorgias'. At the time both his wife and his daughter are present; and it is certainly more likely that he is here addressing his wife, especially as elsewhere he consistently ignores his daughter. But for the purpose of an English production a name is entirely necessary for Cnemon's daughter, and unnecessary for his wife. So I have let Sostratos woo her as Myrrhine.

Then there is Sostratos' mother. She unquestionably appears on the stage, for Sostratos speaks to her in line 867. At the beginning of Scene 3 there are several separate lines which seem to fit neatly the character already given her by both Sostratos and Getas. Yet she is given no name; she is not included in the dramatis personae; and not a word is allotted to her.

Her dubious position is shared by her daughter and by the mother of Gorgias. At line 842 this daughter is betrothed to Gorgias, and it seems reasonable to assume that she is present on the stage at that moment. She plainly would arrive with her mother; and it is possible that she is the Plangon who is told to hurry. Gorgias' mother, who also is denied a place in the dramatis personae, is equally surely on the stage at line 867, where Sostratos presents her, and Cnemon's daughter, to his mother. But there is no line in the manuscript which can suitably be assigned to her. The opening of Scene 3 also gives us two other shadows: the flute-girl Parthenis; and the person who rudely complains that Sostratos' mother has kept everyone waiting. The latter surely cannot be the family slave Getas, and must therefore be a guest; though it is possible that Sostratos' mother is not on stage at all, and that the complaint is made by Sicon the cook to Getas.

*

Menander in the course of his fifty-two years wrote more than a hundred plays. Of this output the plays and fragments we now possess amount to about five per cent; so that, while we may feel that we have a fair idea of his style and language, we cannot pretend to guess whether the majority of his work reached or exceeded this level of quality; still less can we attempt any estimate of the range of subjects he treated, or of his development as a commentator on human nature. We do know that for centuries after his death he was regarded by ancient writers with something akin to reverence, and that his plays were widely known, often performed, and constantly quoted. The Loeb edition, for example, selects well over two hundred quotations, varying from one to twenty-odd lines, taken from unidentified plays, besides a further large selection from those for which their quoters gave a reference.

What qualities make a writer an inexhaustible mine for other writers? I take at random the first four quotations from *Hamlet* that occur to me:

There is nothing either good or bad, but thinking makes it so.

There are more things in heaven and earth, Horatio, than are dreamt of in your philosophy.

Use every man after his desert, and who would 'scape whipping?

Conscience doth make cowards of us all.

Every one of these might have come from Menander (the last, indeed, is in Menander, Fragment 632, page 298). They are not, perhaps, either profound or specially dramatic; they are, as we say, 'on the nail'; that is, true and universal; and such perceptions are, we recognize, very much in place in the tragedy of *Hamlet*. Menander wrote comedies, and in his comedies such perceptions are equally in place. His commentary on life covers many fields. His tirades against matrimony ('In marriage no survivor has ever yet been known') stand side by side with the occasional picture of an ideal state of mutual trust. His observations on the possession, use, and pursuit of money, on pride of birth, on the decay of quality, on the prosperity of the wicked or the inevitability of sorrow, on old age or friendship, on the impartiality of chance, on gratitude, guilt, servility, giving advice, getting drunk, and a hundred other topics, all show that combination of directness of thought with limpidity of expression which we are apt to call Shakespearian. Menander was not a tragedian; he did not present man face to face with time and the cosmos, with death and the depths of his own soul; but he was a poet of humanity, with an eye of genius both for detail and for the universal in human experience, and an ability on occasion to reach greater heights, such as may be seen in Fragments 481 and 552. If our five per cent remnant contains jewels like these, what a treasure must have been lost!

It is unfortunate that the term by which Menander is technically referred to is 'the comic poet'; such a phrase can only be misleading to the general reader. He is an endlessly entertaining writer; but only a small proportion of his entertainment can be called 'funny'. The greater part of it is comedy of character, which entertains by portraiture from life. The development from the stock figures of *Dyskolos* to the portraits given in *The Arbitration* and *The Samian Woman* is remarkable. Sostratos and Gorgias are simple types with little individuality; Cnemon at least reacts to experience, but cannot gain sympathy; the pretty girl in the story has virtually no existence; the fun is provided chiefly by the vivacity of the slaves. *The Arbitration*, on the other hand, immediately introduces us to an individual: Smicrines is a businessman with a legal turn of mind; as the father of the young wife in the story he might well be a stock figure; but the fragments we have of his conversation suggest that he is no more a stock figure than – to choose a Shakespearian counterpart – Polonius. In *The Samian Woman* Demeas, as an over-indulgent father and a somewhat obtuse and censorious male, has features which might belong to a stock figure; but his remarkable mixture of unlikely qualities – he is priggish, sincere, egocentric, fussy, violent, cruel, tender-hearted – makes him as close a parallel to Capulet as could be found anywhere. Slaves, like Onesimos in *The Arbitration*, we may naturally expect to be stock figures, since they are there largely to lay crazy plots, speak out of turn, get beaten and call each other names; but Onesimos has a quite personal selection of qualities to distinguish him: an itch for meddling, a preoccupation with dodging trouble, a delight in philosophical discourse and psychological diagnosis, a susceptible heart for the kind guitar-girl whom he in turn lets down, champions in her absence, mistrusts, and bargains with. Yet another surprise is offered in the small fragment of *The Farmer*, which opens with a sympathetic picture of a slave in love; while it is hard to believe that the Parmenon (certainly a slave's name) to whom Fragment 481 was spoken was one whom we could think of as a stock figure.

Besides the penetration of his commentary on life and the skill and variety of his character-drawing, there is a third quality in Menander which helps to explain the unique position given to him as a writer in the ancient world. This is the claim which he makes, albeit with a disarming diffidence, to be in some sense a successor to the tragedians, and in particular to Euripides. It is true that of the plays of his maturity there are only three of which we possess a substantial part; but the general character of the hundreds of short fragments supports the supposition that these three plays are typical of his work. When we find, therefore, that these plays, while various in their setting, characters, and plot, all deal with the same moral theme, we are surely justified in concluding that this theme was one which especially interested Menander; and we may perhaps go further and say it was a theme which evidently interested his audience. By many references to tragedy, and by quotations, especially from Euripides, Menander shows his familiarity and sympathy with tragic themes and with a reflective approach to moral situations.

Man's thoughts about the problem of living with his neighbour and his family are all included in the Greek word *dike*, which means 'right' or 'justice'. Many of the most famous tragedies are stories of revenge; and revenge is simply the crudest way of seeking justice. These stories (as in Aeschylus' Oresteian Trilogy, or Euripides' *Medea*) usually show the act of revenge as being more wicked than the crime which provoked it; and the result is that the feud continues. In only two plays of Euripides do we find a more hopeful solution to the problem of a wrong which has been inflicted. The final scene of *Alcestis* at least leaves a possibility that Alcestis has forgiven her husband Admetus; and in the final scene of *Hippolytus* Theseus receives full absolution and forgiveness from the son whom he cursed. But *Alcestis* is largely comedy; and Euripides did not, so far as we know, ever again after *Hippolytus* show forgiveness in action, though his characters often reproach those who refuse to forgive.

In each of the three mature plays of Menander which remain to us, a woman of good character and sympathetic personality is hastily misjudged and wronged by a husband or lover. In the first two the man recognizes his mistake, reproaches himself bitterly, and by sincere and practical repentance earns forgiveness; in the last, *The Samian Woman*, the situation has now proved (since the publication of the latest *Codex Bodmerianus*) to be more complex, and will be given special attention presently; much is to be learnt from the way in which the new material has contradicted previous conjecture. The actual bestowing of forgiveness has survived only in *The Unkindest Cut*; but it is performed there with a subtle charm that removes all embarrassment – a finesse of which the author of *The Bad-Tempered Man* gave little promise.

Now of course the making-up of a quarrel is an easy and obvious theme for comedy, and it might be said that to compare Menander's tales with those of Euripides is making much out of little. It is true that Menander works on the domestic level, not on the heroic; but both levels concern humanity (Euripides himself did not despise the domestic level), and there are several indications that Menander took seriously this aspect of his writing. First, there is the large number of surviving quotations which attest a deep concern with the human condition. Secondly there are his own frequent references to Tragedy, often implying a – perhaps self-deprecatory – claim to be similarly concerned with the real predicaments of human life. A third pointer is the whole structure of *The Arbitration*; and a fourth is a short passage in *The Unkindest Cut*. Let us look particularly at the last two.

In the first surviving scene of *The Arbitration* two slaves ask a passing citizen to settle a dispute for them. This might seem at first to an English reader somewhat far-fetched; but Theophrastus corrects this impression – see Characters 5 and 24, which show that such appeals, even to a casual passer-by, were an everyday matter. This fact in itself, as well as the important place that litigation held in the average citizen's life, reflects the passionate interest Greeks felt in questions of right and wrong. When Syriscos argues

> Justice ought to prevail
> Everywhere and on all occasions. The passer-by
> Ought to feel it's his duty to see justice done,

Daos, who has the weaker case, derides him as a 'speechifier', but the educated citizen Smicrines takes him seriously and accepts the position of arbiter. Even though the actual point in dispute – the possession of the birth-tokens – is not at the centre of the plot, the issue of just dealing certainly is. The characters are convinced that a just solution exists, and are determined to find it.

Next we see the slave Onesimos in a quandary. He has in his possession the ring found with the exposed child, which he recognizes as the ring his master lost nine months ago. Is he to show it to Charisios or not? He consults the guitar-girl Habrotonon; and his selfish mistrustfulness lights up the goodness of the slave-prostitute. She, in her exit-line, invokes a deity who has been one of the principal handmaids of *dike* ever since *The Eumenides*, and who has already in this play presided unseen over the arbitration between Syriscos and Daos:

> Holy Persuasion, help me! Bring my words success!

Hasty-tempered free-born men may go about trying to impose solutions by force; the slave-girl, whose only resources are her kind heart and a belief in right, appeals to Persuasion. The central scene of this play is in Act 4, where first Onesimos reports the agonized self-reproach of Charisios, and then Charisios himself appears, to tell us of his wife Pamphile's nobleness of mind, contrasted with his own unjust thoughts of her.

> After myself doing what I did ...
> I was such a brute and savage that I neither felt,
> Nor offered her, one shred of forgiveness – although she
> Had suffered the very wrong that I was guilty of.

A few lines later, when Habrotonon and Onesimos come to bring him the information that will deliver him from his misery, he blunders straight into injustice again, hits Onesimos and threatens Habrotonon. Unhappily the MSS fail us before the scene ends. Then in Act 5, because this is a comedy, the last word on justice is given to Onesimos, who delivers an admirable sermon to Smicrines, exhorting him to deserve a happy life.

ONESIMOS: Smicrines, do you consider
It right for a man to take his daughter from her husband?
SMICRINES: Right? No one says it's right; but in this case it's necessary.
ONESIMOS [*appealing to audience*]: You see? This chap reckons what's wrong is necessary.

Greeks in general were a passionate, revengeful, unjust race; but they knew what they were doing, and reverenced justice even while they outraged it. Onesimos' banter assumes a vital moral awareness in his audience.

The Unkindest Cut gives us a similar picture. Polemon, the hot-tempered soldier, is torn with love and with penitence for his cruel act; there is again a legally-minded older man, Pataicos, to set the rights and wrongs of the matter in perspective; and Polemon is told that the way to win back Glycera's love is not by taking the law into his own hands, but 'by persuasion'. Glycera, trying to make up her mind to forgive Polemon, finds herself face to face with her long-lost father, who now remembers with shame the selfishness which had made him expose his children in infancy. Glycera forgives her father; and in her happiness at the reunion is anxious to forgive Polemon too, since she has learnt from Pataicos how contrite he is. Pataicos says to her,

> When you've enjoyed good fortune, to be ready then
> To accept honest amends – that proves you a true Greek.

There is a moving irony in this; for if history proved anything about the 'true Greek' character, it was that Greeks chose revenge rather than forgiveness. But Menander is not being ironical. He reserves irony – of the gentlest kind – for Glycera's line,

> And that, of course, is why I forgive you!

She thus improves on Pataicos' picture of true Greek generosity, by cancelling his clause, 'When you've enjoyed good fortune'; and shows that she would have forgiven Polemon in any case, for love. The exact subtlety of these exchanges is comedy in the sense which we call Shakespearian.

The text of *The Samian Woman* now runs to 737 lines; which means that we have probably four-fifths of the play; the missing parts are almost all in the first two Acts, the last three being virtually complete. A few puzzles remain; but a rich and eminently stage-worthy dramatic pattern has emerged; and Demeas is clearly the most fully-rounded character so far met in Menander. One of the surprises of the new passages was the discovery that the part of Chrysis is hardly developed at all; the play does not end with her bestowal of forgiveness on the unconscionable Demeas. It is clear that Demeas' love for his adopted son Moschion is a ruling factor in his life; and yet his soliloquy at the beginning of Act III, and his mistress's words in Act I, both establish that his relationship with Chrysis is anything but shallow; while the very harshness with which he rejects and abuses her bears all the signs of self-torture. That he is capable of repentance, self-reproach, and reconciliation is shown by the subtle balances of his final adjustment with Moschion; but this adjustment can be observed in detail, because his relationship with Moschion has been given full expression at every stage; while between him and Chrysis there are not two lines of communication in the extant portions of the play (there may possibly have been a brief dialogue somewhere in the gap which follows 166). Here, then, is a deeply emotional relationship which expresses itself always in acts and attitudes, never in words. Chrysis appears after all to be barely a character; and yet she is the catalyst in the plot. She is simply the one woman in Demeas' always passionate life, and this is her claim to the title-role. In Act III he ill-treats her savagely; in Act IV, having learnt his error, he puts up his fists to a stronger man in her defence, shouts, 'You get indoors, damn it!'; and she accepts this abrupt invitation to return, content with the apology of deeds because she knows her man. She is there, happily in her place (and happily putting others in theirs) in the final wedding-festivities.

The danger of speculating about missing passages in a play is well illustrated by what the present translator wrote about the probable resolution of this play in the first edition. The new material has narrowed the area left open for guessing; and it is worth while now to scorn hazard and try again with the gaps in Acts I and II. It seems probable that the conversation between Demeas and Niceratos at the end of Act I represents their first appearance on the stage, though it is not their actual arrival home, since this has already been reported to Moschion by Parmenon;[1] and the brief exchange between father and son at the beginning of Act II can hardly be their first greeting after months of absence. Therefore it seems likely that in the gap which ends at line 90 Moschion tells the audi-

1. It is also possible that Parmenon reported seeing them in Peiraeus, before they came up to Athens.

ence that he has just welcomed his father home, and that he had intended to speak about his marriage at once, but his nerve had failed him – or possibly that Niceratos had arrived to talk to Demeas just as Moschion was coming to the point. This last suggestion would explain why the two older men enter together at 96; they emerge from Demeas' house in the middle of their conversation.

The next problem occurs at 129–142; the whole passage must be taken together, for it is fairly plain that 142 summarizes the argument, which is about legitimacy and bastardy. What is Demeas angry about? 'It seems that, without knowing it, I have a mistress who is a wedded wife' – this is the literal meaning of his words; but what is his implication? He had told Chrysis, who was pregnant when he set out, that her child was to be exposed, not kept. Why had he given this harsh instruction? Surely because Chrysis, being a Samian, was not his wedded wife, and could never be; her child must be illegitimate, and this is what Demeas is resolved not to have. That is why the missing first word of line 135 is likely to be the word meaning 'illegitimate'; and this assumption is made in the translation. By the same token, the participle in 134 rendered 'Plague take him' must be masculine, not feminine; and Demeas in 133 says 'He shall go', not 'She shall go'. This puts Moschion in the dramatically desirable position of championing his own son, rather than his father's concubine, and neatly points the moment at which he loses his timidity and becomes a man because he is a father. When Demeas says, 'I have a mistress who is a wedded wife', he means that Chrysis has had the boldness to behave as if she were a wife, by disobeying him and keeping her child; his love for her makes the situation a poignant one. In answer to Moschion's next question, Demeas, lashing himself to anger, says that 'a secret son' has been born to him. This phrase would usually, or at least often, mean a son secretly begotten by an adulterer; but if Moschion had thought Demeas meant this, he would unquestionably have said something in reply to such a serious imputation against Chrysis. Annoyance makes Demeas use a vicious word; but he means, and Moschion knows he means, merely that the son has been secretly preserved, and that he, Demeas, instead of being told about the baby in the first moment of his return, has only just had the news broken to him. In this situation Moschion, faced with nothing more serious than intense annoyance (all Demeas' feelings are intense), is not out of place in arguing somewhat academically about legitimacy; and the gap following 142 is the only passage in which we can assume that the happy atmosphere was established which Demeas refers to in 212, 'everything was working out just as I wished'. In that passage, then, Moschion must have told his father that he is only too ready to fall in with Demeas' wish that he should marry Plangon, and completely persuaded Demeas to agree that Chrysis should be allowed to keep the baby. It is possible that in the only major gap now remaining (after 166) Demeas communicates this decision to Chrysis, who refers in 412–416 to some such dialogue.

The play is full of subtle balances of various kinds. The mistress and the adopted son are both alike too nervous to tell Demeas immediately on his return what they know they have to tell him. Chrysis in her first appearance earns her coming tribulation by a clear instance of *hamartia*, 'error': she relies too easily on Demeas' love for her. Her certainty of Demeas' feelings confirms our perception of the reason why in the end words were not necessary to bring them together. Again, Moschion, who at first has no courage at all (69, 93), as soon as he hears the proposal to turn his infant son out of doors, discovers that he can after all face his father boldly (425 ff.). Then in Act V he overdoes it; he has not observed how deep and painful was his father's repentance, and tries to take advantage of it; nor has he learnt how much his father loves him, for he thinks it possible that Demeas will call his bluff. When

Demeas instead lays himself at his son's mercy, Moschion cannot say a single word to implement the hollow tableau of the cloak and sword; but he neutralizes for them both any embarrassment left after Demeas' pleading speech by referring to it playfully as 'that impressive lecture'. Again and again some moment of painful feeling is immediately balanced by a comic entry, as when Niceratos comes with his scrawny sheep to find Chrysis weeping. Demeas, when told by Moschion that nobility and legitimacy are not the same thing, coldly assumes he is joking (137–8); but in 346–7 he utters a similar sentiment himself. This closely-patterned texture combines with inventiveness of dialogue to make an entertainment of incessant and compelling vivacity; but more than that, it illustrates yet again the instinctive recognition of a principle of balance in human behaviour and experience, and in human destiny, which echoes the multiple balances of the natural world.

This belief in *dike*, both as a fact and as an ideal – the conviction that it is possible to find a principle of behaviour which will enable men and women to deal successfully with their own and other people's errors of impatience, ignorance or folly – this belief is a direct inheritance from the moral searchings of Aeschylus and Euripides; what is new in Menander is the application of the principle to unheroic and personal issues in common life. But between the vanishing of tragedy and the rise of Menander's comedy the search has passed through another phase.

Within ten years after the last productions of Euripides – *Phoenissae, Orestes, The Bacchae* – a court of Athenian *dicastae* had sat to dispense justice in the trial of Socrates, and had condemned him to death. Socrates had spent a generation and more, as a fellow-citizen of Euripides, in pursuit of the meaning of justice and goodness. During the generation after his death, Plato recorded and developed this pursuit in *The Republic*. In the generation after that, Plato's pupil and critic Aristotle took up the trail. He classified different types of justice; he distinguished the bond that joins a friend with a friend, from that which joins son to father or husband to wife; he distinguished guilt for a wrong done in anger from guilt for a wrong done with malice aforethought, or unwittingly, or against the better judgement of a good disposition. Menander was a pupil of Aristotle's successor Theophrastus; and when Charisios refers to himself as a 'student of ethics', or Onesimos with mock-pomposity proposes 'essay-questions' in the theory of behaviour, we can see the line of inheritance clearly drawn. Aristotle's studies were written down, not primarily for the guidance of lawyers or litigants, but for the intellectual and emotional satisfaction of thoughtful men who found it natural to reflect about their own moral instincts and the society in which they lived. Such men were in Menander's audience, probably in a larger proportion than would be found in a theatre audience today; and what Menander had studied under his teachers he gave to his audience, translated into living terms, in the conversation of Comedy.

*

Lastly, a word about Menander's metre. Most of his dialogue is written in a relaxed form of the same six-beat line that the tragic poets use. A longer line of eight beats, also found in Tragedy, is used by Menander in several extant passages; and near the end of *Dyskolos* appears a seven-beat line peculiar to comedy. In each case the metre is approximately reproduced in the English translation.

*

For the *Characters* of Theophrastus I have used the text and commentary of R. G. Ussher (Macmillan 1960). For the four principal fragments of Menander I have used the text and commentary of E. Capps (Ginn 1910), with some help from the text of F. G. Allinson (Loeb Library 1921). The translation of *Dyskolos* was made soon after the publication of the first text of the play, with the special purpose of a sound-radio production. This consideration influenced to some extent decisions about the allocation of parts; lines tend to be broken up among different speakers more often than is warranted by the exact balancing of probabilities which scholars have since had time to carry out. I do not feel, however, that these liberties at any point give a false impression either of the Greek text or of the play as a whole; I have therefore left them as they stand. I received at the time much generous help from Mr Raymond Raikes as Producer and from Professor Hugh Lloyd-Jones. I have also been helped by Professor E. W. Handley's edition (Methuen 1965) to make a few desirable alterations. Finally, I am deeply indebted to Professor Handley for his kindness in supplying me with his detailed notes on *The Sicyonian*.

I also acknowledge with thanks permission kindly granted by the Editor of The Loeb Classical Library and by the Harvard University Press to quote twelve lines from page 448 of the Loeb edition of Menander.

P. H. V.

THE CHARACTERS

Theophrastus

Irony, if summarily defined, would appear to be an affectation of the worse in word and deed.

The ironical man is one who goes up to people he detests and is ready to chat with them without any sign of dislike. He praises to their face men whom he has attacked behind their backs, and sympathizes with them when they are meeting ill-success. He is indulgent towards those who slander him, and unconcerned about what is being said. He talks blandly with people who are being ill-treated and who resent it. When people want to see him urgently, he tells them to come back another time. He never admits to anything he is doing, but says he is thinking of it. He pretends that he 'has only just arrived', that he 'was too late', or 'was not well'. To those who ask for a loan or a subscription he replies that he is not a rich man. When he has something to sell, he 'is not selling', and if in fact he is not selling he says he is. He pretends he didn't hear, when he did; that he hasn't seen, when he has; when he has made an admission, that he doesn't remember making it. 'I thought about that', he says; or, 'I've no idea'; or, 'That surprises me'; or, 'I once reached a similar conclusion myself.' In short, he is always using phrases of this kind: 'I don't believe it', 'I don't understand', 'You astonish me'; or, 'You give a different account of it; that wasn't the story he told *me*'; or, 'I think the whole thing's absurd'; or, 'Tell that to someone else'; or, 'I don't see how I can either disbelieve you, or condemn him'; or, 'All the same, don't be in a hurry to believe it.'

2. THE TOADY, OR FLATTERER

Flattery may be thought of as an attitude or relationship which is degrading in itself, but profitable to the one who flatters.

The toady is the sort of person who will say to the man he is walking with, 'Do you notice how people look at you? You're the only man in Athens they study in that way.' Or perhaps, 'You were being complimented yesterday in the Arcade. There was a group of thirty or more sitting talking; and the question cropped up, Who was our best citizen? Starting from that, we all came back finally to your name.' While he is going on like this, he picks a stray thread off the other's cloak; or if a bit of chaff has blown into his hair, he takes it out, and says with a laugh, 'Look at that! Because I haven't seen you for two days, you've got a beard full of grey hairs; though, if anyone's hair keeps its colour in spite of years, yours does.' Then he will tell the company to keep silent while the great man is speaking; he will praise him when he is listening; and when he pauses in his talk he will back him up with 'Hear, hear!' When his patron makes a feeble joke he laughs, stuffing his cloak into his mouth as if he couldn't contain his merriment. He asks people they meet in the street to wait until 'He' has passed. He buys apples and pears, brings them in and gives them to the children when their father is watching, kisses them and says, 'Well, youngsters, you've got a splendid father.' If he goes with his patron to help him buy some shoes, he remarks that the foot is more shapely than the shoe. If the other is on his way to visit some friend, the toady will run ahead and tell the friend, 'He's coming to see you,' and then turn back and say, 'I have announced you.' He is even capable of running errands, at a moment's notice, to the women's market. At a dinner-party he is the first to praise the wine, and he may be relied on to exclaim, 'How delicate your food is!' Then he picks up something from the table, and says, 'Now, isn't that choice?' He will ask his friend if he is cold and if he would like to put something more on; and while still asking he puts a wrap round him. What's more, he leans over to whisper in his ear; or, when talking to other guests, keeps glancing at their host. Then in the theatre, he will take the cushions from

34

the slave, and himself arrange them on his patron's seat. His patron's house, he will say, is beautifully built; his land has been nicely planted; and his portrait is an excellent likeness.

3. THE CHATTERER

Chatter is the churning-out of long-winded, unconsidered talk.

The chatterer is the sort of man who sits down beside someone he doesn't know and begins by delivering a panegyric on his own wife; continues with an account of his dream of the night before; then describes in detail what he had for supper. Next, getting into his stride, he remarks how far inferior men of the present day are to the ancients; how reasonable wheat is now in the shops; how full of foreigners Athens is getting. He observes that since the Dionysia it has been good sailing weather; and that if only Zeus would send more rain it would be better for the farmers. Then he tells you what part of his land he will put down to crops next year; and how difficult it is to live; and that Damippus has set up an enormous torch at the Mysteries; and 'How many columns has the Odeion?' and 'I was violently sick yesterday'; and 'What day of the month is it today?' Then he tells you that the Mysteries are in September, the Apaturia in October, and the Rural Dionysia in December. In fact, if you put up with him, he will never stop.

4. THE BOOR

Boorishness I would define as uncivilized ignorance.

The boor is the sort of man who drinks barley-brew before going into the Assembly; who asserts that garlic smells as sweet as any perfume; wears shoes too big for his feet; and can't talk without bellowing. He won't trust his friends and relations, but he'll consult his slaves about his most important business; and he'll retail all the affairs of the Assembly to the labourers he employs on his farm. He sits down with his clothes hitched above the knee, exposing his nakedness. In the streets, other sights arouse in him no interest or surprise whatever, but if he sees a cow or a donkey or a goat he stops and inspects it. He can't fetch a bit of food from the cupboard without nibbling at it on the way; he drinks his wine neat. He quietly tries to rumple the bakery-maid, after he's helped her to do the grinding for the whole household, himself included. He feeds his horses while still eating his own breakfast. He answers the front door himself; and calls his dog and takes hold of it by the nose, and says, 'This fellow guards the house and the whole place.' When he has been paid by someone with a silver coin, he rejects it, saying it is worn too smooth, and takes another instead. If he has lent his plough, or a basket, or a sickle, or a bag, he remembers it as he lies awake and goes to ask for it in the middle of the night. On his way down to town he asks anyone he meets what price hides or bloaters were fetching, or whether the new-moon festival is being held today. And in the same breath he tells you he's going down to get his hair cut; and while he's passing that way he means to call at Archias's for some fish. He sings in the public bath; and he drives hobnails into his shoes.

5. ANXIETY TO PLEASE

Anxiety to please (to compass it in a definition) is a quality designed to give pleasure, but whose impact does not make the best impression.

The ingratiating man is, shall we say, the sort who greets you from fifty yards off with 'My dear man', gazes at you full of admiration, holds you by both hands and won't let go, and then after accompanying you a little way and asking when he is to see you next, finally departs on a note of eulogy. When he is called in to an arbitration he is anxious to please not only the man he is supporting but also his opponent, so as to appear impartial. In a dispute between foreigners and Athenians he will say the foreigners are in the right. When invited out to dinner he will ask his host to call the children; and when they come in he will say they are as like their father as so many peas in a pod. Then he pulls them towards him, kisses them and makes them stand by him. Then he romps with them, and sings the words of the game himself –

> Atishoo, atishoo,
> We all fall down!

– and he lets some of them fall asleep on his stomach, in spite of the cramp it gives him.

6. THE OUTCAST, OR THE DEMORALIZED MAN

The quality of an outcast is the ready submission to what is degrading, both in act and word.

The demoralized man is one who will take an oath at a moment's notice, being well able to carry a bad name and accept vilification; a man of coarse nature, disreputable habits, and no principles. He is capable, if you will, of dancing the Kordax,[1] sober and without a mask, in a comedy chorus. At street-corner shows he will be the man to go round and collect the coppers, missing no one, and battling with those types who always have a 'pass' and want to see the show for nothing. He is very likely, too, to go in for inn-keeping or brothel-keeping or tax-farming; he shrinks from no disreputable trade – town-crier or hired cook; he gambles, and lets his mother starve; he gets arrested for petty theft, and spends more time in prison than at home.

[2] [In addition, he would seem to be one of those who collect a ring of people, then call up a whole crowd, and carry on abusive arguments in a loud, grating voice; meanwhile some join in the gathering, others wander off before hearing him

1. An obscene dance. 2. This paragraph is probably spurious.

out; some of them get the beginning of his rigmarole, others a resumé, others a fragment; and for making this kind of exhibition he always chooses a time when the town is crowded for some special occasion.]

In the law-courts he is perfectly at home, either conducting his defence, or denying knowledge on oath, or simply appearing with a file of documents tucked into his gown and clusters of memoranda in his hands. It's not beneath him to be a little king among the barrow-boys, lend them money for the asking, and charge twenty-five per cent per day; or to make the rounds of the pie-and-pasty shops, the wet-fishmongers and the dried-fishmongers, and collect the interest due to him straight out of the customer's hand into his mouth[1].

7. THE TALKER

Loquacity, should you want to define it, would seem to be an incontinence of talk.

The talker is the sort of man who, when you meet him, if you make any remark to him, will tell you that you are quite wrong; that he himself knows all the facts, and if you listen to him you shall learn what they are. When you reply, he interrupts you with 'You've already told me, remember, what you're just going to say'; or 'What a good thing you reminded me!' or, 'It's so valuable to have a talk'; or, 'Oh, I just forgot to mention –' or, 'You saw the point at once'; or, 'Yes, I've been watching you to see if you'd come round to my view.' He gives himself openings like this, one after the other, so that you never have time to take breath. Then, when he has talked the hind legs off individual victims, nothing will stop him advancing on groups and gatherings, and making them leave their business in the middle and take to flight. He will even walk into schools or sports-grounds, and hinder boys in their exercises, by talking in this endless way to their

1. A convenient way to carry a coin – as we put a pencil behind the ear.

trainers and teachers. When people say, 'We must go now', he likes to keep them company on the way and see them safely home. When he hears what has happened in the Assembly, he tells you about it; and adds, for good measure, the story of the battle in Aristophon's year, and of the Spartan victory under Lysander; and of the speech he himself once made, which drew some applause from the Assembly; at the same time throwing into his discourse some derogatory remarks about 'the masses'. The result is that his audience either let their attention wander, or drop off to sleep, or desert him in mid-course and vanish. When he is on a jury he prevents his fellow-jurors from reaching a verdict; in a theatre he won't let you follow the play, at a dinner he won't let you eat. 'A talker finds it hard to stop,' he says; and adds that his tongue runs on of itself, and he couldn't stop it, even if people thought him worse than a nest of swallows. He is actually ready to let his own children make fun of him, when they are feeling sleepy and say to him, 'Daddy, talk to us and send us to sleep!'

8. THE INVENTOR OF NEWS

Newsmaking is the fabrication of false reports, which the inventor wants to have believed, about things said and done.

The newsmaker is the kind of man who, on meeting someone, counters his friend's glum look with a smile and asks, 'Where have you come from? and what's your news? Can you give me the latest about this business?' And then, pressing his attack. he asks, 'No new developments? Well, certainly the reports are splendid.' And giving you no chance to reply he goes on, 'What's that? You haven't heard? I can see I'm going to regale you with news.' And he has some soldier, or perhaps a slave of the flute-player Asteios, or it's the contractor Lycon, arrived straight from the battle, from whom he says he has heard all this. In fact, the credentials of his statements are of a kind that no one could possibly check. Quoting his sources, he recounts how Polyperchon and the king have won a battle[1], and Cassandros has been taken prisoner. And if someone asks him, 'Do you believe this?' he will say, 'Why, the whole town's buzzing with it, confirmation keeps coming in, all accounts agree. There's been an almighty mash-up.' For evidence, he says, you have only to look at the faces of men in the Government, and note the change in every one of them. He has heard incidentally, he says, that they have an informant (whom they are keeping hidden) who knows everything. As he unfolds his tale, you will hardly believe how convincingly he moves tears with his 'Poor Cassandros! What a tragic end! Doesn't it make you think – what Chance can do to us? Well, he was a great man once!' And he adds, 'You must be the only one to know this' – when he has already trotted it all round Athens.

[2]What I don't understand about men like this, is why they do it. Not only are they liars, but they show a loss on their day's work. Some of them, as often happens, while holding an audience in the public baths, have had their cloaks stolen; some have lost lawsuits by default while winning victories by land and sea in the Stoa; others, while verbally capturing cities, have missed their dinner. These men's occupation is entirely pitiable; in every public place, in every factory, in every corner of the Agora, they are busy all day long boring their hearers to death and exhausting them with their fabrications.

9. THE SHAMELESS MAN

Shamelessness may be defined as indifference to ill repute for the sake of gain.

The shameless man is one who will go to borrow money from the very person he is defrauding; one who after sacri-

1. See Introduction, page 9.   2. See Introduction, page 11.

ficing to the gods will himself go out to dinner with someone else, and then salt down the meat and store it. At his host's table he calls his slave, then picks up meat and bread from the table and gives it to him, saying so that everyone can hear, 'Make a good meal, Tibeios!' When he goes shopping he reminds the butcher of any little service he may have done him; and he stands near the scale and slips on to it some meat if possible, otherwise a bone to make soup; and if he gets away with it he's happy, and if not, he whips a bit of tripe off the table and chuckles as he hurries away with it. When he has guests from another city he buys (with their money) seats for a theatre performance, and thus sees the play without paying his share; and the next day he even brings his sons, and their tutor. If you are carrying something you've bought at a bargain price, he will always ask you to share it with him. He will go to a neighbour's door and borrow barley, or perhaps bran, and then get the person who has lent it to carry it over to his house. In the public baths, what he likes to do is to go over to where the jugs are kept, fill one (while the bath-man bawls at him), throw water over his own head, and then announce that he has had his bath, adding as he goes out, 'And no thanks to you!'

10. THE SKINFLINT, OR STINGY MAN

Stinginess is a disproportionate avoidance of expense.

The stingy man is the sort who will come to your house in the middle of the month and ask you for half a month's interest on his loan. When he is at table with others, he will count how many cups each person has drunk; and of the whole company at dinner, he will pour the smallest libation to Artemis. If you buy anything for him, however cheaply, he will say, when you send in your account, that it has taken his last penny. If a servant breaks a jug or a dish, he stops the price of it out of his allowance. If his wife has dropped a threepenny-bit, he is the sort of person to start moving the furniture, shifting couches and cupboards, rummaging among rugs. If he has anything to sell, he will only let it go at a price which means a bad bargain for the buyer. He would never let you eat a fig out of his garden, or walk through his land, or pick up one of his windfall olives or dates. Every single day he inspects his boundaries to see if they have been tampered with. He is a terror, too, for enforcing the right of distraint, and for charging compound interest. When it is his turn to give the parish dinner, he cuts the meat into tiny slices to serve out. He goes off to market, and comes home again without buying anything. He forbids his wife to lend salt, or lamp-wick, or herbs, or barley-grains, or garlands, or holy-cakes. 'These things all mount up, you know,' he says, 'in a twelvemonth.'

II. THE ABOMINABLE MAN

Abominable behaviour is not hard to define: it is blatant and offensive levity.

The abominable man is one who on meeting respectable women will lift his clothing and display his private parts. In the theatre he claps when the rest have stopped; and hisses players whom everyone else is enjoying; and when there is a silence he will lift his head and belch, to make the audience turn round. Just when the market is most crowded he goes to the stalls where they sell nuts, or myrtle-berries, or fruit, and stands there nibbling away while he chats to the stall-keeper. In company he will address by name someone with whom he is not acquainted. If he sees that people are in a hurry, he insists on their stopping a little. If you have just lost an important lawsuit he comes up as you leave the court and congratulates you. He goes out to do his own shopping, hires a couple of flute-girls, and then if you meet him shows you what he has got and invites you to come and share them.

He will stand talking outside the barber's or the myrrh-shop, and announce that he intends to get drunk. When his mother has just come in from visiting the fortune-teller he deliberately uses unlucky words. When prayers or libations are going on, he drops his cup and then laughs as if he had done something funny. When he is being played to on the flute, he will be the one person to tap the tune with his fingers and to whistle an accompaniment, and then severely ask the flute-girl why she didn't stop at once. When he wants to spit, he spits across the table at the slave who is pouring wine.

12. THE UNSEASONABLE MAN

Unseasonableness is an annoying faculty for choosing the wrong moment.

The unseasonable man is the kind who comes up to you when you have no time to spare and asks your advice. He sings a serenade to his sweetheart when she has influenza. Just after you have gone bail for somebody and had to pay up, he approaches you with a request that you will go bail for him. If he is going to give evidence he turns up when judgement has just been pronounced. When he is a guest at a wedding he makes derogatory remarks about the female sex. When you have just reached home after a long journey he invites you to come for a stroll. He is certain to bring along a buyer who offers more, when you have just sold your house. When people have heard a matter and know it by heart, he stands up and explains the whole thing from the beginning. He eagerly undertakes a service for you which you don't want performed but which you have not the face to decline. When people are sacrificing and spending money, he arrives to ask for his interest on a loan. When a friend's slave is being beaten he will stand there and tell how he once had a slave who hanged himself after a similar beating. If he takes part in an arbitration, he will set everyone at blows again just when

43

both sides are ready to cry quits. And after dancing once he will seize as partner another man who is not yet drunk.

13. OVERDOING IT

Well, of course, overdoing it will be something like well-meaning presumption in word or act.

The presumptuous man is one who makes the kind of promise he will not be able to keep. When a matter is generally admitted to be just, he raises objections, and is then overruled. He insists on his slave mixing more wine than the company can finish. He tries to separate two men fighting, even when he doesn't know them. He begins to show you a short cut, and presently has no idea where he is going. He will walk up to the colonel and ask him when he intends to put the troops in battle-formation, and what will be his orders for the day after tomorrow. He will go to his father and tell him that his mother is still fast asleep in their bedroom. When the doctor has forbidden an invalid to be given wine, he says he wants to try an experiment, and makes the patient tipsy. When a woman relative has died, he inscribes on her tombstone her husband's name, and her father's and her mother's, as well as her own name and her place of birth, and adds, that 'they were all estimable people'. And when about to take an oath he remarks to those standing round, 'I've done this scores of times.'

14. FECKLESSNESS

Fecklessness, if we are to define it, is slowness of wit in word and action.

The feckless man is one who, after working out some figures on his reckoner, and finding the total, asks the man sitting next to him, 'What does it come to?' When he is defendant in a lawsuit, and the case is due to come on, he forgets and goes off for a day in the country. When he goes to see a play, he gets left behind all alone in the theatre fast asleep. After a heavy supper he gets up in the night to go to the lavatory, and is bitten by his neighbour's dog. He buys something, puts it carefully away himself, and later looks for it and can't find it. When someone informs him that a friend of his has died, so that he can attend the funeral, he says, with a mournful expression and tears in his eyes, 'Well, that's fortunate.' When he receives back money that is owed to him he will insist on having witnesses present. In the middle of winter he has a row with his slave for not buying cucumbers in the market. He compels his own children to wrestle and run even to the point of exhaustion. In the country, if he is going to cook pease-pudding for himself, he puts salt into the pot twice, and makes it uneatable. When it is raining he remarks, 'What a lovely smell from the stars' – when other people would say, 'from the earth'. And when someone asks, 'How many dead bodies do you suppose have been carried out through the Sacred Gate?' he answers with 'I only wish you and I had as many.'

15. THE HOSTILE MAN

Hostility is harshness showing itself in words.

The hostile man is one who, when asked where so-and-so is, replies, 'Don't come bothering me'; or who, when spoken to, will not answer. When he has something to sell, instead of telling the buyers what he will let it go for, he asks them, 'What am I getting for this?' To those who politely send presents when he holds a feast, he says that he wants none of their gifts. If you have accidentally pushed him or trodden on his foot, he never forgives you. When a friend has asked him to contribute a donation, he first says he won't give one; then later he brings it, with the remark, 'More money thrown away.' When he stubs his toe in the road he invariably curses the stone. He can't bear to wait long for anyone. He will never consent to sing, or to recite, or to dance. Probably too he never prays to the gods.

16. THE SUPERSTITIOUS MAN

Ah, yes, superstition: it would appear to be cowardice in face of the supernatural.

The superstitious man is one who, if anything dirty touches him, will wash his hands, sprinkle himself with water from a holy fountain, and walk about all day with his mouth full of bay-leaves. If a weasel crosses his path, he will not go a step further until someone else has overtaken him, or until he has thrown three stones across the road. Should he see a snake in his house, if it's a harmless one he invokes Sabazios; but if it's a venomous one he immediately builds a shrine to Heracles on the very spot. When he passes the smooth stones at a cross-roads he pours oil on them from his flask, and won't leave the place till he has fallen on his knees and kissed them. If a mouse gnaws through a leather bag of barley, off he goes to the expounder of omens and asks what he ought to do. If the reply is that he should take the leather bag to the cobblers and get it patched, he pays no heed to this advice, but turns on his heel and performs an expiatory sacrifice. He likes to purify his house at frequent intervals, saying that something has occurred to attract Hecate. If, when walking, he hears owls hoot, he is alarmed, and will only go on when he has pronounced the words, 'Athene is greater.' He will never set foot on a tomb, or come near a corpse or a woman in childbirth, but says it is important for him to avoid pollution. And on the fours and sevens of the month (i.e., the fourth, seventh, fourteenth, seventeenth, etc.) he instructs his household to put wine on to boil, and goes out and buys myrtle-berries, incense and honey-cakes, and when he comes in again spends the rest of the day putting garlands on the images of Hermaphroditos. When he has had a dream, he is off again to the interpreters, the fortune-tellers, the bird-watchers, to ask which of the gods or goddesses he should pray to. When he is contemplating initiation he visits the Orphic instructors month by month, and takes his wife with him (if she can't spare the time he takes the nurse) and even his children. I should say he will be one of those who meticulously sprinkle themselves with salt water on the sea-shore. And if ever he catches sight of cross-road offerings to Hecate wreathed with garlic, he goes away and washes his head thoroughly, and calls in some wise women and gets them to purify him by walking round him with a lily-bulb or a puppy for sacrifice. If he sees a madman or an epileptic he shivers, and spits into the fold of his gown.

17. A CHIP ON THE SHOULDER, OR THE MAN WITH A GRIEVANCE

To have a 'chip on the shoulder' means to complain unduly about the lot which life has assigned to one.

The man with a grievance is the kind of man who, when a friend has sent him his share of a banquet, remarks to the slave who brings it, 'He doesn't invite me to dinner: that way he saves my share of his soup and his nasty wine.' When his sweetheart is caressing and kissing him he says to her, 'I wonder if you genuinely love me as much as you seem to.' He is resentful against Zeus, not for sending rain, but for sending it too late. If he finds a purse in the road, he says, 'But a fortune – no! I've never found *that*.' When he has bought a slave cheap after much haggling, 'I wonder, now,' says he, 'whether for that money I can have bought anything worth having.' When someone comes to him with the good news, 'You've got a son,' he replies, 'If you add to that, "And away goes half my property," you'll be telling the truth.' When he has won a lawsuit by a unanimous vote, he finds fault with the man who wrote his speech, for omitting a number of strong points. When his friends have contributed to provide him with a loan, and one of them says, 'Now you can feel cheerful,' 'Can I indeed,' he answers, 'when I've got to give every one of you his money back, and on top of that show gratitude, as if I'd been done a favour!'

18. THE DISTRUSTFUL MAN

Lack of trust is the assumption that everyone is cheating you.

The distrustful man is the sort who, after sending a slave to buy provisions, sends another whose job is to find out how much he paid for them. He carries his money himself, and sits down twice in a quarter of a mile to count how much he has. When he's lying in bed he asks his wife if she locked the safe, if the sideboard is sealed, and the front door bolted. If she says Yes, he none the less gets out of bed, naked and barefoot, lights the lamp, and trots round checking everything; and finally with some difficulty gets to sleep again. If you owe him money, he asks for his interest in front of witnesses, to remove all chance of your saying you were not asked for it. He likes to send his coat for cleaning, not to the cleaner who does the best work, but to the one who has a reliable guarantor. When someone comes to borrow silver cups, he refuses if he possibly can; if it is a relative or a close acquaintance, he lends only after taking every precaution short of testing and weighing the metal, or even getting a third party to go bail. When his slave attends him in the street, he orders him to walk in front instead of behind, so that he can keep an eye on him and see that he doesn't run away. If you have bought something from him, and say, 'How much? Put it down to my account, as I haven't time just now to send the money,' he replies, 'Don't put yourself to that trouble; I'll come along with you – until you *have* time.'

19. OFFENSIVENESS

Offensiveness is a neglect of one's personal condition such as to cause annoyance.

The offensive man is one who walks about with eczema or scabs or misshapen finger-nails, and says that he was born with these afflictions; his father and his grandfather, he says, had them just the same – and it's no easy thing to be smuggled into *their* family. And of course it's just like him to have ulcers on the front of his shins, and whitlows on his fingers, and not to look after them but let them fester. He has arm-pits like a bear's, and the hairiness extends across half his body; and his teeth are black and decaying, so that talking with him is thoroughly unpleasant.

Things like this too: he wipes his nose while eating; while engaged in a sacrifice he chews; spits while talking to you; and belches at you in the middle of a drink. He does not wash before getting into bed with his wife. He uses rancid oil in the bath, so that he stinks. He puts on a thick vest and a flimsy cloak covered with stains, and goes off to the market-place like that.

20. THE TIRESOME MAN

Tiresomeness – to attempt a definition – is a quality whose impact causes annoyance rather than actual harm.

The tiresome man is the kind who will walk in when you have just dozed off and wake you up to have a chat with you. When people are on the point of setting sail he will hinder their departure. He will arrive for an appointment, and then ask you to wait till he has taken a walk. He will take his child from its nurse, bite up its food and feed it himself, cooing and clucking at it and calling it 'Daddy's little imp'. When you sit next to him at a meal he will describe to you how he took a dose of hellebore which gave him a thorough

49

clean-out; 'You should have seen the colour of the bile in my excreta,' he says, 'darker than that gravy you've got.' He's a terror for asking his mother, in front of relations, 'Tell me, Mummy, when you were in labour with me, was it an easy birth?' Then he answers for her, and says that childbirth is pleasurable, but that it is not easy to conceive a human being without experiencing both pleasure and pain. He tells you that in his house he has cold water laid on from a reservoir; that he has a garden with many kinds of vegetables, young and tender; that he has a cook who is very clever with fish; that his house is a regular hotel, and his friends are like the proverbial sieve: 'The more you do for them, the less they're satisfied.' When he gives a dinner, he draws his guests' attention to his parasite,[1] commenting on the man's personal qualities. And as he stands over the wine-bowl he announces encouragingly that provision has been made for the pleasure of those present: they have only to ask and his slave will fetch her at once from the agency. 'Then,' he says, 'she will supply us all with music and merriment.'

21. PETTY AMBITION

Petty ambition will be familiar as an undignified craving for marks of respect.

The man of petty ambition is one who, when asked out to dinner, sets great store by sitting next to the host himself during the meal. He takes his son off to Delphi for his ceremonial hair-cut.[2] He takes trouble to have a black slave to attend him in the street. When he returns a loan of one silver mina he makes his slave pay it with a new coin. He has his hair cut very frequently; keeps his teeth white; changes his clothes while they are still good; and uses scented ointment instead of oil. In the Agora he frequents the banking

1. Compare Character 2; and Chaereas in *The Bad-Tempered Man*, page 66.
2. i.e., at his coming of age.

quarter; in the gymnasia he spends his time where the young men are exercising; in the theatre, when there's a performance he chooses a seat near the Strategoi. He buys – for himself, nothing; but all kinds of things for friends abroad; he sends off pickled olives to Byzantium, Spartan hounds to Cyzikos, Hymettos honey to Rhodes; and at the same time lets the whole town know about it. And naturally it's he who must keep a pet monkey, and have a short-tailed ape and some Sicilian doves, and dice made of gazelle-horn, oil-flasks of the round variety from Thurioi, twisted walking-sticks from Sparta, a curtain with a woven design of Persians; and a private wrestling-ground with sand in it, and a hand-ball court. And he goes around lending this place to philosophers, to sophists, to drill-sergeants, to musicians, for giving displays. And when the displays are in progress he himself walks in, rather late, so that spectators turn to each other and say, 'That's the man who owns this place.' Of course he keeps a jackdaw at home; and he must buy a toy ladder for it, and make a tiny bronze shield for the jackdaw to hold while it hops up the ladder. When he has sacrificed an ox, he nails up the forelock, wreathed with enormous garlands, just inside his house opposite the door, so that everyone who comes in can see that he has sacrificed an ox. When he has taken part in a procession of the Knights, he hands all the rest of his equipment to his slave to take home, and then walks about the Agora in his spurs, constantly tossing back his cloak. If his little Maltese terrier has died, he sets up a memorial tablet to it, with the inscription, 'A Scion of Malta'. If he has dedicated a bronze ring in the Temple of Asclepios, he wears it thin with polishing and oiling it every day. And of course he manages to obtain from the Presidents the privilege of announcing to the public the result of a sacrifice. Arrayed in a gleaming cloak, and wearing a wreath, he steps forward and says, 'Athenians! We, the Presidents, have performed the sacrifice of the Galaxia to the Mother of the gods, and the omens are auspicious;

therefore receive her blessing.' After making this proclamation he goes off home and recounts in detail to his wife how exceedingly well everything is going with him.

22. MEANNESS

Meanness is the absence of desire for honour where expense is involved.

The mean man is the sort of person who after winning, as Choregos, first place with his tragedy, then dedicates to Dionysos a wooden tablet, inscribing on it only his own name. When voluntary contributions to public finance are being made in the Assembly, he gets up and quietly slips out. When he is giving his daughter in marriage he sells all the meat of the sacrifice except the portions for the priests, and to attend and serve at the wedding banquet he hires staff who feed at home. When he is trierarch he spreads the helmsman's blankets on the bed for himself, and puts his own blankets away. He has a way of keeping his sons home from school when there is a festival of the Muses, so that they will not have to contribute; and sends a message that they are unwell. When he has been shopping he carries the vegetables from the market himself in a fold of his gown. He stays indoors while his coat is at the cleaner's. If a friend of his is raising a public subscription and has mentioned it to him, should he see him coming he will turn down a side street and go home by a roundabout way. If his wife has brought a dowry, instead of buying a maid for her, he hires from the women's market a slave to attend her when she goes out. He wears shoes that are patched, and says they are as strong as horn. When he gets up he tidies the house and sweeps out the dining-room; and as he sits down he hitches aside the cloak which is the only garment he wears.

23. THE BOASTER

Put plainly, boastfulness would seem to be pretension to advantages which one does not possess.

The boaster is a man who will stand on the jetty talking to foreigners about the vast sums he has at sea; describing the wide extent of his investment in overseas trade, with details of his own gains and losses; and while shooting a great line on this topic, he will send off his boy to the Bank, where his balance is one drachma. If you travel with him, he has you at his mercy; he loves to tell you how he campaigned with Alexander;[1] how he got on with him; how many jewel-encrusted cups he brought home. Then he talks about Asiatic craftsmen, maintaining that they are better than the European; and all this he will say, without having ever travelled outside Attica. He will tell you he has had letters – three in succession – from Antipater[1] inviting him to Macedonia; that he has been offered a licence for tax-free export of timber from Macedonia, but has refused it, so that no one may cast aspersions on him as a pro-Macedonian. In the famine, he says, his outlay in gifts to distressed citizens amounted to more than five talents – 'I never could say No.' Then, though the men sitting next to him are strangers, he tells one of them to work it out in writing; and reckoning in sums of six hundred drachmae or one mina, and speciously assigning a name to each gift, he finally makes it as much as ten talents. He points out that this is the amount contributed by himself to charities, mentioning that it does not include the trierarchies[2] or other public expenses he has undertaken. He will go up to a dealer in horses of quality, and pretend that he wants to buy. He will go into a clothing-store, and ask to see clothing priced at anything up to two talents, and then browbeat his slave for coming without his money. And when he is living in a rented house he will assert,

1. See Introduction, page 9.
2. An undertaking to equip a ship for the navy at one's own expense.

to someone who doesn't know this, that it is the family resi-
dence; but he intends to sell it. 'It's a bit small,' he says; 'I do
a lot of entertaining.'

24. ARROGANCE

Arrogance is the habit of despising everybody except oneself.

The arrogant man is one who will say, to someone who is
in a hurry to speak with him, that he will see him after dinner
when he takes his walk. If he has done you a favour, he will
mention that he recalls the occasion. If a passer-by asks him to
arbitrate a dispute, he gives a quick judgement on the spot.
When he is being elected to some public office he declines to
stand, stating on oath that he cannot spare the time. He will
never make the first approach to anyone. To people who have
something to sell, or whom he has employed, he always says,
'Come and see me in the morning.' If he passes you in the
street he will not speak to you, but keeps his head bent down,
or, when he chooses, looks up in the air. When he entertains
friends he does not dine with them himself, but makes one of
his servants look after them. When he goes visiting he sends
someone ahead to say he is coming. He will allow no one to
visit him while he is oiling himself, or washing, or eating.
When he is casting an account with someone, you can be sure
he will tell his slave to scatter the counters, make a rough total,
and book the debt. When sending a business letter, he doesn't
write 'I shall be obliged if you will...', but 'I want this done',
and 'I wrote expecting to receive . . .', and 'Make sure my
instructions are followed', and 'As quickly as possible'.

25. COWARDICE

Cowardice, let us say, is a sort of shrinking of the soul due to
fear.

The coward is the sort of man who, when at sea, is sure that the cliffs just sighted are pirate vessels; or on meeting a heavy swell, asks if there is any uninitiated person on board; or looks up at the steersman to ask if he is on mid-course, or what he thinks of the weather; and explains to the man next to him that his fear is due to a dream he had; and takes off his tunic and gives it to his slave, and begs him to help him to the shore. On military service, when the infantry are marching out to battle, he calls his fellow-townsmen and tells them to stand near him and have a look round first, and remarks that it's a job to tell which lot are the enemy. Then when he hears shouting and sees men falling, he tells those standing next to him that in his hurry he forgot his sword; and he runs back to the tent, and sends his slave out, telling him to look and see where the enemy are; and meanwhile he hides his sword under his pillow, and then spends a long time looking for it; and while he's in the tent he sees a wounded man being brought in – one of his friends; so he runs to him, tells him to cheer up, and lends a hand to carry him. Then he looks after him, washes him, sits down beside him, and flicks the flies off his wound – in fact, anything rather than fight the enemy. When the trumpet sounds the advance, he remains sitting in the tent, and says, 'To hell with you! Can't you let the man get a bit of sleep – always blaring away!' Then, covered with blood from the other man's wound, he meets the men as they come back from the battle, and recounts how – at some risk to himself – he has 'saved one of our comrades'; and he brings the men of his tribe in to see the patient, and describes to each of them how with his own hands he brought the man back to the tent.

26. THE AUTHORITARIAN

Authoritarianism, or the oligarchic temperament, may be described as an arrogant relish for power and profit.

The authoritarian is the sort of person who, when the Assembly is discussing what men to appoint as assistants to the

Archon in organizing the procession at the Great Dionysia, will come forward and state his opinion that those appointed should be given unconditional powers; and if someone else proposes ten assistants, he will answer, 'One is enough, but he must be a *man*.' Of the poems of Homer there is one single line he has made his own:

From many rulers no good comes; let one man rule.

Of all the rest of Homer he knows nothing. Typical of him are utterances like this: 'We must get together by ourselves and discuss these matters, out of reach of the rabble and the street-corner. It's time we stopped kow-towing to every jack-in-office, and ourselves accepting kicks or compliments from them. Either they or we must run this city.' He will go out about midday, with his cloak thrown well back, his hair taste-fully trimmed, his nails precisely pared, and strut about de-claiming statements like this: 'These blackmailers make Athens impossible to live in'; or, 'In the law-courts we are simply slapped down by corrupt juries'; or, 'People who meddle in politics – I can't imagine what they want'; or, 'The working classes – they're always the same: ungrateful, and ready to obey anyone who offers a bribe or a bonus.' Or he will tell you how ashamed he feels in the Assembly, when some mean-looking, scruffy citizen sits down next to him. 'The rich are being bled to death,' he says, 'with subsidizing the navy, the theatre, the festivals, and everything else. When is it going to end? Democratic agitators – how I detest them!' Then he names Theseus as the original cause of the country's deterioration; for it was he who concentrated the twelve small States in one, thus elevating the lower classes, putting power into the hands of the majority, and destroying the monarchy. He adds that Theseus got his deserts; for he was himself the first victim of democracy. And many other such assertions he bestows on foreigners and on Athenians whose temperament and policies are similar to his.

27. LATE LEARNING

Late learning would seem to be a love of difficult tasks which is excessive in view of one's age.

The late learner is the sort of man who, at sixty, learns by heart speeches from the tragedies, and when reciting them over the wine forgets them. He gets his son to instruct him how to do a 'right wheel' or 'left wheel' or 'about turn'. At heroes' festivals he competes with boys in the torch-race. And of course, if he is invited somewhere to a feast of Heracles and asked to choose a victim, he throws off his cloak and chooses the bull, so that he can bend back its neck for slaughter. He goes into the wrestling-schools and submits to training. At a variety show he will sit through three or four performances, learning the songs by heart. When undergoing initiation in the mysteries of Sabazios, he is determined to acquit himself the best in the eyes of the priest. He falls in love with a girl of the town, and when caught by a rival client in the act of forcing her door with a crowbar, and given a beating, he then brings an action for assault. He rides out to the country on a borrowed horse, practises horsemanship on the way, falls off, and breaks his head. At a tenth-day festival he collects a group to sing with him. He plays at 'Long John' with his own slave. He competes at archery and javelin-throwing with his children's tutor, whom he advises to learn from *him* – as if the tutor too knew nothing about it. When wrestling at the baths he wriggles his bottom rapidly, so that people may think he has been properly trained; and when there's a performance of women's dancing, he too practises the steps, whistling the tune for himself.

28. THE SLANDERER

The habit of slander is a bias of the mind towards evil-speaking.

The slanderer is the sort of man who, when asked who so-

and-so is, replies, 'Well, then, shall I begin, like the genealogists, with his parentage? His father was a man who was originally called Sosias; in the army he was known as Sosistratos; and on being enrolled in his deme changed to Sosidemos. His mother is a nobly-born lady of Thrace – at least she answers to the name of "Sweetie"; and I'm told that ladies of that kind are regarded as noble in their own country. The man himself – as you would expect from his antecedents – is a bad lot – a thorough jail-bird.' Or he will say to someone in a nasty tone, 'Oh, I know that kind of trash well enough, that you've come all this way to plead for.' Then he goes on to give details: 'These women grab men out of the street as they pass the door'; or, 'In that house you'll always find them with their feet up. Oh, it's not such nonsense as you might think; why, the women couple in the street like dogs.' Or, 'They talk nothing but men'; or, 'They sit just inside the front door, listening for callers.' Then if other people are talking slander, naturally he'll join in with, 'Yes, I hate him too, more than anyone. You can tell from his face he's a criminal. His wickedness is unique – I'll give you an instance. His wife brought him a good dowry – several talents; she has given him a son; yet her allowance for sweets is three-halfpence, and he makes her wash in cold water in mid-winter.' If he's sitting next to you he always makes remarks about anyone who has just left; and once he has begun, he will not stop short of abusing even his relations. In fact he will utter all manner of slander against friends, relations, even against the dead. And he miscalls his behaviour 'plain speaking' or 'democratic freedom', and makes it his chief pleasure in life.

29. LOVE OF EVIL

By 'love of evil' I mean a partiality for the criminal character.

The 'lover of evil' is the sort of man who contacts those

who have lost lawsuits or been found guilty in criminal cases, and reckons that by associating with them he will become more experienced and more formidable. If someone is referred to as honest, he adds, 'To all appearance', and goes on to say that there is no such thing as an honest man; that all men are alike; indeed he uses the phrase 'What a good man' as a joke. A criminal type he will describe as 'Independent-minded, if you look at him fairly. Many of the things people say of him,' he admits, 'are true; but there are some things they don't know. He's naturally talented; he sticks to his friends; and he's no fool.' He insists emphatically that he has never met a more capable person. He will take the side of a man who is making his defence in the Assembly, or on trial in a law-court; and he will probably tell the jury that 'They must judge the case and not the man.' He will describe the defendant as a 'watchdog of the people, one who keeps his eye on wrong-doers. Unless we value such men,' he says, 'we shall have no one left who cares what goes wrong in public life.' He can't resist championing worthless men; on a jury he organizes a pressure-group in a bad cause; when judging a case he takes the statements of the opposed parties in the worst sense.

30. THE AVARICIOUS MAN

Avarice is the craving for sordid gain.

The avaricious man is one who when giving a party will not put out enough bread for his guests. He borrows from a man of another city who is spending a night with him. When distributing shares at a club feast, he says it is right that a double share should be given to the distributor – and immediately helps himself. When he has wine for sale, he sells it to his friend watered. If he travels on a public commission, he leaves at home the money provided by the State for his expenses, and borrows from his fellow-deputies; he loads his servant with a heavier pack than he can carry, and gives him smaller rations than anyone else in the group; and if any presents are given by their hosts, he demands his full share – and sells it. When he is anointing himself at the baths, he says to his slave, 'Here, this oil you've bought is rancid,' and uses someone else's. If his slaves find a bag of coppers in the street, he cries out, 'Luck's for all,' and claims his share. He sends his cloak to the cleaner's, borrows another from an acquaintance, and trails it round for days afterwards, till the owner has to ask for it back.

Other little ways of his are: he measures out the rations for his household with his own hands, using a 'thrifty' can with the bottom knocked in, and brushing off the top very close. He beats down a friend who thinks he is selling something reasonably, and once he has got it, goes and sells it. And you may be sure, when he is paying a debt of thirty minas, that he will pay it four drachmas short. If his sons have missed some days from school through illness, he deducts from the month's fee a proportionate sum; and during the month Anthesterion, because there are so many festival days, he saves the fee by not sending them to their lessons at all. When he has hired out his slave, and is receiving from him the money due, he asks for the discount as well; and when holding an audit he makes the same demand from the administrator under question. When entertaining the men of his clan, he begs a dish from the common table for his own slaves; and he makes a list of the half-radishes that are left over, so that the waiters won't get them. When he is travelling with a party of acquaintances, he uses their slaves, lets his own slaves out on hire, and does not contribute the hire-money to the common fund. When his club meets at his house for dinner, it is just like him to put aside for himself a portion of the provisions contributed, such as firewood, lentils, vinegar, salt, or lamp-oil. If a friend, or a friend's daughter, is getting married, some time before the wedding he goes travelling abroad, to avoid sending a present. And the things he borrows from acquaintances are the kind of things one would never ask to have back, or would hardly accept even if they were offered.

THE SPURIOUS PREFACE[1]

My dear Polycles,

I have often wondered, when I have given the matter thought – and it may be I shall never stop wondering – why it is that we Greeks, living as we do in a country with a uniform climate and all receiving the same education, don't all happen to have the same character. I have studied human nature for a long time, and am now ninety-nine years old; moreover, I have mixed with many people of all nationalities and have very closely compared good characters with bad; and therefore I felt it was my duty to write down the different habits of life displayed by both kinds. I shall set before you, one by one, all the various types into which men are divided, and show how they manage their affairs. For I believe, my dear Polycles, that our sons will be the better men for having had bequeathed to them such object-lessons, which they may study as examples, and which will teach them to choose the company and conversation of the men of highest principles, and to endeavour not to fall below their level. Now I will turn to my theme; and it is for you to follow my argument and judge if I am right. I will dispense with prelude and preamble; and I will begin with Irony and those who make irony their aim. I will define it, and then I will describe the ironical man, showing the sort of person he is, and the sort of life his nature makes him lead; and then I will try to illustrate other conditions one by one, as I have set out to do.

1. See Introduction, page 10.

PLAYS AND FRAGMENTS

Menander

*

DYSKOLOS

OR

THE BAD-TEMPERED MAN

DYSKOLOS

OR

THE BAD-TEMPERED MAN

CHARACTERS

PAN, *the god of country life*
SOSTRATOS, *a rich young man from town*
CHAEREAS, *his parasite*
PYRRHIAS, *a young slave of Sostratos*
CNEMON, *a bad-tempered old farmer*
MYRRHINE, *his daughter*
DAOS, *an old slave of Gorgias*
GORGIAS, *Myrrhine's half-brother*
SICON, *a hired cook*
CALLIPPIDES, *Sostratos' father*
GETAS, *his slave*
SIMICE, *an old woman, slave of Cnemon, and Myrrhine's nurse*
Sostratos' mother and sister; Gorgias' mother; various guests

*

Scene: Phyle in Attica. In the centre of the stage is the entrance to a rustic shrine. On the right is Cnemon's house, on the left Gorgias'. By the entrance to the shrine is a statue of Pan.

SCENE ONE

Enter PAN *from the shrine.*

PAN: Imagine that this place is Phyle in Attica;
  That this cave from which I have come is a shrine of the
      Nymphs,
  A well-known holy place belonging to the people of Phyle –
  Those of them who manage to cultivate these rocks.
  This farm on my right is the home of Cnemon, an old man
  Who prefers his own to anyone else's company;
  Surly-tempered to everybody; detests crowds.
  Crowds, did I say? He has never yet in all his life –
  And that's a good many years – uttered a pleasant word
  To a single soul; never opened a conversation;
  Except that, being my neighbour, he will speak in passing
  To me, Pan, because he's obliged to; but I'm sure
  A moment later he wishes he hadn't.

                                          Yet this man,
  This surly creature, married a widow, whose first husband
  Had newly died, leaving her with one little boy.
  Joined to her in the state of holy acrimony
  He spent his days, and a great part of his nights as well,
  In quarrelling – an unhappy life. When a girl was born
  Things became worse; until at last they reached a point
  Where misery beggared all comparison, and the woman,
  Finding her life intolerable, left him and went back
  To live with her son by her first marriage, Gorgias.
  He, now grown up, has this little farm next door, where he
      keeps
  His mother and one faithful slave who belonged to his father.
  They are poor; but the lad has common sense beyond his
      years;
  For hard experience quickly matures a man.

67

Old Cnemon, with his daughter, and an aged crone
To serve them, lives a lonely life, fetching in logs,
Digging, toiling away; and loathing every soul
Without exception, from his own wife and his neighbours
   here
To the villagers of Cholargos further down the valley.
But the girl does honour to her simple upbringing;
She is pure, good-hearted; serves with devoted piety
The Nymphs, who are my companions. So she inspires in
   us
A wish to help her.

                    Not far from here a wealthy man
Farms an estate worth many talents. This man's son,
A town-bred youth, happened to come here with a friend
Hunting. He saw Cnemon's daughter. I made him fall
Madly in love. So that's the outline of the plot;
The details you can hear if you choose – and please do
   choose!
I think I see him coming, this lover – and his friend,
Both deep in conversation about this very thing.

          [*Exit* PAN. *Enter* SOSTRATOS *and* CHAEREAS.]

CHAEREAS: What was it you said, Sostratos? You saw a girl,
   A free-born girl here, bringing garlands for the Nymphs,
   And you fell in love at once?

SOSTRATOS: At once.

CHAEREAS: Fast work. Surely
   You'd made your mind up, when you first set out from
      home,
   To fall in love with someone?

SOSTRATOS: You laugh, Chaereas;
   But I'm in a bad way.

CHAEREAS: I believe you.

SOSTRATOS: And that's why
   I've brought you here to help me. You're my friend, I'm
      sure;

68

And you always know what to do.

CHAEREAS: In such matters, Sostratos,
This is the way I go to work. Say, one of my friends
Is keen on a girl, asks me to help. If she's one of that sort,
I act in a flash – I simply allow no argument;
I get drunk, burn her door down, swoop and carry her off.
Before I even ask who she is, she must be had.
The longer he waits, you see, the more he falls in love;
While if he enjoys her soon he soon gets over it.
But if it's marriage he talks of, with a free-born girl,
I take a different line; enquire about her family,
Her life, the sort of girl she is; for in this case
I leave my friend a souvenir for the rest of his life
Of my own efficiency in these matters.

SOSTRATOS: Excellent –
[aside] But not exactly what I wanted.

CHAEREAS: Now I must hear
The whole story.

SOSTRATOS: You know Pyrrhias, the boy who hunts
with us?

CHAEREAS: Yes.

SOSTRATOS: Well, early this morning I sent him off with a
message.

CHAEREAS: A message – yes, who for?

SOSTRATOS: I told him to see her father,
Or whatever man's in charge of the house –

CHAEREAS: Oh, Heracles!
You didn't do *that*?

SOSTRATOS: It was a mistake. It's hardly the thing
To send a *slave* on such a business. When you're in love
It isn't easy to know what's best. I wonder, now,
What can have kept Pyrrhias all this time. I told him
To find out how the land lay there, and come straight
back.

        [*Enter* PYRRHIAS, *running and breathless.*]

PYRRHIAS: Look out! Get away quick, everyone clear out!
   He's mad,
  There's a madman after me.

SOSTRATOS: What's all this?

PYRRHIAS: Get out of his way!

SOSTRATOS: Whose way?

PYRRHIAS: I'm being pelted with sods and rocks. I'm
   wrecked.

SOSTRATOS: Who's pelting you? – Here, where are you off to?
        [SOSTRATOS *seizes* PYRRHIAS, *who thus has time to*
        look round and see that he is not being pursued.]

PYRRHIAS: Perhaps he isn't
  Chasing me any longer.

SOSTRATOS: He isn't.

PYRRHIAS [*mopping his brow*]:   I thought he was.

SOSTRATOS: What *are* you talking about?

PYRRHIAS [*nervously*]:   Look here, now – let's get away.

SOSTRATOS: Where to?

PYRRHIAS: Away from that door, as far as possible.
  He's a son of mischief, the devil's in him, he's lunatic –
  The man who lives there, in that house you sent me to.
  The brute! O gods, my toes! I've pretty near broken them
   all
  On these rocks.

SOSTRATOS: Chaereas, he must have been rude to the man.

PYRRHIAS: I'm sure he's coming back here to set on me again.
  By Zeus, I tell you, Sostratos, we'll all be murdered.

SOSTRATOS: You won't be murdered. Now just tell me
   carefully
  Exactly what you said when you spoke to him.

PYRRHIAS: I can't.
  I'm shaking, and I'm out of breath.

SOSTRATOS [*getting hold of him*]:   You'll tell me now.

PYRRHIAS: Well, first I knocked at the door, and said I
   wished to see

The master. A wretched hag came out, and stood over there,
Where I was talking just now, and pointed him out to me
Up on that hillside, prowling round his blasted pear-trees
Collecting wood enough for a gallows made to measure.

SOSTRATOS: How terrifying! Go on, go on.

PYRRHIAS: Well, then I went
Into the field and walked towards him. And I thought
I'd show him I was a really friendly, capable sort
Of chap; so I called out to him – still quite a long way off –
'I've come to see you on urgent business, sir,' I said,
'Of moment to yourself, sir,' I said. 'Damn you,' says he,
'Who told you to walk into my field?' With that he picks
    up
A lump of turf and slings it slap into my face.

CHAEREAS: Hell! To the crows with him!

PYRRHIAS: And as I blinked, and yelled
'Poseidon drown you!' he picked up a stick this time, and
    beat me
With it, and bellowed, 'What business have you got with
    me?'
At the top of his voice, and, 'Don't you know the public
    road?'

CHAEREAS [to Sostratos]: This farmer friend of yours is a
    plain lunatic.

PYRRHIAS: In the finish, I ran. He chased me best part of two
    miles,
Right round the hill, then down here through the thorn-
    bushes,
Pelting me first with sods and stones, then with his pears
When he hadn't anything else. He's a proper old savage,
A holy terror. Come away, plea . . . se!

SOSTRATOS: I'm not afraid of him.

PYRRHIAS: You don't know what a beast he is. He'll eat us
    raw.

CHAEREAS: Perhaps he's feeling a bit upset today. I think

You might do well to put off meeting him, Sostratos.
There's always a right time for everything; and that's
A good practical rule, you take my word for it.

PYRRHIAS [*fervently*]: You're so right.

CHAEREAS: Penniless peasants are almost all like that –
Vicious tempered; he's not the only one. Tomorrow,
First thing, I'll come here alone, now that I know the house,
And talk to him. Now I'm off home; you go home, too,
And wait a bit, see? Everything's going to be all right.

     [*Exit* CHAEREAS.]

PYRRHIAS: Yes, let's go home.

SOSTRATOS: Ha! Chaereas jumped at the excuse.
It was obvious he disliked coming here with me,
And disapproved my plan to marry. As for you, Pyrrhias,
You wretch, may all the gods blast you as you deserve!

PYRRHIAS: What, *me*? What have *I* done, Sostratos? Eh?
    What have I done?
I didn't do any damage in the man's field, or steal –
Not a single thing.

SOSTRATOS: No? So the man was beating you
For doing nothing?

PYRRHIAS: Look! He's coming! That's the man!
I'm going, I am, sir! You talk to him yourself.

     [*Exit* PYRRHIAS.]

SOSTRATOS: Oh, but I can't. I never make a good impression
When I start talking. What do you *say* to a man like this?
He certainly looks anything but kind. By Zeus,
What a rage he's in! Here, I'll stand back from the door a
    bit –
That's better. Why, as he walks he's mumbling to himself.
He doesn't look sane to me. Apollo and all the gods!
I'm frightened – that's the truth, I may as well confess it.

     [*Enter* CNEMON.]

CNEMON: Now Perseus was a famous man. What luck he had!
First, he had wings – could fly about in the air. That meant

He never had to meet a soul that walks on earth.
Second, he had an invaluable possession, with which
He could turn everyone who annoyed him into stone.
If only I had that power now! There'd be nothing
More plentiful anywhere than fine stone statues.
As it is – by Asclepios, life grows impossible.
People come trespassing on my ground and chat to me.
I've taken to spending my days on the public highway,
   have I?
Why, I don't even *work* this bit of land any more,
I've given it up, to avoid the people who pass by;
And now – they hunt me up to the hill-tops. Curse them all,
There are too many *people*! – Oh, for pity's sake, there's
   another,
Standing at my front door!

SOSTRATOS: Is he going to hit me now?

CNEMON: Where can one get away from *people*? Even if a man
   Wanted to hang himself he couldn't do it in private.

SOSTRATOS: It's me he's angry with. – Excuse me, sir, I'm
   waiting
For someone here; I've made an appointment.

CNEMON [*choking with rage*]:   Didn't I say so?
   Do you take this for a public square or a market-place?
      [*He advances on* SOSTRATOS, *who retreats.*]
   Go on, then! If there's anyone you want to see,
   Come to my door – why not? Do all your business here!
   While you're about it, bring your favourite arm-chair!
   Build a committee-room, just here at my front door!
      [*He leaves* SOSTRATOS *and turns back to his house.*]
   Sheer, shouting rudeness – that's the trouble nowadays.
      [*Exit* CNEMON *to his house.* PYRRHIAS *creeps back,
      but keeps out of Sostratos' way.*]

SOSTRATOS: It seems I've taken on no ordinary job;
   This plainly calls for special measures. Should I go
   And fetch my father's slave Getas? By God, I will.

There's a spark about him; and he's seen a lot of the world.
Let the old man rave – Getas will be a match for him.
I don't believe in wasting time; a lot can happen
In one day. – Why, here's someone coming out of his house.
[*Enter* MYRRHINE *from Cnemon's house.*]

MYRRHINE: Oh, what shall I do now? Isn't that just my luck?
Nurse dropped the bucket down the well!

SOSTRATOS: O Father Zeus!
Saviour Apollo, and Heavenly Twins! What loveliness!
She's ravishing!

MYRRHINE: Father told us when he left the house
To get hot water ready.

SOSTRATOS [*appealing to audience*]: Athenians! Did you
    ever . . . ?

MYRRHINE: If he finds out, he'll beat her terribly. Oh, dear!
By the two goddesses, there's not a moment to lose –
    [*She turns towards the shrine, hesitating.*]
Dear Nymphs, I'll have to take some water from your spring.
    [*She sees Sostratos.*]
There's someone in there making an offering. I daren't
Disturb him.

SOSTRATOS: Please, give *me* your jug; I'll dip it in
And bring it to you.

MYRRHINE [*handing him the jug*]: Will you? Very well, please
    do.

SOSTRATOS [*aside*]: What charm, what breeding! – and a
    country girl!

MYRRHINE [*turning suddenly round*]:   Oh, gods!
What sound was that? Is it father coming? How terrible!
He'll beat me if he finds me here.
        [*The door of the house on the left opens and* DAOS *comes
        out.* MYRRHINE, *relieved, turns to the shrine to look
        for Sostratos.*]

DAOS [*speaking back into the house, addressing Gorgias' mother
    inside*]:   Now look: I know

That you're my mistress; but I've stayed in long enough
Doing chores for you, while your son Gorgias is out
In the field digging, single-handed. I'm going to help him.
        [*He slams the door.*]
Oh, hateful, damnable Poverty, why did we get
So large a share of you? Why have you come to stay
So many years in our house, a guest who never leaves?
SOSTRATOS [*to Myrrhine*]: Here's your jug. Come nearer,
    take it.
        [MYRRHINE *takes it and goes towards her door.*]
DAOS [*looking from one to the other*]: What's *he* doing there?
SOSTRATOS [*to Myrrhine*]: Good-bye now, and attend to your
    father.
        [*Exit* MYRRHINE.]
                              Oh, she's gone,
And I'm in misery.
        [PYRRHIAS *comes forward.*]
PYRRHIAS: Now stop moaning, Sostratos.
SOSTRATOS: Oh, *you*'ve come back.
PYRRHIAS: Everything'll turn out all right.
SOSTRATOS: Turn out all right? How?
PYRRHIAS: Never worry. Simply do
What you were going to do: find Getas, and explain
The whole thing to him clearly; and then come back
    here.
        [*Exeunt* SOSTRATOS *and* PYRRHIAS *together.*]
DAOS: Now, what the mischief? I don't like the look of this.
A young man making up to Myrrhine? Most improper.
Cnemon, may the gods punish you for the fool you are!
This innocent girl – instead of keeping guard on her,
You leave her alone out here, with no one else about.
This fellow, I'll bet, as soon as he heard the coast was clear,
Blessed his good luck, and flew straight to her. Well, I'd best
Tell Gorgias immediately what's going on;
Then we can both keep a more careful eye on her.

I think I'll go and talk to him now.

    [*Voices are heard approaching, talking and singing.*]

                        There are people coming,

With offerings for Pan. They've had a drop to drink;

This is no time to get involved with *them*. I'm off.

    [*Exit* DAOS.]

FIRST CHORAL INTERLUDE

SCENE TWO

GORGIAS *and* DAOS *come from the field.*

GORGIAS: And you mean to say you dealt with such a situation
In this off-handed, feeble manner?

DAOS: What do you mean?

GORGIAS: I mean, by Zeus, when you saw this fellow go up
to her,
You ought to have thrown him out on the spot, whoever
he is,
And warned him not to let anyone catch him at it again;
Not stand aside as if it were no concern of yours.
You've duties to our family, Daos, that you can't shirk.
Myrrhine's still my sister, and I'm concerned for her.
I know her father wants to have nothing to do with us;
But why should we copy his ill nature? If Myrrhine finds
Herself in trouble, *I*'m going to be blamed as well.
Neighbours don't know whose fault it is; they see what's
happened
To the girl, and nothing else.

DAOS: I tell you, Gorgias,
The old man frightens me. The moment he sees me coming
Anywhere near his door, he shouts, 'I'll have you whipped!'

GORGIAS: Yes, you'll find him an awkward customer to argue
with.
Nobody knows how to *compel* him to reform;
Nobody can give him advice or win him over.
He's got the law on his side – so he can't be compelled;
And he's got a devil in him – so he won't be advised.

DAOS: But soft – what have we here?[1] We're in the nick of
time –
I said he'd soon be back.

---

1. This line in Greek has a distinctly conventional rhythm, suggesting the
style of tragedy.

GORGIAS: Is that him in the fancy cloak?

DAOS: That's him.

GORGIAS: He's up to no good, you can tell that at
one glance.

[*Enter* SOSTRATOS *with* PYRRHIAS.]

SOSTRATOS: I couldn't get hold of Getas, he was out. My
mother
Is going to hold a sacrifice to some god or other
And she's asked her friends. Oh, yes, she does that every day –
Tours the whole district celebrating sacrifices;
And she's sent Getas out to hire a cook. So I
Said, 'To hell with the sacrifice,' and came back here.
I've had enough of this roundabout way of doing things;
I'll talk to the man myself. I'll knock at his door, before
I've time to consider it further.

GORGIAS: Would you mind, young man,
Listening a moment to something important I have to say?

SOSTRATOS: Certainly. What is it?

GORGIAS: I believe that everyone,
Rich or poor, comes to a point where his luck will end,
And a change set in. The successful man, I believe, will find
His affairs continue to prosper just so long as he
Can carry his luck without doing wrong to anyone.
But, once his good luck leads him to do wrong, why then
He'll meet a change for the worse. And so with poor men
too:
If they are not led by poverty into wrong-doing,
But bear their bad luck bravely, they may hope, with time,
To come to the end of trouble and see happier days.
You take my meaning, then? Don't, just because you're rich,
Rely too much on that; and don't look down on us
Because we're poor. Let people see, by what you do,
That you deserve to keep your good luck all your life.

SOSTRATOS: And what crime do you imagine I'm committing
now?

78

GORGIAS: I'd say you'd set your mind on doing a rotten thing:
  You want to tempt a free-born girl to her disgrace,
  Watching your chance to do a thing that you'd deserve
  To die for ten times over.

SOSTRATOS: Well, I'm ... !

GORGIAS: It's not fair,
  When *you*'ve got leisure, and *we* haven't, you should use it
  To injure us. When a poor man feels an injury,
  Remember this, there's no one can turn nastier.
  First he feels sorry for himself; but soon he takes
  The wrong he's suffered for insult more than injury.

SOSTRATOS: Now, lad, as you hope for luck, just listen –

PYRRHIAS: Bravo, master!

SOSTRATOS: I tell you I wish you every kind of luck. You've
    had
  Your say; now let *me* talk a little. I saw a girl
  Who lives here. I'm in love with her. So, if *this* is
  The injury you speak of, I suppose I'm guilty.
  What should I say? I've come here now not to meet *her*,
  But to see her father. I'm a free man, pretty well off;
  But I'm ready to take her without a dowry, and give my
    oath
  To love her faithfully. If I came here to do any wrong,
  Or scheming anything underhand against any of you,
  May this god Pan, and all the Nymphs as well, my friend,
  Strike me helpless, here and now in front of your house.
  I tell you it upsets me deeply that you should think
  I was that sort of fellow.

GORGIAS: If I spoke too strongly,
  Please don't let it upset you any more. You have
  Convinced me I was wrong; what's more, you can count
    on me
  As a friend – and when I say that, bless you, I have the right:
  I'm Myrrhine's half-brother; and from now on, by Zeus,
  I can be of help to you.

SOSTRATOS: What sort of help?

GORGIAS: Listen –
  I see you're a good-hearted fellow. I don't want
  To disappoint you with empty promises; instead,
  I'll tell you plainly how things are. Myrrhine's father –
  There's never been another like him, past or present.

SOSTRATOS: You mean old Sour-guts? Yes, I've had a taste
    of him.

GORGIAS: It's a very difficult situation. He owns this farm,
  Which is worth perhaps two talents; and year in year out
  He works the place alone – won't have a soul to help.
  He keeps not a single man in the house; he won't employ
  A local farm-hand; even neighbours can't get near;
  He does the lot himself. His greatest pleasure is
  To see no one at all. Most of the time he keeps
  His daughter by him as he works. He talks to her,
  And it's hard work to make him talk to anyone else.
  She shall marry, he says, when he finds a husband for her
    who's
  Another one like himself.

SOSTRATOS: Well, that means never.

GORGIAS: My friend,
  Don't take the job on; you'll get nowhere. He's *our* burden,
  As luck would have it – we're his family.

SOSTRATOS: Good gods!
  Lad, have you never been in love?

GORGIAS: No, friend, I can't
  Afford it.

SOSTRATOS: Why? What stops you?

GORGIAS: Simple arithmetic.
  Adding up bad luck leaves no time for falling in love.

SOSTRATOS: So I gather: you talk like a man who knows
    nothing about it.
  You say, 'Give it up' – but I no longer have any choice:
  The god has chosen for me. [*He points to the statue of* PAN.]

GORGIAS: Well, you do *us* no harm;
  You simply go through misery and get nothing for it.
SOSTRATOS: What if I win the girl?
GORGIAS: You won't win her. – Unless,
  Perhaps – I'm going up to the hill – you could come too
  And stand beside me; *he* works the next field to ours.
SOSTRATOS: How would that help?
GORGIAS: I'll drop a casual word to him
  About his daughter getting married. That's a thing
  I'd be very glad to see –
DAOS: You try: he'll start a war
  Straight off on everyone, hurling insults at the way
  His neighbours live. [*To Sostratos*] And if he sees *you* idling
    there
  Keeping your hands clean, he'll not stand the sight of you.
SOSTRATOS: Is he there now?
GORGIAS: Not now, but in a little while
  He'll go out by his usual way.
SOSTRATOS: Do you say he takes
  Myrrhine with him? My dear man, for the chance of that
  I'll gladly come as you suggest. I beg you, now,
  Throw all your weight in on my side.
DAOS [*sourly*]:   Just how do you mean?
SOSTRATOS: How? [*To Gorgias*] Come on, let's be going as
    you said.
DAOS: Now look:
  We're going to work. Are you going to stand next to us
  Wearing that fancy cloak?
SOSTRATOS: Why not?
DAOS: He'll pick up clods
  And throw them at you, and call you a lazy pest. You've got
  To dig along with us. If he saw you doing that
  Who knows but he might condescend to hear a word
  Even from you, if he thought you were a poor farm-hand
  Earning your living.

SOSTRATOS: I'll do anything you say. Lead on.

GORGIAS [*aside to Daos*]: Why are you forcing him to go through agony?

DAOS [*aside to Gorgias*]: I tell you what: we'll do the heaviest day's work

You ever saw, and make the young fool rupture himself.

That'll stop him coming around and getting in our way.

SOSTRATOS: Fetch me a hoe.[1]

DAOS: You'd better take mine. I'll spend the time

Mending the wall – that's got to be done too.

SOSTRATOS: Give it me.

DAOS [*aside to Sostratos*]: You've saved my life. [*To Gorgias*]

I'm going down to the wall, master;

You'll find me there.

[*Exit* DAOS.]

SOSTRATOS: My mind's made up: either I die

Now, or I win Myrrhine and live.

GORGIAS: If what you say

Is what you really mean, why then I wish you luck.

SOSTRATOS: By the holy gods! Every discouragement *you* think

Will stop me, doubles my resolution to go on.

[*Exit* GORGIAS.]

– She's a girl who wasn't brought up in a crowd of women;

She knows nothing of the sins and sorrows of this life,

Was never frightened by any aunt or nurse; she has lived

With this old father of hers – he's a bit rough, but gives her

A free-born home, and hates bad characters. Well, then,

Surely to win this girl would be a wonderful thing? . . .

This hoe weighs half a ton, it'll kill me. All the same

No weakening now! I've begun – I must go through with it.

[*Exit* SOSTRATOS *following Gorgias to the field.*

SICON *the cook enters dragging a sheep by a rope.*]

1. This hoe was a two-pronged tool apparently used for a variety of purposes – as will appear later.

SICON: This ruddy sheep's enough to break your ruddy heart.
  Ah, go to hell! If I pick it up and carry it,
  It gets its teeth on the branch of a tree and chews the leaves
  And tears the branch off. Same if I put it down on the
    ground,
  It won't get moving. Talk about slaughter! – it's not the
    sheep,
  It's me, the cook, gets slaughtered, dragging this battleship.
  Well, gods above be praised, here's the shrine of the
    Nymphs,
  Where the banquet is. My greetings to great Pan!

      [GETAS *appears from the direction of the town, carrying*
      a bundle of cushions.]

                                          Here, Getas!
  What sort of time is this to arrive?
GETAS: Those damned women –
  Look at the load they strapped on me: enough to break
  Four donkeys.
SICON: Seems there must be a lot of people coming –
  That's an enormous bundle of cushions you've got there.
GETAS: Cushions? What haven't I got?
SICON: Pile them up here.
GETAS: There. Whew!
  You know that Pan at Paeania, fifteen miles away?
  She's only got to dream about him – whhtt!! – we're off –
  You mark my word – we've got to hold a sacrifice.
SICON: What? *Who's* been dreaming?
GETAS: Oh, you make me tired.
SICON: Come on,
  Tell me, who was dreaming?
GETAS: My mistress.
SICON: Well, what was the dream?
GETAS: You'll drive me up the wall. She dreamt that Pan –
SICON: Which Pan?
  This one?

GETAS: Yes, him.

SICON: Well, what did he do?

GETAS: Why, he got hold
Of Sostratos my master –

SICON: Oh, such a nice young man!

GETAS: – and put chains on his ankles ——

SICON: Apollo! You don't say!

GETAS: Then gave him a leather jacket and a hoe, and told him
To get into that next field and start digging.

SICON: No!!

GETAS: Why, yes! That's what the sacrifice is for, to turn
This 'dreadful portent' into something good.

SICON: I see.
Well, now, pick all those up again and take 'em in;
We'd better rig up the couches, put the place to rights.
Once they get here, I don't want nothing unfortunate
To hold up the sacrifice; everything must go along smooth.
And look here – brighten your face up, can't you, misery?
You'll get your share – I'll stuff you right and proper today.

GETAS: Didn't I always say you was a wonderful man,
And a wonderful cook too? [*Aside*] I don't trust you, all the
same.

[*They both go into the shrine.*]

SECOND CHORAL INTERLUDE

SCENE THREE

CNEMON *comes out, turning to speak to Simice inside.*

CNEMON: Simice, lock the door; and don't you open it
  To anyone till I come back; and I reckon *that*
  Won't be till after dark.
        [*He is going off to his field when he sees Sostratos' mother
        and sister arriving with friends and some slaves. He watches
        them.*]
MOTHER [*to her daughter*]: Come on, you, Plangon, hurry.
  We ought to have got the sacrifice over by now.
CNEMON: Now what on earth's going on here, blast it?
    People again!
  To the crows with them all!
MOTHER: Now, Parthenis, play the Hymn to Pan.
  They say you shouldn't come near Pan without a tune.
        [*The girl plays.*]
A GUEST: Well, so you've all arrived at last. By Heracles,
  We were getting bored; we've sat about waiting here for
    hours.
MOTHER: Is everything ready for us?
GETAS: Ready? I should say it is.
  That sheep's pretty near died of old age; can't wait for you,
  Poor beast.
MOTHER: Well, come in, everyone; get the baskets ready,
  The holy water, the cakes, the incense!
        [CNEMON *grunts contemptuously.*]
GETAS [*to Cnemon*]:   Well, old man,
  Have you been struck by lightning? What are you gawp-
    ing at?
        [*They all crowd into the shrine, leaving* CNEMON
        alone.]
CNEMON: You trash! Damn you to blazes! Can't get on
  with my work.

How can I leave the house, with all that crowd about?
Having this shrine of the Nymphs next door is such a
    plague,
I reckon there's only one thing for it: pull down my house
And build another somewhere else. Look at these thieves
At their sacrifice! They bring in beds, wine by the cask –
For their own pleasure, not the gods'. A bit of incense
Makes a pious gift, or a cake; you offer it in one piece
On the altar, and it all goes to the god. Those gentry there
Offer the gods the inedible scraps – the stump of the tail
And the gall-bladder – and guzzle down all the rest
    themselves.
– You, Simice! Here, open the door again; be quick.
I reckon I'd best keep eye on everything here at home.

> [CNEMON *goes into his house.* GETAS *comes out of the
> shrine, holding a slave-girl by the arm.*]

GETAS: You tell me you've forgotten the kettle, eh? You're
    drunk,
All of you, snoring drunk. *Now* what are we going to do?
> [*The girl runs in.*]
It seems I'll have to bother the god Pan's next-door
    neighbours.
> [*He knocks at Cnemon's door.*]
Hullo, there! – Of all the measly sluts I ever met –
Gods! this lot takes the prize. [*He knocks again.*] Hullo,
    there! – The only thing
They know all about is bed-wrestling. – Anyone in?
– *And* how to blackmail anyone who catches 'em at it.
> [*He continues knocking.*]
Hullo, hullo! – Now what the hell's wrong here? – Hullo!
Isn't there a single slave about? – Ah, that's better;
Someone seems to be coming.
> [CNEMON *opens the door.*]
CNEMON: How dare you touch my door, you cur? How
    dare you, eh?

GETAS: Now, now, don't bite me, there's a good chap.

CNEMON: I will, by God,
   I'll eat you alive.

GETAS: Now, don't, please.

CNEMON: You can't come to *me*
   For money, you damned offal, I don't owe you any.

GETAS: Money nothing – I haven't come to collect a debt;
   Nor have I brought the bailiffs along. I want to borrow
   A kettle.

CNEMON: A kettle?

GETAS: A kettle.

CNEMON: Do you imagine *I*
   Go in for all this nonsense, sacrificing bulls?

GETAS [*aside*]: *You* wouldn't sacrifice a winkle! – *Good*
      afternoon!
   My compliments! The women told me just to knock
   And ask. So I did. It doesn't matter. I'll go back
   And tell them. – Holy gods! Have you ever seen an adder
   With grey hair? Well, here's one.
         [*Exit* GETAS *to the shrine.*]

CNEMON: These brutes, these savages!
   They walk right up and knock at your door like an old
      friend.
   Just let me catch any of you coming to my door again!
   If I don't make him a warning to the whole neighbourhood
   You can call me Simple Simon. That type who came just
      now –
   Whoever he is – how *he* got away with it I don't know.
         [CNEMON *goes back into his house. Enter* SICON *from the
         shrine followed by* GETAS.]

SICON: Damn it, he was telling you what he thought of you.
      Then I'll bet
   You asked him like a stinker. Some people never learn
   To manage a thing like that. Now, *I*'ve mastered the art.
   I go and cook for thousands of people up in town;

I pester their neighbours, borrowing saucepans right and
   left.
If you want anything, you've got to butter 'em up.
   Suppose
An old man answers the door, I say, 'How are you, Dad?'
Or, 'Grandad'; if it's a hag, I call her Ma; or if
She's middle-aged, 'Priestess'; a kitchen-maid I call
   housekeeper.
But you – you're only fit for the rope: you're ignorant.
GETAS: All right. [*He knocks.*] Hullo there, hullo hullo hullo!
   It's me.
Come out here, Dad, I've knocked five times.
CNEMON [*opening the door*]:   What, you again?
GETAS [*dodging behind Sicon*]: Same thing again.
CNEMON: I believe you're plaguing me on purpose.
   Didn't I tell you not to come near my door? Here, Simice!
   Hand me that strap.
          [GETAS *side-steps, and* CNEMON *beats* SICON.]
SICON: Oh, no! no! Stop!
GETAS [*laughing*]:   Let him go, old boy!
SICON: Let go, for God's sake!
CNEMON: Just you come here again!
SICON: Poseidon
   Drown you!
CNEMON: Are you still talking?
SICON [*with an effort, mildly*]:   Listen, I came to ask you
   For a large stew-pot.
CNEMON: I haven't got a large stew-pot;
   Nor a chopper either; nor salt, vinegar, or anything else.
   I've told everyone round here it's absolutely forbidden
   To come to my door.
SICON: Not me, you haven't.
CNEMON: I'm telling you now.
SICON [*aside*]: You are, plague rot you. [*To Cnemon*] Please,
   now, listen: wouldn't you just

Inform me where I might get one?

CNEMON: Didn't you hear what I said?
Are you still nattering at me?

SICON: Well, good afternoon.

CNEMON: I can do without 'Good afternoon' from any of
you.

SICON: All right, then, do without it.

CNEMON: Intolerable pests!

[*He goes in, slamming his door.*]

SICON: Whew! Well, he's forked me over properly.

GETAS: See what it is
To ask for things politely. Makes a world of difference.

SICON: Should we knock at another door? If all the people
here
Out clubs as quick as *he* does, I'm going to find things
difficult.
Perhaps I'd best *roast* all the meat. Anyway, I've got
A frying-pan of sorts. Hell to this Phyle crowd!
I'll just use what I've got.

[*Exeunt* SICON *and* GETAS *to the shrine. Enter*
SOSTRATOS *limping and covered with dirt and sweat.*]

SOSTRATOS: If anyone's running short of trouble, just let
him
Come out to Phyle hunting. Oh, my lumbar joints!
They're agony! Oh, my back! My neck! My whole body!
I was a young man, I thought. I threw myself at the work
As soon as I got there, swinging my hoe high in the air
Like any labourer trenching a good crop; I worked –
I gave it all I'd got – for a little while. And then
I began looking around, to see when the old man
Would come with his daughter. And, by Zeus, I took the
chance
To rub the small of my back – without their seeing at first.
As time dragged on and on, I'd bend right over back-
wards –

I was gradually going as stiff as a wooden post.
Nobody came. The sun blazed down. And Gorgias
Watched me out of the corner of his eye, as I gingerly
Straightened up, then over again – up and down
Like a pump-handle. 'Seems to me, young man,' he says,
'Cnemon won't come now.' 'Right,' I said; 'then what do
    we do?'
'Leave it for now,' he said; 'we'll wait for him tomor-
    row.'
Then Daos came to take my place at digging. So –
End of Scene One. Well, here I am – though God knows
    why.
There's something about this business draws me to the
    place.

> [*Enter* GETAS. *He does not at first see Sostratos; he is
> talking to one of the slaves inside the shrine.*]

GETAS: Now what the – here, you! Do you think I've got
    ten pairs of hands?
I make the fire up for you, wash things, carry things,
Cut up the liver, knead the bread, shift everything round,
Keep an eye on the cook. On top of all that I'm blind with
    smoke.
In this feast I reckon I've got the donkey's share.
SOSTRATOS: Getas!
    Hullo there!
GETAS [*rubbing his eyes*]: Who's that?
SOSTRATOS: Me.
GETAS [*pretending not to recognize him*]:   You? Who?
SOSTRATOS: Can't you see me?
GETAS: Why,
    Young master!
SOSTRATOS: Tell me, what are you all doing here?
GETAS: Doing?
    We've just had a sacrifice. Now we're getting a meal
    ready –

90

For *you*.

SOSTRATOS: Mother here?

GETAS: Long ago.

SOSTRATOS: Father?

GETAS: We're expecting him.

SOSTRATOS: Getas, come over here a moment. In one way
This feast comes in the nick of time. I'm going now
Straight away to find this Gorgias and ask him along,
And his servant too. Once they've shared in our sacrifice,
From then on they're my allies – they'll be much more
use
To me in winning Myrrhine.

GETAS: Here, what's this? You'd like
To go and fetch some extra people in to lunch?
Why not? Oh, don't mind *me*. Just make your number
up
To a round three thousand. *I'll* never get so much as a
bite –
Why should I? I've known that all along. Make it a mass
Meeting. You've sacrificed a splendid animal,
Well worth looking at. But what will our ladies have to
say?
They're very particular. What do you think *they'd* give
away
To anyone? Not a pinch of kitchen salt.

SOSTRATOS: Getas,
Don't worry. Today is going to be a great day. I feel it
In my prophetic soul, O Pan! – You see, I always
Say a prayer to you every time I pass your shrine. –
I'll give you a fair deal, Getas.

[SOSTRATOS *goes to fetch Gorgias and Daos.* SIMICE
comes out of Cnemon's house.]

SIMICE: Oh, did anyone ever
Have such bad luck? Oh dear, oh dear!

GETAS: Oh, go to hell!

Who's this? Some slut of the old man's.

SIMICE: What'll he do to me?
That bucket that fell down the well – I thought I'd try
To get it out myself, if I could, without saying
Anything to the master. So I got the hoe, to hook
The bucket up with, and let it down on a piece of cord.
Oh dear, the cord was weak and rotten, and it snapped
Straight off.

GETAS: Good work!

SIMICE: So now I've dropped the hoe down there
To join the bucket. Oh dear!

GETAS: All you've got to do now
Is chuck yourself down.

SIMICE: Well, the master, as luck would have it,
Was going to shift a heap of muck out of the yard;
So now he's running in circles, shouting himself hoarse,
Looking for his hoe.

GETAS: That's him coming out. Run for it, now,
You old so-and-so, run! He'll kill you! – Wait; better
stand your ground.

CNEMON [*bursting out*]: Where is she, the old thief?

SIMICE: I didn't mean to, master;
I dropped it down by accident.

CNEMON: Get back indoors.

SIMICE: Now what are you going to do to me?

CNEMON: I'm going to let
You down on a cord.

SIMICE: No, no, no, please!

CNEMON: What's more, by God,
I'm going to use the same cord *you* used for my hoe.
And if it's rotten right through, so much the better.

SIMICE: Help!
I'll call the neighbours, I'll shout for Daos.

CNEMON: Shout for Daos,
Will you, as well as ruin me, you old heathen? Here,

What did I say? Get moving, take your old bones indoors.

    [SIMICE *goes in.*]

CNEMON: What a curse, living alone! – All right, then, *I*'ll go
down

As soon as the next man. There's no other way.

GETAS: Oh, sir,

I should be very happy to provide a rope.

CNEMON: You dare provide me anything. I hope the gods
Make catsmeat of you.

    [CNEMON *goes indoors.*]

GETAS: Serve me right, too, if they did.

Well, Jack's back in his box. Poor devil, what a life!

Now, there's pure Attic peasant for you, if you like:

He fights the stones, for growing nothing but thyme and
sage,

And gets no good from it; his only crop is misery.

    [*Enter* SOSTRATOS *with* GORGIAS *and* DAOS.]

Why, here comes my young master bringing his two
guests.

[*With disgust*] Oh! They're just village farm-hands. How
unsuitable!

Well! Why does he bring *them* here *now*? And where on
earth

Can he have met them?

SOSTRATOS [*to Gorgias*]: Of course you'll come, I insist.

We've plenty of everything.

Heracles! What do you call a man who refuses flat

To come to a feast with his friend after a sacrifice?

Listen, this is the exact truth: I am your friend,

And have been since before I first set eyes on you.

Now, take these hoes and things indoors and then come
back.

GORGIAS: Oh, but I couldn't. Leave my mother alone at
home?

SOSTRATOS: Well, do whatever you need to do for her;
then come.
I'll meet you here in a minute.

> [*Exit* SOSTRATOS *to the shrine,* GORGIAS *to his
> house.*]

THIRD CHORAL INTERLUDE

SCENE FOUR

SICON *is busy.* SIMICE *runs out of Cnemon's house.*

SIMICE: Help, help! Oh dear, oh dear! Oh gracious me!
　　Help, help!
SICON: For Heracles' sake, and all the gods and goddesses!
　　Can't you leave us to offer our holy wine in peace?
　　All this swearing, beating, screaming – what a house!
SIMICE: My master's down the well!
SICON [*in a dead-pan voice*]: Oh; why?
SIMICE: 　　　　　　　　　Why? He was climbing
　　Down to fetch out the hoe and the bucket; and he slipped
　　Just at the top, and down he went.
SICON [*with delight*]: 　　　　　Here – you don't mean
　　Old Belly-Ache? Not him?
SIMICE: 　　　　　　Yes, him.
SICON: 　　　　　　　　You holy gods!
　　He never did a better thing. My dear old hag,
　　It's up to you now.
SIMICE: 　　　What do you mean?
SICON: 　　　　　　　　　Just run and find
　　A millstone, or a horse-trough – something nice and heavy,
　　And tip it down on top of him.
SIMICE: 　　　　　Oh, please, please, my friend,
　　Climb down.
SICON: 　　What, *me*? Poseidon! Like the fool in the
　　　proverb,
　　Fight with a mad dog down a well? Not on your life!
SIMICE: Gorgias! Gorgias! Wherever are you?
　　　　[*Enter* GORGIAS *from his house.*]
GORGIAS: 　　　　　　　　Where am I?
　　Why, what's the matter, Simice?
SIMICE: 　　　　　　Haven't I told you once?

95

My master's down the well.

[SOSTRATOS *appears at the entrance of the shrine.*]

GORGIAS: Sostratos, come out here.

SOSTRATOS: Right: into his house, then; lead the way. Go on, hurry.

[*Exeunt both into Cnemon's house.*]

SICON: Well!! Is there a god in heaven! For Dionysos' sake!

Cnemon, you temple-robber, who won't even lend a kettle

To people who come to sacrifice, you're so damned mean –

Good: now you've fallen down your well, just drink it dry;

Then you won't even have *water* to share with anyone.

The Nymphs have punished him for me, just as he deserved.

No one ever wronged a cook and got away scot-free;

There's something sacred about our art. Now a head-waiter

You can do what you like to, and nothing to fear.

[MYRRHINE'*s voice is heard indoors.*]

MYRRHINE: Oh dear, oh dear!

He isn't dead, is he? Father darling, are you all right?

SICON: Somebody seems upset. I wonder why. I'm not

The least upset at Cnemon getting soused. What does

Disappoint me is that just when the gods are doing their best

And have brought off something most appropriate, in rush those

Two impious fools to undo it all. I'll bet you, now,

They get a rope and haul the old curmudgeon up.

Eh, gods! What sort of a sight do you think he'll be, all drenched

And shivering? A very pretty sight, you take my word –

And one, friends, that will give me pleasure. Yes, by
    Apollo!
– You ladies, pour libations for them; pray to the gods
For this old man, that he may be spared to end his days
A one-legged cripple. That's the way he'll give least
    trouble
As neighbour to the god Pan and all his worshippers.
It matters to me, in case I'm hired as cook again.

      [*Exit* SICON. *Enter* SOSTRATOS.]

SOSTRATOS [*to audience*]: Athenians! By holy Demeter and
    Asclepios,
By all the gods, I never yet in my whole life
Saw any man half-drowned at a more opportune moment.
Oh, we've been having a lovely time! Soon as we got in,
Gorgias jumped straight down the well with a rope, and
    we –
That is, Myrrhine and I – we were above, just doing
Nothing. Well, what was there to do? Except that she
Kept tearing her hair, weeping bitterly, beating her
    breast.
I stood beside her – oh, this is my golden day! –
For all the world as if I'd been her guardian,
Begging, beseeching her to stop, gazing at her –
A vision not of this world. As for the wretched old man
Sputtering away below there, I didn't give him a thought;
Except, of course, that I had to keep hauling on the rope –
And that, I tell you, went dead against the grain. In fact
I very nearly put paid to him: I kept looking
At Myrrhine, and three times or so let the rope slip.
But Gorgias, like the hero that he is, held on,
And in the end I just managed to hoist him up.
Once he was safe, I came out here; I simply couldn't
Control myself any longer – I was on the point
Of going and kissing Myrrhine, I'm so frantically
In love with her. And what I mean to do is this –

There now! I hear them at the door.

[*Enter* GORGIAS *with* CNEMON, *followed by* MYRRHINE *and* SIMICE.]

O Saviour Zeus!
What an apparition!

GORGIAS: Tell me, Cnemon, what can I do
For you?

CNEMON: I don't know. I'm in a terrible state.

GORGIAS: Cheer up.

CNEMON: It's too late to cheer up. You won't have Cnemon
on your hands
Much longer.

SIMICE: This is what comes of living all alone.

MYRRHINE: You see – you were within an inch of being
killed
Just now.

GORGIAS: You're an old man. From today on we'll need
To keep an eye on you.

CNEMON: I'm decrepit, yes, I know.
Gorgias, call your mother here as quick as you can.
[*Exit* GORGIAS.]
It seems bad luck's the only thing that can teach us sense.
Daughter, take hold of me, please; help me on to my feet.

SOSTRATOS: Oh, lucky man!

CNEMON: Why are you standing there? Can't you see I'm
ill?

SOSTRATOS: I'm waiting . . .

CNEMON: I know, that's what you said before. Clear
off!

[SOSTRATOS *retires to corner of stage.* GORGIAS *returns with* CNEMON'S WIFE.]

GORGIAS: Here she is, Cnemon, my mother.

WIFE: Oh, dear, is he badly hurt?

CNEMON: Is that my wife?

WIFE: Yes, here I am.

CNEMON: Don't chatter, then. I want to say
Several things to all of you together, while they're on my
   mind.
Listen, wife, and Myrrhine and Gorgias. I tell you this:
I'd much rather have been killed outright –
      [*They make deprecating noises.*]
                                Yes! Nor could any of you
Ever make me change my mind about it; so agree with me.
One mistake, perhaps, I *have* made – thought I could do
   everything
For myself, be independent, ask no help from anyone.
Now I've seen that life may have a swift and unexpected
   end –
Well, I know I was mistaken. Every man needs someone
   near,
Needs a friend he knows will help him. But, when I saw
   people's lives
All absorbed in making money, watched them scheme and
   calculate,
By Hephaestos, I grew bitter. Not a single man, I thought,
Ever has true kindly feeling towards another. This idea
Paralysed me. Only now has one man proved the con-
   trary –
Gorgias, whose action shows a generous and noble heart.
There I was – I even forbade him ever to come near my
   door;
Never raised a hand to help him; never even talked to him,
Never said Good morning. Yet, from mere good will, he
   saved my life.
Others would have said – and justly, 'Since you've told me
   to keep out,
Right, I'll keep out; since you've never helped me – right,
   I won't help *you*.'
Now look here, my boy; whether I die now, as I think I
   shall –

I'm in a bad way – or whether I get over it, I adopt you now

As my son. My money, and my whole estate, consider yours.

As for my daughter Myrrhine, I entrust her to you. You must find

A husband for her. I should never manage to find her one myself,

Even if I had my health – there isn't one that I should ever like.

You just let me live my own life. Take the whole place over, son.

You've got sense; and good luck to you. You're the natural guardian

For your sister. Reckon up the value of my property;

Give her one half for her dowry; take the other half yourself,

And look after me and your mother.

                                        Lay me down now, Myrrhine.

Talking more than necessary is no occupation for a man;

But there's just one thing I'd like to say to you, son, in defence

Of myself, my way of living. In a word, if everyone

Followed *my* way, did as I do, soon there'd be no courts of law,

Nor would men put men in prisons, nor fight wars; but each would have

What he needed, and be satisfied. Ah, well; people like it best,

I suppose, the way things are now; carry on, then, as you were.

One cantankerous old man will soon be well out of your way.

GORGIAS: Father, thank you for all you've said. Now the first thing we have to do,

With your help, is find a man for Myrrhine – if you agree.

CNEMON: I've told you what *I* want. Don't fuss *me* about it,
for God's sake.

GORGIAS: Here's a young man wants to meet you –

CNEMON: For the gods' sake, *no*!

GORGIAS: – to ask
You for leave to marry Myrrhine.

CNEMON: Who? – I'm finished with all that;
Can't be bothered.

GORGIAS: It's the man who helped to save your life.

CNEMON: Who's that?

GORGIAS: Here he is. Come, Sostratos.

    [SOSTRATOS *comes forward.*]

CNEMON: He's sunburnt. Is he a farmer, then?

GORGIAS: I should think so! He's not soft; he's not the sort of
man you'll find
Ambling round all day doing nothing.

CNEMON: Very well. You'll find indoors
One gold talent: that's her dowry. Give her to this man.
Arrange
For a decent, proper wedding. Carry me indoors.

GORGIAS: I will do
Everything you say. Here, Simice, take him in; look after
him.

    [SIMICE *helps* CNEMON *back into the house.*]

SOSTRATOS: Gorgias: to complete the pattern, take *my* sister
for *your* wife.

GORGIAS: Let's consider that another time, my friend.

SOSTRATOS: Why, Gorgias,
There's no obstacle; my father won't oppose me in anything.

GORGIAS: Well . . . At least I here betroth and give you,
before these witnesses,
Myrrhine; so take and keep her, brother, as your lawful
wife.

When you came to court her, you used no pretence. You
   were prepared
Honestly to do anything to win her. Though your hands
   were soft,
You took a hoe, and dug – went through it willingly. A
   thing like that
Shows what stuff a man is made of, when he can forget his
   wealth,
Take his coat off, and work side by side with a poor
   countryman.
Such a man will bear the ups and downs of life with a good
   heart.
You've shown clearly enough what sort of chap you are.
   Well, stay like this
All your life.

SOSTRATOS: I hope to be a *better* man than I am now.
   Still, self-praise is in poor taste. – Why, look! How very
   fortunate!
Here's my father.

GORGIAS [*recognizing him*]: Callippides! Is *he* your father?

SOSTRATOS: Certainly.

GORGIAS: Is he, now? He's a rich man, by Zeus; and he de-
   serves to be.
He's a first-rate farmer.

        [*Enter* CALLIPPIDES; *he does not at first see the others.*]

CALLIPPIDES: I've arrived too late, no doubt. They've all
   Long ago devoured the sheep, and vanished round the
   countryside.

GORGIAS [*aside to Sostratos*]: Why, he's starving, by Poseidon!
   Is this quite the moment to –
Talk to him?

SOSTRATOS [*aside to Gorgias*]: No; let him eat first – he'll be
   more amenable.

        [GORGIAS' MOTHER *and* MYRRHINE *retire into*
        Cnemon's house.]

CALLIPPIDES: Sostratos! Well, what's going on here? Have
  you eaten?

SOSTRATOS: Yes, father;
  But there's plenty left for you, so come on in.

CALLIPPIDES [*going towards the shrine*]:   I will indeed.

GORGIAS [*aside to Sostratos*]: Go in with him. Say what you
  have to say between the two of you.

SOSTRATOS: Will you wait for me indoors, then?

GORGIAS: Yes, yes, I'll not leave the house.

SOSTRATOS: Right you are, then. Won't take long. I'll come
  and call you very soon.

  [*Exeunt* SOSTRATOS *and* GORGIAS.]

FOURTH CHORAL INTERLUDE

CALLIPPIDES *and* SOSTRATOS *come out of the shrine.*

SOSTRATOS: Father, your attitude leaves me not quite
    satisfied;
  In fact, a little disappointed.
CALLIPPIDES: Why? Haven't I
  Agreed that you shall marry the girl you love? I mean it;
  And I insist upon it.
SOSTRATOS: *I* don't think you mean it.
CALLIPPIDES: Now by the gods I do. You're young; I see
    this marriage
  As helping you to settle down – if it is love
  That leads you to your choice.
SOSTRATOS: Well, since I'm going to marry
  Gorgias' sister, because I think him worthy of
  Our family, why do you now say you won't give *him*
  My sister in return?
CALLIPPIDES: It's a frightful suggestion!
  What? Get a daughter-in-law and a son-in-law together
  Both penniless? I've no wish to. One is quite enough.
SOSTRATOS: You talk of money: money's unpredictable.
  If you are certain money's going to stay by you
  All through your life, then guard it close, let no one else
  Touch any of it, keep control in your own hands.
  But if it all belongs to Fortune, not to you,
  Father, why should you grudge a share to anyone?
  Fortune herself may well rob you of all you have
  And give it to someone else who perhaps doesn't deserve
    it.
  So I say, as long as you possess your money, father,
  You ought to use it generously yourself, and put it
  At everyone's disposal, and make as many people

Rich as you possibly can. That's something permanent;
And when *you're* in trouble, that's where you'll find help
   in turn.
A friend for everyone to see is worth far more
Than money shut out of sight or buried down the garden.

CALLIPPIDES: Look here, my son, you know me. The
   money I've put together
I don't keep buried away for myself. Well, what do you
   think?
It all belongs to you. So, if you want to invest
In a friend for the future, use your judgement, go ahead,
And I wish you all good luck. Why moralize to me?
Go and be generous; give away, or share; I've changed
My mind, I'm with you, willingly.

SOSTRATOS: Yes? Willingly?

CALLIPPIDES: Indeed, yes; have no qualms.

SOSTRATOS: Then I'll call Gorgias.

GORGIAS [*appearing*]: I was just at the door, on the point of
   coming out,
And I heard every word you said, right from the start.
Now, Sostratos, I know you're a warm-hearted friend;
And I'm extremely fond of you. But I don't want
A style of life above my own; even if I did
Want it – by Zeus, I couldn't stand it.

SOSTRATOS: I don't see
Quite what you mean.

GORGIAS: Don't you? I'm giving you my
   sister
To be your wife. But as for *my* marrying *your* sister –
It's kind of you, but –

SOSTRATOS: Why not?

GORGIAS: Well, I don't much care
To live like a rich man on what someone else has earned.
I'd rather earn it for myself.

SOSTRATOS: Why, Gorgias,

You're talking nonsense. Do you think you're not good
    enough
To marry my sister?

GORGIAS: Yes, I think I'm good enough;
But it's not right for a man who only has a little
To take a lot.

CALLIPPIDES: By Zeus almighty, I like the tone
Of the rubbish you talk.

GORGIAS: How?

CALLIPPIDES: You're a have-not, and you mean
To appear a have-not. However, since, as you see, my
    son
Has managed to persuade me – come, use common sense.

GORGIAS: Your arguments convince me from two sides at
    once.
If a man has neither money to show nor common sense
Folk soon think there's no hope for him. – All right, I
    agree.
It only remains to make our contract formally.

       [CALLIPPIDES' WIFE *and* DAUGHTER *enter from
       the shrine.*]

CALLIPPIDES: Young man, I now solemnly promise and
    betroth
My daughter to you, to bear you lawful sons; and give
With her a dowry of three talents.

GORGIAS: And I have
One talent to give as dowry with Myrrhine.

CALLIPPIDES: You have?
Now, don't offer too much.

GORGIAS: I have it.

CALLIPPIDES: Well, I accept
The talent as her dowry. Don't divide the farm;
Keep it yourself, Gorgias, intact. Now fetch your mother
And sister here to meet our womenfolk.

GORGIAS: Yes, of course.

SOSTRATOS: Good. Now, tonight we'll all stay here and have
a feast.
Tomorrow we'll have the weddings. – Oh, and Gorgias,
bring
Old Cnemon here too. He needs looking after; perhaps
We can do more for him.

GORGIAS: No, he won't come, Sostratos.

SOSTRATOS: Oh, but persuade him.

GORGIAS: If I can.

>   [*Exit* GORGIAS.]

SOSTRATOS: Now, father dear,
We must arrange a splendid drinking-party for *us*,
And keep the ladies awake all night.

CALLIPPIDES: On the contrary,
The ladies'll do the drinking, of that I'm very sure,
And *we*'ll be kept awake all night. Oh, well; I'll go
And get ready what's necessary for you.

SOSTRATOS: Do.
[*To audience*] There isn't any single thing an honest
worker
Ought ever to despair of. Diligence and hard work
Will get you everything. Look at *me*, now: in one day
I have achieved a marriage beyond all men's dreams.

>   [GORGIAS *approaches with his* MOTHER *and*
>   MYRRHINE.]

GORGIAS: Come on, now, quickly, both of you.

SOSTRATOS: Yes, please come. Mother,
Will you receive these ladies? Where's Cnemon?

GORGIAS: Sostratos,
Cnemon still won't come. He was even begging us
To send old Simice away, so that he could be
Entirely alone and by himself.

SOSTRATOS: Well, what a man!

GORGIAS: He's like that.

SOSTRATOS: Then forget him. Come on, let's be going.

GORGIAS: I'm much too shy to meet these ladies, Sostratos.

SOSTRATOS: Oh, nonsense! Come on. Mother, this is
  Gorgias.

  [*To Gorgias*] Remember, from today we're all one family.

>   [*They all go into the shrine.* SIMICE *comes out of
>   Cnemon's house, shouting back at him.*]

SIMICE: I *am*, by Artemis, I'm going too. Just you
  Lie there and stew in your own bad temper, all alone.
  These gentlefolk all want to take you to the shrine,
  And you say No. By the two goddesses, you'll have
  Another dreadful accident, much worse than this.
  . . . Well, I hope you'll be all right.

>   [GETAS *comes from the shrine.*]

>   Why, Getas, where are you going?

GETAS: I'm going in to the old man, to see if he needs anything.

>   [*The sound of flute-music comes from the shrine.*]

  Now, damn you, what's the use of playing the flute to *me*,
  I ask you?
  I've no time yet to go and dance. They've sent me here to
  visit
  The patient, see? Keep quiet.

SIMICE: That's right, *you* sit with him. It's high time
  For someone else to take a turn. I'm going to my young
  mistress
  To say good-bye, and kiss her and talk to her, and give my
  blessing.

GETAS: Of course you must; trot off. Meanwhile *I*'ll give him
  proper treatment.

>   [*Exit* SIMICE.]

  I've long been wanting such a chance, but couldn't see how
  to work it.
  No one can come out yet awhile, they're all too busy
  drinking.

>   [*He goes to the door of the shrine and calls softly*.]

Hey, cook! Hey, Sicon! Come out here, come quickly!
    [SICON *appears*.]

                                       O Poseidon!

Guess what a treat I've got for you.

SICON [*rather drunk*]:   You called me?

GETAS: Yes, I called you.
The things *he* did to you just now – do you want to get your
    own back?

SICON: Did things to me just now? What things? You're
    talking through your arse, boy.

GETAS: Old Belly-Ache's asleep, alone.

SICON: And what is his [*hiccup*] condition?

GETAS: Not half so sick as he might be.

SICON: Could he get on his feet and beat us?

GETAS: Couldn't even get on his feet, I reckon.

SICON: Sounds delightful!
I'll go right in and ask for something; that'll send him
    raving!

GETAS: Wait; first let's lug the man out here; then, when
    we've got him planted,
Let's bang like blazes on his door, and ask for things, and
    drive him
Into a flaming temper. That will be some pleasure, I tell you.

SICON: It's Gorgias I'm afraid of; if he catches us he'll flay us.

GETAS: Hark at the row in there – they're drinking; no one's
    going to hear us.
In fact, it's up to us, now that the old boy's a relation,
To teach him family manners. If his present style continues
It's no joke to put up with.

SICON: It is not.

GETAS [*opening the door*]:   Be very careful
To get him out in front here without anybody seeing.
    [*He pushes Sicon in front of him.*]
Go on a bit, now.

SICON: Wait, I implore you – now don't go and leave me;

And for the gods' sake don't make noises.

GETAS: I never made no noises.
    Swear by the earth I didn't.
        [They carry Cnemon out asleep in his chair.]
                To your right.

SICON: There we are.

GETAS: Put him down now.
    Now's the moment.

SICON: I'll go first. Look – you repeat my rhythm.
        *[He knocks as follows: tum-túm-ti-tum, tum-túm-ti-tum,
        tum-túm.]*

CNEMON *[muttering in his sleep]*:   Oh, help, I'm done for!

GETAS: Now me.
        [He knocks, in the same rhythm.]

CNEMON *[waking]*: Oh, help! I'm done for! *[He sees Sicon.]*
    Who's that? You're one of that crowd, I can see you are.
    Now what are you after?
        *[SICON is shouting into the house, not looking at
        CNEMON, who is outside.]*

SICON: Please, sir, I want to borrow a kettle *and* a pudding-
    basin.

CNEMON *[growling ominously]*: Oh, someone help me up.

SICON: You've got one, I know for sure you've got one.
    And I want seven saucepans, *and* twelve tables. Slaves, look
    sharp now
    And take my message, I'm in a hurry.

CNEMON: I've got nothing.

SICON: Nothing?

CNEMON: Nothing, I've told you a thousand times.

SICON: I'm off, then.

CNEMON: Plagues and devils!
    How did I get out here? Who stuck me down out here?
    Clear off, you!

GETAS *[knocking twice as loudly]*: Now my turn. Porter!
    Butlers!

Housemaids! PORTER!!

CNEMON: You – you madman!
You'll smash my door in.

GETAS: Lend me nine hearth-rugs.

CNEMON: Where from?

GETAS: I want too
Some woven Persian hangings – thirty yards.

CNEMON: I wish I had 'em.

GETAS: You've got them.

CNEMON: Where? Simice! Oh, where's that old crone?

GETAS: I'm going
To try at another door.

CNEMON: Clear off, then. Simice!

[SICON *comes up again.*]

You devil,
May all the gods torment you! What do you want?

SICON: I want to borrow
A large bronze stewing-pan.

CNEMON [*nearly bursting*]: Oh, someone help me up!

GETAS [*coming back*]: I'm certain
You've got those Persian hangings, Dad, quite certain of it.

CNEMON: I haven't.

SICON: No? nor the stew-pan neither?

CNEMON: I'll kill that Simice.

[SIMICE *suddenly reappears from the shrine.* GETAS *and*
SICON *run to hide at the edge of the stage.*]

SIMICE [*derisively*]: Go to sleep, now;
Stop growling. Look at you – a man who avoids his fellow
creatures,
Hates his own wife –

[GETAS *and* SICON, *seeing Simice is on their side,*
return.]

– and won't join in at a sacrifice or a party.
So take your medicine, all of it.

SICON: There's no one here to help you.

GETAS: Sit there and stew in your own juice.

SIMICE: And listen to your misdoings
All set out in order.

CNEMON: I won't listen. I've done nothing.
I only ask to be left alone to live the way I want to.
I interfere with nobody. Although I'm ill and helpless
I didn't even make my daughter stay at home to attend
   me.
In any case, what good have she and her mother got from
   going?

SIMICE: They're being congratulated and embraced by all the
   neighbours –
A most delightful experience for your poor wife and
   daughter.

SICON: Why, over there I was laying out a feast for all those
   people –

GETAS: You listening, hey? Now don't drop off.

CNEMON: Drop off! Great gods!

GETAS: What about it?
Will you come to the party?

SICON: Listen, I'll tell you some more.
   We were in a hurry;
And I was strewing the ground with mats and cushions,
   setting the tables –
Yes, me. Are you listening? That's my business, I'm a cook
   by profession.

GETAS: Don't you remember?

SICON: The man's no spirit.

GETAS: Someone else was lifting
And tipping into the mixing-bowl a jar of Jolly Bacchos
Of ancient vintage; stirring in water from the Nymphs'
   fountain,
And drinking healths with the men –

SICON: – while someone else filled up for the women;
Like pouring wine into sand, it was.

SIMICE: Ah! Can you picture it, Cnemon?
A little slave-girl, rather merry, wearing a wreath of ivy
To crown the flower of her young face; her feet already
    restless
With the rhythm; shyly hesitating, fluttering with excite-
    ment:
Another girl joins hands with her, and away they dance
    together!

GETAS: Cnemon, you've had a terrible time – now come on,
    join the dancers!
    [He takes Cnemon by the arm to lift him up.]

CNEMON: What are you up to? Hit me, would you?

GETAS: No! Just come and join them.

SICON: You've got no manners!

CNEMON: I won't, I swear.

GETAS: All right – do we have to carry you?

CNEMON: Oh, what can I do?

SICON: Dance, man!

CNEMON: I suppose perhaps it'll be less painful
To dance in there than endure you here.

GETAS: You're right! We've won! It's a triumph!
Here, Donax, Sicon, Syros, all you slaves, come here!
    [A number of slaves run up.]
Right: pick him up and carry him in.
    [They pick Cnemon up in his chair.]
                Cnemon: look out
For yourself, if ever we catch you making trouble for
    us;
I swear we'll give you the *full* treatment another time.
    [Some guests come out to welcome them in.]
Give us garlands, someone, and a torch.
    *[A garland is put on Cnemon's head, a torch in his hand.
    Guests form a procession round him.]*
                Now, up with him!
    [They lift him high and carry him in to the dancing.]

So, now we've brought to heel this troublesome old man,
Congratulate us, all of you, both young and old,
And give us a hearty clap. May noble Victory,
The laughter-loving maiden, stay our friend for ever!

EPITREPONTES

OR

THE ARBITRATION

CHARACTERS

ONESIMOS, *a slave of Charisios*
DAOS, *a shepherd*
SMICRINES, *father of Pamphile, wife of Charisios*
SYRISCOS, *a charcoal-burner, slave of Chaerestratos*
HABROTONON, *a guitar-girl*
CHAERESTRATOS, *a rich Athenian, father of Charisios*
PAMPHILE, *wife of Charisios*
SOPHRONE, *Pamphile's nurse, an old slave of Smicrines*
CHARISIOS, *a young man*
CHORUS *of Banqueters*
Syriscos' wife; an infant in arms

*

The place is near Athens; and the scene shows two houses. One is that of Charisios, where Pamphile is now living; the other belongs to Chaerestratos, and here his son Charisios is living with Habrotonon.

Act 1[1]

SCENE ONE

ONESIMOS *and* DAOS *meet.*

DAOS: I say, Onesimos, do tell me: is it true
    That your young master Charisios, who is living here
    With this guitar-girl Habrotonon, is in fact
    A quite recently married man?
ONESIMOS: I'm sorry to say
    That's perfectly true.

---

1. Of this Act only three lines are preserved.

Act 2

SCENE ONE

SYRISCOS *enters from the country with his wife, who is carrying a baby; they are met by* DAOS, *who is coming from Athens. Syriscos has just demanded of Daos the ornaments which, he has been told, were found with the child; and Daos has refused to give them up.*

SYRISCOS: You're evading your duty.

DAOS: And you're trying to swindle me, You perisher.

SYRISCOS: You've no right to keep what isn't yours.

DAOS: Look – arbitration! That's the thing! We must get someone
To arbitrate for us.

SYRISCOS: I'm ready.

DAOS: Good; let's get this settled.

SYRISCOS: Who shall we ask?

DAOS: Anyone you like will do for me.
– Shall I get my rights, though? Oh, why on earth did I ever
Tell you about it?

[SMICRINES, *who has been visiting his daughter Pamphile in Charisios' house, now comes out.*]

SYRISCOS: Would you agree to have *him* as judge?

DAOS: That's lucky. Yes, have him.

SYRISCOS [*to Smicrines*]: My good sir, excuse me, sir!
Could you, if you please, spare us a few moments, sir?

SMICRINES: Spare you a few moments? What's it about?

SYRISCOS: You see, we're having
A bit of an argument.

SMICRINES: What has that got to do with me?

SYRISCOS: Why, this: we're both looking for some fair-minded person
To decide it for us. If nothing urgent calls you away
This moment, you arbitrate for us!

SMICRINES: You slippery rogues!
So you parade the streets making lawyers' speeches, do you?
Hob-nail boots and all, eh?

SYRISCOS: Well, what if we do?
It's quite a simple argument, Dad, won't take you a minute.
Come on; we'd be greatly obliged to you. And please don't say
A thing like this doesn't matter. Justice ought to prevail
Everywhere and on all occasions. The passer-by
Ought to feel it's his duty to see justice done.
It's one of life's obligations – comes to everybody.

DAOS [aside]: Eh, now I've got tangled up with a right speechifier.
Why did I ever say a single word to him?

SMICRINES: Now tell me, are you both going to abide by my decision?

SYRISCOS: Certainly we are.

SMICRINES: I'll hear you then; why shouldn't I?
[To Daos] Well, you've said nothing so far. Come on, you speak first.

DAOS: I'll have to begin a little way back, before my quarrel
With him began, so that you can get the whole thing clear.
Well, sir: about a month ago I was with my sheep
On the heath not far from here; on that particular day
I was all alone. And there, lying on the scrub, I found
A little new-born child, with tokens round its neck,
Ornaments, and such things.

SYRISCOS: Those are what the quarrel's about.

DAOS: See? He won't let me speak!

SMICRINES: If you interrupt again
You'll feel my stick, see?

DAOS: Quite right, too.

SMICRINES: Speak on.

DAOS: I will.
I picked the child up; took it home, with all its things.

119

I'd a mind to rear it – seemed a good idea just then.
But in the night I had second thoughts, as people do.
'Children mean trouble; what about the expense?' I thought,
'And all the worry?' That's the way I looked at it.
Next morning, out with the sheep again. *He* comes along
To the same place – he's a charcoal-burner – to saw logs.
I'd known him a long time. We started talking. He
Saw I was gloomy. 'What's the matter, Daos?' he says.
'You've something on your mind.' 'I'm a busybody,' I
    said;
And I told him all about it; how I'd found the child
And taken it home. Then straight away, before I'd finished
'Please now,' he said, 'if ever you hope for blessing, Daos,' –
Those were his very words – 'if you hope for luck, for
    freedom,
Give *me* the child. I've got a wife,' he said; 'she had
A baby, who died.' That's his wife there, holding the child.

SMICRINES [*to Syriscos*]: Did you say this?

SYRISCOS: I did, yes.

DAOS: Why, he gave me no peace
The whole day long, begging and arguing. At last
I agreed; gave him the child; and off he went, praying
For blessings on me – kissed my hands as he took the kid.

SMICRINES [*to Syriscos*]: Is that true?

SYRISCOS: Quite true.

DAOS: That was that. But now today
He happens to meet me here, with his wife, and suddenly
He wants the things I found laid out beside the child –
Just worthless bits and pieces – demands them as his right;
Very indignant that I refuse to give them up.
By right, I say, they're mine. He asked for the child, and
    got it;
He ought to be grateful. Why should I be put on trial
For not giving him everything? If he'd been there
With me, and shared the luck of the find, then naturally

Part would have gone to him, and part to me; but I
Found it alone. Now, do you think you should have the lot,
And me nothing at all, when you weren't even there?
It comes to this: I made you a free gift of what
Was mine. If you're contented, keep it. If you're not,
If you've now changed your mind, give the child back to
   me.
That means no injury or loss to you. But if
You claim the lot, part as a willing gift, and part
By forcing me, you're in the wrong. Well, that's my case.

SYRISCOS: Has he finished?

SMICRINES: Didn't you hear? He's finished.

SYRISCOS: Good, my turn.

His story's quite true – he alone found the child; no doubt
Of that, that's how it happened, sir, I don't dispute.
I asked and begged him for it; and he gave it me –
All true. Now, he told one of his mates, another shepherd,
That he'd found certain tokens with the child. This man
Told me. Now, sir, this infant – Give him to me, wife –

    [*Syriscos takes the child from his wife.*]

Comes here himself to claim them. Daos, he demands
His necklace, and the other tokens of his birth.
They were put on him, he says, to bring him credit, not
To keep you fed. By giving him to me, you yourself
Made me his guardian. As his guardian, then, I join
With him in asking for his rights.

    [*He gives the child back to his wife.*]

                    So now, sir, this,
I reckon, is what you must decide: whether this gold,
Or whatever the tokens are, ought to be kept for him
Until he grows up (since his mother, whoever she was,
Gave them with that intention) or whether this man here,
Who robbed him of them, ought to keep what isn't his
Because he found him first. – You, Daos, may wonder why
I didn't ask for these tokens at the time, when you

Gave me the child. Why, at that time I had no right
To speak for him. Even now I ask nothing for myself.
You say you 'shared the luck of the find' with me. You
    call it
A 'find'? You stripped this body! That's no 'find'; that's
    theft.
   A further point, sir: this young boy here is, perhaps,
Of noble birth, and will in time look far beyond
Us working folk that reared him; rise to his own level,
Perform some exploit worthy of his blood; hunt lions,
Bear arms in battle, run in the Olympic games.
You've seen plays in the theatre – you know all those tales
By heart – Neleus and Pelias, how they were found
By an old goat-herd wearing the kind of leather coat
I'm wearing now; when he saw the boys were of better
    stock
Than himself, he told them the whole story, how he'd found
And taken them home; and he gave them the little leather
    bag
Of tokens, from which they learnt the truth about their
    birth;
And so, brought up as goat-herds, they became both kings.
Now, suppose Daos had grabbed those tokens and sold the
    lot
To put twelve drachmas in his pocket: the two princes,
Both noble heroes, would have lived their whole lives
    unknown.
   Now, sir: is it right that *I* should house, clothe, feed this
    child,
While Daos takes and throws away his only hope
Of a good life? Tokens like these have held men back
From incest, helped them recognize and save from death
Parent or brother. Danger's a part of human life;
Then, sir, we should take care, and value every means
To overcome it. 'Give the child back,' Daos says,

'If you're not satisfied.' Now there he thinks he has
A powerful argument. It's not a just one, though.
Because you owe this child his property, do you now want
To take the child himself? Perhaps you think you'd feel
Safer for the next piece of dirty work – selling
The bits and pieces Fortune has preserved for him?
    I've finished. Give whatever decision you think right.

SMICRINES: The case is clear. All articles exposed with the child
Are the child's property. That's my judgement.

DAOS: Good; but who
Is to have the child?

SMICRINES: Certainly not the man who now
Wrongs him, but his defender and champion against you
Who tried to rob him.

SYRISCOS: Bless you, bless you, sir!

DAOS: What? Zeus!
That's a disgraceful judgement! I found everything,
I alone; and now I'm stripped of everything; this man
Found nothing, takes the lot! Must I hand over, then?

SMICRINES: You must.

DAOS: It's scandalous, damned if it isn't.

SYRISCOS: Come on, quick now.

DAOS: Outrageous! Heracles!

SYRISCOS: Untie that wallet, show us the things –
That's where you carry them. [*To Smicrines, who is going*]
    Sir, I beg you, wait here a minute
To make sure he hands over.

DAOS: Oh! Why did I ever agree
To let him judge?

SYRISCOS: Come on, now, handcuffs, part with it.

DAOS [*giving the wallet*]: It's shameful.

SMICRINES: Is it all there?

SYRISCOS: I think so.

SMICRINES: So do I –

Unless he swallowed this or that while I was giving
Judgement against him.

SYRISCOS: I hardly think he could do that.
Well, best of luck, sir! If only all judgements were as just!
          [*Exit* SMICRINES.]

DAOS: Heracles! Of all the stupid, scandalous decisions!

SYRISCOS: You're a bad lot.

DAOS: You thief! I'll keep an eye on you
Day and night from now on, to see you guard those things
And keep them safe for the child.

SYRISCOS: Shog off and drown yourself.
          [*Exit* DAOS *towards the country.*]

Wife, hold this wallet; take it into my master's house.[1]
Right. Now we'll wait here for Chaerestratos. Tomorrow,
When I've paid my monthly dues, we'll set off back to work.
But first let's make a note of these things one by one.
Got a basket? Well, hold out your gown.

          [SYRISCOS *tips the contents of the wallet into his wife's
          gown.* ONESIMOS *enters from Chaerestratos' house; he
          looks up and down the road.* SYRISCOS, *who is busy
          looking through the articles from the wallet, does not see
          him at first.*]

ONESIMOS: Cooks always arrive late. This one's the worst
I've known.

Yesterday by this time the meal was finished with.

SYRISCOS: This seems to be a sort of chicken. A tough one
too.

Take it. What's this now? Something set with stones. And
here's

A toy axe.

ONESIMOS [*to himself*]: What's going on?

SYRISCOS: Look, here's a signet-ring;
Gold-plate on iron; and the device, a bull or goat –

---

1. Does he want them given to Chaerestratos, or Charisios, for safe-keeping?

I can't tell which ... Some letters – here's the maker's name,
Cleostratos.

ONESIMOS [*excited*]: Here! Show me.

SYRISCOS: There. Who are you?

ONESIMOS: It is!
The very one.

SYRISCOS: What is?

ONESIMOS: This ring.

SYRISCOS: Is what? I don't
Know what you're talking about.

ONESIMOS: This is Charisios' ring,
My master's.

SYRISCOS: Oh, you're crazy.

ONESIMOS [*slipping it on his finger*]: The one he lost.

SYRISCOS: Look here,
Give that ring back, you miserable –

ONESIMOS: Give it back, eh? It's ours!
And where did you get it from?

SYRISCOS: You twister! Holy gods,
It's a lovely job, looking after an orphan's property!
First man you meet'll rob you as soon as look at you.
Give me that ring, I tell you. Are you being funny with
me?

ONESIMOS: This is my master's ring, I swear it by all the gods.

SYRISCOS: I'll be hanged, drawn and quartered before I
haggle with you.
All right, then, let 'em all come. I'll take every man of them
To a court of law. It's not my property, it's the boy's.
Wife, take this necklace; this red wrapper. Now, indoors!
        [*His wife goes into Chaerestratos' house, taking the child
        and the rest of the tokens.*]
Now, you: what have you got to say?

ONESIMOS: This ring belongs
To Charisios my master. He lost it when he was drunk,
So he told me.

SYRISCOS: I see. Well, I belong to Chaerestratos.
   Either keep that safe, or give it to him; whichever you like.
ONESIMOS: I've got it safe; I'd rather take charge of it myself.
SYRISCOS: It doesn't matter to me. In any case we both
   Seem to be going to the same house.
ONESIMOS: But at this moment
   Guests are arriving – not a good time, perhaps, to mention
   This to my master. Tomorrow.
SYRISCOS: I can wait. Tomorrow
   I'm ready to put my case before any judge you like.

      [*Exit* ONESIMOS *into Chaerestratos' house.*]

   Well! Didn't come off too badly with him either. These days
   You've got to set everything else aside, and go to law.
   Seems it's the only way a man can assert his rights.

      [*Exit* SYRISCOS *to the house in pursuit of Onesimos.
      Some of Charisios' guests arrive and present the* SECOND
      CHORAL INTERLUDE; *after which they too retire into
      the same house.*]

Act 3

SCENE ONE

Enter ONESIMOS *from Chaerestratos' house, furtively; he is keeping out of Syriscos' way.*

ONESIMOS [*to the audience*]: See this ring here: five times or
    more I've started off
  To show it to Charisios my master; I go to him,
  And then, as soon as I'm standing right in front of him,
  I shirk it. I wish now I'd never told him anything
  About his wife having a child while he was away.[1]
  Ten times a day I hear him muttering, 'Blast the man
  Who told me that!' I'm terrified that he and his wife
  Will make it up; and since I'm the man who knows what
    happened,
  And tipped him off, he'll just make a clean sweep of me.
  Well, then, I'd best brew up some other kettle of fish; –
  Yet that, again, involves a terrible risk for me.

      [HABROTONON *appears at Chaerestratos' door, pro-
      testing to some young men inside who are molesting her –
      no doubt guests of Charisios.*]

HABROTONON: Let go, now, please! Stop! Will you please
    leave me alone?

      [*The young men vanish.* HABROTONON *speaks to the
      audience, standing on the opposite side of the stage to*
      ONESIMOS, *who is still looking at the ring and does not
      notice her.*]

  Well, of all the wretched luck! I've made a fool of myself.
  How was I to know? I expected to be made love to;
  But the man hates me – it's unnatural, the way he hates me!
  Why, now he won't even have me next to him at dinner;

---

   1. This line is not in the Greek; since much of the play is missing it is
necessary to add some explanation here.

I'm put at a distance.

ONESIMOS: Am I to give it back again

To the fellow I've just taken it from? Ridiculous!

HABROTONON: But why does he pour out money for nothing
  so recklessly?

For all he's done, poor chap, I could this very moment

Carry a holy basket in the Panathenaea;

I've been here three days now, and I'm still, as the priest
  says,

A pure and untouched virgin.

ONESIMOS: And if I don't, then how on earth, for the gods'
  sake – ?

        [*Enter* SYRISCOS *from a side door of Chaerestratos'
        house.* HABROTONON *listens unseen.*]

SYRISCOS: I'm chasing him round in circles. Where's he got
  to? [*Seeing Onesimos*] Hey!

You in the porch there!

        [ONESIMOS *turns and comes up to him.*]

                Listen, friend: either give that ring

Back to me now, or show it without more waste of time

To the man you want to show it to. I've got things to do;

Let's settle the matter.

ONESIMOS: Look, mate, this is the position.

This ring's my master Charisios' ring, I know it is;

But I don't want to show it him. If I hand him this,

Found with the foundling child, why, I as good as make

Him the child's father.

SYRISCOS: How do you mean, you fool?

ONESIMOS: Listen.

He lost this ring last year at the Tauropolia –

An all-night song-and-dance for women. It's pretty clear

What happened was, a girl got raped, and had this child;

And then, of course, exposed it. Now, if someone could

First find the girl, and then produce this ring, he'd have

Clear proof; but now, showing the ring would only cause
Suspicion and confusion.

SYRISCOS: Well, that's up to you –
Do as you like; but if you're making all this fuss
Hoping I'll give you a little something for yourself
In exchange for the ring, you're barmy. I'm not going shares,
Not on your life.

ONESIMOS: I didn't ask for anything.

SYRISCOS: Look – I must run; I've several things to do in
town.
I'll soon be back; we'll see then what seems best to do.

[SYRISCOS *goes off towards Athens.* HABROTONON
comes up to Onesimos.]

HABROTONON: Onesimos! This baby the woman's nursing
now
Indoors – was it the charcoal-burner who found it?

ONESIMOS: Yes,
He says so.

HABROTONON: Poor little mite, it's very sweet.

ONESIMOS: What's more,
This ring was on the child; and – it's my master's ring.

HABROTONON: Well, then, if he's in fact your master's son,
you couldn't
Surely stand by and see him brought up as a slave?
Why, that's as bad as murder!

ONESIMOS: I was just telling you,
No one knows who the mother is.

HABROTONON: He lost the ring,
You say, at the Tauropolia?

ONESIMOS: Yes; he was drunk, or so
The boy attending him told me.

HABROTONON [*reflectively*]: He'd be alone, of course,
When he came across the women dancing at dead of night.
– Why, just such a thing happened under my very eyes!

ONESIMOS: Under your . . . ?

HABROTONON: Yes, at last year's Tauropolia.
  I was there to play for the dances. There was this young girl
  Dancing with all the rest – it never occurred to me
  At the time; I didn't know then about men, you see –
  That's true, by Aphrodite.

ONESIMOS: Well, who was this girl?
  Do you know?

HABROTONON: No, but I could find out. She was a friend
  Of the women I was with.

ONESIMOS: Did you catch her father's name?

HABROTONON: Nothing; but I would know her if I saw her
    again.
  She was simply lovely; and they mentioned she was rich.

ONESIMOS: It might be her.

HABROTONON: I don't know. While she was
    there with us
  She wandered off; then suddenly came running back
  Alone and sobbing, tearing her hair; her pretty dress
  Of finest Tarantine silk all ruined, torn to shreds.

ONESMIOS: Did she have this ring?

HABROTONON: Perhaps; she didn't show it me,
  To be quite truthful.

ONESIMOS: Well, then, what must I do now?

HABROTONON: Look here, if you'll be sensible and listen to
    me,
  Go to your master; lay all the facts in front of him.
  Suppose this child's the son of a free-born girl; then why
  Should not Charisios know what happened?

ONESIMOS: Yes – but first
  Let's find out who the girl is; that's where you come in.
  Now, think . . .

HABROTONON: Oh, no, I couldn't; not until I know
  For certain who the man is who assaulted her.
  What frightens me is the thought of giving a false lead

To the women I told you of. Who knows? Some other man
May have happened to lay a bet with him and win the ring
And then lose it again at dice. Or he paid it down,
Perhaps, as earnest of his share in a Club dinner.
Or else he made some agreement, and handed over the ring
To get himself out of a tight corner. A thing like that,
Once men get drinking, can easily happen a thousand ways.
Until I know the guilty man, I don't intend
To look for the girl, or breathe a word to anyone.

ONESIMOS: That's not a bad bit of reasoning. Well, what shall
 we do?

HABROTONON: I've thought of a plan, Onesimos; see what
 you think of it.

It's this: I will pretend the whole thing happened to me.
I'll take this ring, and go in and see Charisios.

ONESIMOS: Yes, go on.

HABROTONON: When he sees I've got the ring he'll ask
 Where I got it from. I'll say, 'At the Tauropolia,
When I was still a virgin' – and I'll tell everything
As my own story; I know the details well enough.

ONESIMOS: A first-rate scheme.

HABROTONON: You'll see, if he's the guilty man,
He'll rush head-over-heels to give himself away.
He's drunk now; so he'll pour out everything at once.
I'll let *him* mention details first, rather than me,
And agree to what he says; I mustn't make any slips.

ONESIMOS: Magnificent!

HABROTONON: To make sure I don't get anything
 wrong
I'll bluff it out with the usual phrases – 'What a brute
You were to me; nothing would stop you!'

ONESIMOS: That's the stuff!

HABROTONON: 'You were so rough,' I'll say, 'throwing me
 to the ground,
Tearing my lovely dress to bits!' But first I'll go

And see the woman who has the baby; I'll pick it up,
And cry, and kiss it, and ask her where she got it from.

ONESIMOS: You're wonderful!

HABROTONON: Then for the final stroke I'll show
This foundling; and I'll tell him, 'There's your baby son!'

ONESIMOS: Perfect, my duck; wickedly clever!

HABROTONON: And if then
It all comes clear, and he's proved father of the child,
We'll take our time to find the girl.

ONESIMOS: There's one thing more
You haven't mentioned: you'll be set free! Once he thinks
You're his son's mother, he'll buy your freedom on the
spot.

HABROTONON: I don't know. Oh, if only . . . !

ONESIMOS: You don't know? You do!
And by the way, who will you have to thank? Why, me!

HABROTONON: Why, heavens, yes! For everything! I don't
know what
I'd have done without you!

ONESIMOS: Now, if you just give up the idea
Of finding the girl – just drop the matter, and let me
down,
What happens then?

HABROTONON: Stupid! Why should I? Do you imagine
I dote on babies? All I want is to be free.
Gods, give me that for my reward!

ONESIMOS: I pray they will.

HABROTONON: Agreed, then?

ONESIMOS: Absolutely. If you play tricks on me –
I'll fight you *then* – I'll have a hold on you. Meanwhile
Let's see how this plan goes.

HABROTONON: You agree then?

ONESIMOS: Certainly.

HABROTONON: Quick, then, give me the ring.

ONESIMOS [*handing the ring*]: Take it.

132

HABROTONON: Dear goddess, hear!
   Holy Persuasion, help me! Bring my words success!
     [*Exit* HABROTONON *into Chaerestratos' house.*]
ONESIMOS [*alone*]: I call that smart! Our little girl no sooner
    sees
   That the trade of love's a blind alley, and not the road
   That leads to freedom, than she tries the other tack.
   But look at me: I'll be a slave my whole life long,
   A snivelling booby – never a thought to better myself.
   However, if she's lucky, perhaps I'll get a share –
   It's only right – Pah! That way of reckoning makes no
    sense;
   I'm a poor fool, to hope for gratitude from a woman.
   I only pray not to be worse off than before.
   My mistress, now, Charisios' wife – things might well
    take
   A nasty turn for her, and soon. Suppose this girl,
   The mother of this infant, should turn out to be
   A free man's daughter: then Charisios will take
   Her, and get rid of Pamphile his present wife.
   For the moment, though, I think I've neatly dodged the
    blame
   For stirring up this present trouble. For the future –
   I've done with meddling, thank you. If anyone catches me
   Minding what's not my business, or speaking out of turn
   Ever again, he's welcome to cut off both my – ears.
     [*He sees Smicrines coming back from Athens.*]
   Now who can this be? Smicrines, on his way back
   From town – and once again all wound up for a row.
   Has someone told him the real reason for the quarrel
   Between his daughter and my master? I'd rather keep
   Out of the way. It's quite possible, I should think,
   He's coming to fetch his daughter home. And *my* cue is –
   Let well alone.
     [*Exit* ONESIMOS. *Enter* SMICRINES.]

At this point a further considerable portion of the play is lost, or survives only in tattered papyri where one or two words at the beginning or end of a line are legible. From these remains a certain amount of conjecture is possible. Smicrines on reaching the stage addresses the audience somewhat as follows:

SMICRINES: I was deceived in that young man Charisios. He is nothing but a profligate. The whole town talks of his scandalous behaviour. It's clear that he's a bad character; he drinks all day, and disgraces his name by the life he leads. And now, I learn, for more than three days he has been living apart from his wife, my daughter. I thought at first I would try to reconcile them; but now, it seems, he has taken a guitar-girl to live with him. This, on top of drinking and gambling, is too much; I've done with patience!

Next, a Cook arrives, probably a similar character to the Cook in *The Bad-Tempered Man*. He has been sent for by Charisios to prepare an extravagant banquet for him and his friends. The sight of such preparations increases the rage of Smicrines at his son-in-law's behaviour. Later Simmias, a friend of Charisios, is on the stage, and a line addressed to him suggests that Habrotonon has succeeded in her interview with Charisios, and that he has now acknowledged the child as hers and his. Smicrines, as always, is the last person to find out what is going on.

SMICRINES: The beggar drinks only the most expensive
    wine.
  That's what puts *me* in a rage. I don't say a word about
  Just getting drunk – which after all's plain greediness,
  Even if you make yourself swill down the twopenny stuff;
  But this is the last straw – he's going to throw to the winds
  His whole fortune! What's that to do with me, you say?
  I tell you once more, he'll be sorry! Four talents
  Of silver my daughter brought him as her dowry; yet
  He's made his mind up not to be his wife's footman.

He sleeps away from home. He pays a pimp three pounds
Per day for a whore, three pounds! He has a marvellous
    head
For business, has Charisios. Now tell me: what sum
Is reckoned enough to keep a man, humanely speaking?
Two shillings a day. – Well, where on earth's the sense in
    paying
More to a hungry man?

> [*Enter* CHAERESTRATOS *with* ONESIMOS. SMI-
> CRINES *at first does not notice them.*]

ONESIMOS: Chaerestratos, I see someone on the look-out for
    you.
CHAERESTRATOS: This man? Bless you, who is he?
ONESIMOS: Your son's father-in-law,
    Raging and cursing at his miserable luck.
SMICRINES: She's pretty, it seems, this guitar-girl he's
    acquired; and so
    This graceless, brainless, heartless son-in-law of mine
    Decides to abandon his devoted, faithful wife . . .

A gap here of some fifteen lines, in which Chaerestratos tries to put
in a plea for his son.

CHAERESTRATOS: . . . So pause, my friend, I beg you, as you
    hope for luck.
SMICRINES: You just keep quiet. You go to hell. You'll
    regret this.
    I'm going indoors now; and when I've found out exactly
    How things are with my daughter, I must then decide
    On the best way of dealing with Charisios.

> [*Exit* SMICRINES *into Charisios' house.*]

ONESIMOS: Ought we to warn Charisios that the old man's
    here?
CHAERESTRATOS: Oh, the young monkey! Turning his
    whole house upside down!

ONESIMOS: I wish he'd turned some others upside down.
CHAERESTRATOS: What others?
ONESIMOS: Next door, for one.
CHAERESTRATOS: *My* house?
ONESIMOS: Yes, yours. Let's go in now
  And see Charisios.
CHAERESTRATOS: Yes, let's go; here comes a crowd
  Of rowdy youths, half soaked. It seems a good idea
  To keep out of their way.
        [*They both go in.*]

The last five lines above are puzzling. They seem to suggest that
the house of Chaerestratos, where Charisios has been living with
Habrotonon, is in fact under lease to Habrotonon's owner, the pimp,
who has accepted Charisios as a tenant as long as Charisios is paying
for Habrotonon. This raises the question, Why didn't Chaerestratos
let his house to his son who was getting married, instead of to a
pimp? Was it accepted that a respectable man might let his property
for a brothel? These are some of the unanswered questions in an
incomplete play.

Act 4

Enter ONESIMOS *alone.*

ONESIMOS: Human life is all peril and uncertainty.
Look at me: what's my city? my safeguard? my law?
My one judge of all right or wrong? My master is
All these to me. At his sole pleasure I must live.
But that old Smicrines, damn him – without a thought for
us . . .

Of the next few scenes only a few lines survive, mostly from
quotations. The next fragment is in the latter part of Act 4, and
discovers Pamphile in conversation with her father Smicrines.

PAMPHILE: . . . But if, while saving me from my husband,
you should fail
To convince me this is best, it would be clear that you
Are not my father but my master now.
SMICRINES [*indignantly*]: Hear that!
That's Pamphile giving utterance! Shouting that she wants
Reason, persuasion, no compulsion! But if I
May be allowed a word, I'd like to make three points
For your reflection. First, your marriage has now reached
A state where there's no hope for either him or you.
He'll go on living in this wild fashion, enjoying himself.
You won't enjoy yourself one bit. Even suppose
You live in his house, will he let you have a servant-girl
If you happen to need one? One of his visiting tarts,
perhaps?
Not likely! Husband first in everything, that's the rule;
Wife nowhere.

After a gap of about twenty-four lines Smicrines is again – or still –
speaking.

And then, see how expensive it's going to be for him,
At festival-time, Pamphile. He'll have to buy
Two tickets for Thesmophoria; *two* tickets again
For Scirophoria – think of the financial strain!
Why, he's as good as bankrupt, never a doubt of it.
Picture what sort of a life *you*'ll have. 'I must be off,'
Says your husband, 'to Peiraeus.' He goes; does duty there.
Not pleasant for you? Just wait. He's back again in Athens –
Drinking, of course, with a whore –

PAMPHILE: I think I'll be going now;
Someone's come out . . .

A gap of perhaps seventy lines, during which this Scene ends and the next Scene begins.[1] The new Scene probably opened with a soliloquy by Habrotonon telling how, as a result of her pretence, Charisios has acknowledged his lustful act at the Tauropolia, and believes the child to be his and Habrotonon its mother. So now it remains for Habrotonon to find the real mother; and she will begin by making enquiries of the women who hired her to play on that occasion.

When she has finished, Sophrone, Pamphile's old nurse, comes with Pamphile to the door of Charisios' house. Habrotonon recognizes Pamphile, who then goes in, while Sophrone comes forward on the stage. During Sophrone's first lines Habrotonon slips back into the house and quickly comes out again with the baby. Then she listens, concealed in the doorway, to what Sophrone is saying, which (though only five lines survive) would probably include words to make it even clearer to Habrotonon that Pamphile is the mother of the child. Sophrone describes the arguments which Smicrines has been using to persuade Pamphile to leave Charisios and return home.

SOPHRONE: My eyes are all burnt up, I've cried so much
       today.
   I'll tell you what her father Smicrines said to her.
   'Pamphile,' he said, 'for a free-born woman to fight a
       whore

1. I have followed E. Capps's reconstruction.

Is courting trouble. A whore's much more unscrupulous,
More knowing; ashamed of nothing; a better wheedler
too ...'

[HABROTONON *comes forward holding the child, who is
crying. At first she speaks only to herself or the child.*]

HABROTONON: I'll take baby for a walk. Poor mite, he will
cry so!

I've had him poorly now for days and days. There, there!

SOPHRONE [*to herself*]: I don't know what to do. If only the
gods would help!

HABROTONON [*to the baby*]: Poor darling, I'm so sorry for
you. We'll go out.

I don't know what to do; but all the same we'll go.

[*To Sophrone*]: Excuse me! Wait for me one moment.

[HABROTONON *now sees Sophrone's face, and recognizes her as having been with Pamphile at the Tauropolia.*]

I'm so glad

I've found you!

SOPHRONE: Found me? Why, then, who do you think I am?

HABROTONON [*to herself*]: It is! I recognize her. [*To
Sophrone*] Glad to see you again!

Bless you, turn round and look, now! Listen to me a
minute.

SOPHRONE: Look here, what are you talking about?

HABROTONON: A year ago

At the Tauropolia I saw you, if I'm not mistaken.

[*Now Sophrone has seen the tokens hung round the child's
neck.*]

SOPHRONE: Tell me – this baby of yours – where did you
get him from?

HABROTONON: Oh, bless you, bless you! You see something you recognize?

Yes, how did he get this? – Please don't be afraid of me.

SOPHRONE: Then you are not its mother?

HABROTONON: I pretended to be;
Not so as to steal him from her, but to give me time
To find out who she is. And now I've found – well –
you.
You're the same person I saw then.

SOPHRONE: But who's his father?

HABROTONON: Charisios!

SOPHRONE: My dear girl, are you sure of that?

HABROTONON [*showing the ring*]: Do you know this ring? Is
it the property of the man
Whose young wife I've just seen indoors?

SOPHRONE: Why, yes, it is!

HABROTONON: The gods must love you! You asked for
help, and here it is.
One of your neighbours is coming out; I heard the door.
Come, take me in with you to your mistress's house;
Then I can tell you the whole story, end to end.

[*They both go into Charisios' house. Out of Chaerestratos' house comes* ONESIMOS; *as he speaks he points
behind him into the house.*]

ONESIMOS: This man's going slightly mad. He *is* mad, by
Apollo.
He's really gone mad, by all the gods. In fact – he's mad.
I allude to my master, Charisios; he's suffering
From neurotic paranoia – something of that sort.
That's only a guess; but what else could it be? Just now
For half an hour he was bending down and listening
At the door of the other house, where his wife's father, it
seems,
Was urging her to leave her husband. Charisios
Turned pale, then red – I really shouldn't give him away.
He was calling aloud, 'Darling, what noble words you
speak!'
Then he beat his head with clenched fists; and after a while

He began again: 'What a wonderful wife I've got,' says he;
'And what a wonderful, miserable mess I've made of
    things!'
At last, when he'd heard everything, he came indoors;
And there he was in his room, groaning, tearing his hair,
Raving incessantly. 'Yes, I'm a criminal,' he'd say
Again and again. 'After myself doing what I did,
And being myself the father of a bastard child,
I was such a brute and savage that I neither felt,
Nor offered her, one shred of forgiveness – although she
Had suffered the very wrong that I was guilty of.'
He loads himself with reproaches, rages at himself
With bloodshot eyes. I'm terrified; my mouth's all dry.
If while he's in this state he catches sight of *me*,
The one who told him his wife's trouble, like as not
He'd kill me. That's why I've slipped out here. What can I
    do?
Where can I go? I'm finished, done for. – That's the
    door;
He's coming out. – O Saviour Zeus, if possible
Save me!

> [*Enter from the house* CHARISIOS; ONESIMOS *remains
> at first unseen.*]

CHARISIOS: I was the faultless man who made honour my
    aim;
I the student of ethics, sifting right from wrong;
My life immaculate, blameless! Now my own folly
Has shown my feet of clay; and the just gods have sent
My fit reward. 'You poor wretch, all conceit and talk,'
I hear them say, 'You reject your wife for a mishap
That was forced upon her; now we'll show the world that
    you
Tripped up on the same wire. And when it all comes out
She'll use you gently – you who now dishonour her.
Then you'll be known as an example to the world –

Not of bad luck, but of sheer crass brutality.
Compare what *she* said to her father, with what *you*
Were thinking about her. "I came to share his life" –
That's what she said – "so certainly I must not try
To step aside from this mischance that's come to me."
But you – you self-conceited prig! – how different
Was your behaviour!'

The next twenty lines of the text are fragmentary, and the translation largely conjectural. Habrotonon enters at some point.

                 Now her father Smicrines
Will think the worst, and treat her as she has not deserved.
Well, what do I care for Smicrines? I'll tell him off!
'Look here,' I'll say to him, 'just you stop making trouble
And pestering Pamphile. My wife's not leaving me!'
      [*He sees Onesimos.*]
What, are you here again?

ONESIMOS [*aside to Habrotonon*]: Things look pretty black to me.
For God's sake don't desert me.

CHARISIOS: You there! You blackmailer!
Are you eavesdropping?

ONESIMOS: By all the gods, I've just come out.

CHARISIOS: You louse, last time you eavesdropped, no good came of it.

ONESIMOS: Why, when do you mean, sir? Where, sir? I assure you, sir –

CHARISIOS: Still jabbering, are you? Right, take that! [*He hits him.*]

ONESIMOS: Oh! – Nothing, sir!
You're doing me a wrong, though, master; you'll soon see.

CHARISIOS: I'll teach you a lesson soon enough.

HABROTONON [*coming forward*]: Charisios!
There's something you don't know yet.

CHARISIOS: Something I don't know?

HABROTONON: That child I showed you wasn't mine. I made
that up.

CHARISIOS: Not yours? Whose then? Quick, tell me.

HABROTONON: Will you set me free
If I tell you?

CHARISIOS: I'll see you whipped and hanged if you don't
tell me
This instant.

HABROTONON: Yes, I'd better tell. That child's your wife's.

CHARISIOS: Are you quite sure?

HABROTONON: Quite sure. Speak up, Onesimos.

CHARISIOS [*to Onesimos*]: Well, what about it? Are you two
just trying me out?

ONESIMOS: *She* put me up to it, by Apollo I swear she did.

CHARISIOS: You'll twist me round, will you, you little
twister, you?

HABROTONON: Now, dear Charisios, have it out with me.
This child
Is your own wedded wife's and no one else's.

CHARISIOS: Oh!
I wish it were!

HABROTONON: It is, by the dear goddess.

CHARISIOS: But –
How can I believe such a thing?

HABROTONON: It's true!

CHARISIOS: You mean, this child
Is really Pamphile's child?

HABROTONON: Yes, her child – and yours too.

CHARISIOS: Pamphile's child? For God's sake, girl, don't
lead me on
With false hope.

HABROTONON: This is true, sir; but I had to wait
Before explaining, till I was sure of all the facts.

Here there is a gap of several lines, in which presumably Habrotonon tells how she carried out her plot. Then Charisios goes into his own house to see Pamphile. End of Act 4.

Act 5

SCENE ONE

CHAERESTRATOS, ONESIMOS.

ONESIMOS: Listen, Chaerestratos. This slave-girl Habro-
   tonon –
   I'll tell you what she said next. 'Onesimos,' she said,
   'It's your duty to stay loyal in all respects –
   And you know what I mean – loyal to Charisios.'
   There now! She's not your ordinary hired girl! People
   Who act like that are not to be met with every day.
   It was her determination that found the child for
      you.
CHAERESTRATOS: You can have your freedom – it's
   settled. Come, don't hang your head!
   And now, first go and find Charisios alone,
   My own son, my beloved boy . . .

Another gap; then a fragment which probably belongs here.

CHAERESTRATOS: You never could mind your own
   business, Onesimos;
   But I love you all the same.
ONESIMOS: There's nothing I love more
   Than finding everything out . . .

After another considerable gap we have these lines, probably ending
the scene.

CHAERESTRATOS: . . . I'm sure now Habrotonon's a decent,
   virtuous girl.
   But – how attractive she is! I know Charisios:

He'd never have kept his hands off, if she hadn't been
The soul of virtue. Well, I'll keep my hands off too.

    [*Exit* CHAERESTRATOS, *perhaps with Habrotonon, to
    go to buy her freedom from her owner.*]

SCENE TWO

Enter SMICRINES *alone.*

SMICRINES [*to himself*]: Sophrone, I'm damned if I won't
  split your skull for you!
  You'll give me a piece of your mind, like all the rest, will
    you?
  I'm in too much of a hurry, am I, because I intend
  To take my daughter away – you nagging old rag-bag,
    you?
  Must I stand by and watch this precious son-in-law
  Eat up my money in my daughter's house? Must I
  Argue with you about things which are *my* concern? Is
    that
  What you'd like me to do? Isn't it better to take the bull
  By the horns? Just you say one more word, and see what
    you get!
  Damn it, am I to plead my case before Sophrone?
  I'm to interview that tart and persuade her to go home,
  Am I? I tell you, Sophrone, as I hope to live:
  You've seen that pond by the side of the road on the way
    home?
  I'm going to duck you in it again and again all night
  And drown you dead. I'll teach you to have your own
    opinion
  And take sides against me.
        [*He tries the door of Charisios' house.*]
                              This door seems to be locked;
  All right, I'll bang. [*He bangs on the door.*]
  Hi, you there, slaves! Are you all deaf? Open this door!
        [ONESIMOS *opens it and stands firmly in the doorway.*]
ONESIMOS: Who's that knocking at the door? Oh, is it
  Smicrines,

147

Old Pepper-pot, come to fetch his dowry and his daughter?

SMICRINES: You know who I am, blast your eyes.

ONESIMOS: Quite right, quite right!
A very rational, sensible intention too:
A real, first-class abduction.

SMICRINES: Oh! You immortal gods!

ONESIMOS: Smicrines, do you imagine the immortal gods
Have so little to do that they can spend their days
Dealing out good and bad to individuals?

SMICRINES: What do you mean?

ONESIMOS: I'll put it simply for you. How many
Cities are there in the whole world? Let's say a thousand.
In each of them three hundred thousand people live.
Do the gods punish or reward each one of them
Separately? That's not how the gods live! The gods
Are at peace. A life like that would be one endless head-
ache!
You'll ask me, Don't the gods then care about us at all?
They do. They assign to each man his appropriate
Character, to command the garrison of his soul.
This inner force drives one man straight to ruin, if ever
He has abused it; leads another to happiness.
Character is our god, which apportions to each man
Good luck or bad. Propitiate this god, by acting
Kindly and decently; and deserve a happy life.

SMICRINES: You snivelling scab! Don't I act decently?
What's wrong
With *my* character, then?

ONESIMOS: It's driving you to ruin.

SMICRINES: Confound your impudence!

ONESIMOS: Smicrines, do you consider
It right for a man to take his daughter from her husband?

SMICRINES: Right? No one says it's right; but in this case it's
necessary.

ONESIMOS [*appealing to audience*]: You see? This chap
    reckons what's wrong is necessary!
  It's not his character letting him down; it's something else.
        [*He taps his forehead.*]
  Only just now you were set on doing a wicked thing;
  And what has saved you? Just the natural course of events.
  Result: all difficulties smoothed away and solved.
  So, Smicrines, don't let me catch you another time
  Acting precipitately; I warn you. For the present
  Consider yourself acquitted on these charges. Now,
  Go in, pick up your grandson and pay your respects to
    him.
SMICRINES: My *grandson*? What do you mean? You're only
  fit for flogging!
ONESIMOS: You've got a thick skin too, Dad – and a thicker
  skull.
  Your marriageable daughter – is that how you took care of
    her?
  So, five-months children are born; we rear them! Miracle!
SMICRINES: I haven't the slightest idea what you're talking
  about.
ONESIMOS: Maybe;
  But I think old Sophrone has. On a certain date my
    master –
  In fact, at last year's Tauropolia –
SMICRINES [*shouting in at the door*]: Sophrone!
ONESIMOS: – my master found your daughter, dragged her
  off by force
  From where the rest were dancing – there you are, you
    see!
SMICRINES: I see.
ONESIMOS: Now he and she have recognized each other;
  And all is bliss.
        [SOPHRONE *has now entered.*]
SMICRINES: Come here, you pocket-picking hag.

Just tell me what he's talking about.

SOPHRONE [*striking an attitude*]: ''Twas Nature's will,
Who respects not man's law. For this was woman born.'

SMICRINES: Have you gone mad?

SOPHRONE: I'll say the whole speech, end to end,
If you still can't put two and two together, Smicrines.
It's from Euripides' *Auge*.

SMICRINES: Oh, you make me sick,
Reciting poetry. Well you know it's preposterous,
What Onesimos said.

SOPHRONE: I know; there were two preposterous things–
And he's made sense of both of them.

SMICRINES [*as understanding glimmers*]: Why, bless my soul!
But this is extraordinary!

SOPHRONE: It's the most wonderful piece of luck
There ever was.

SMICRINES: If what you're saying's really true,
Why, then, this child is . . .!

PERICEIROMENE

OR

THE UNKINDEST CUT

CHARACTERS

POLEMON, *a Corinthian soldier*
GLYCERA, *his mistress*
SOSIAS, *Polemon's slave*
DORIS, *Glycera's maid*
The goddess IGNORANCE, *or Imperfect Knowledge*
DAOS, *Moschion's slave*
PATAICOS, *a Corinthian merchant*
MYRRHINE, *a wealthy Corinthian woman*
MOSCHION, *son of Myrrhine*
HABROTONON, *a guitar-girl*
CHORUS *of tipsy guests*

*

Scene: A street in Corinth. There are three houses, belonging respectively to Polemon, Pataicos and Myrrhine.

Act 1

SCENE ONE

Almost the whole of the first scene is missing. The following is a conjectural summary:

Glycera lives in the house of her lover Polemon, who is away on military service. Moschion, the son of her neighbour Myrrhine, sees her at her door, comes up to her, and embraces and kisses her. She does not protest or resist. At that moment Sosias arrives to announce that Polemon is back from the war and will soon reach his home. Sosias interrupts Glycera's encounter with Moschion; Moschion vanishes, and Sosias goes off to tell Polemon what he has seen. Polemon arrives and challenges Glycera; she does not deny the fact, and is hesitant in her answers. Polemon, convinced of her infidelity, storms at her. She runs into the house; Polemon follows her, and there in his rage cuts off her hair. Then Glycera reappears shorn and weeping, followed by Polemon full of remorse and guilt and baffled jealousy. Of this scene only three lines survive.

POLEMON: Don't cry, Glycera! I swear to you by Olympian Zeus
  And by Athene – dearest, dearest Glycera –!
GLYCERA: I've heard you swear you love me a thousand times already!

After this, Polemon in despair goes into the house of his friend and neighbour Pataicos. Glycera and her maid Doris discuss what is to be done. Glycera says she is too much afraid of Polemon to stay in his house. She returns there to pack her belongings.

SCENE TWO

The next scene opens with the appearance of the goddess Ignorance. A dozen lines are lost from the beginning of her speech. She tells how, many years ago, Pataicos' wife had twin children, a boy and a girl; and how she died soon after their birth. Pataicos at about the same time lost all his fortune; and feeling unequal to the burden of bringing up two children, decided to expose them. A poor woman found them and took them home. Here the MS begins.

IGNORANCE: ... One of these infants, the girl, she resolved
 to keep
And love as her own child; the other she would give
To a wealthy woman who was longing for a baby,
Who lives here in this house.
   [*She points to Myrrhine's house.*]
          So that was what she did.
Eighteen years passed. War came; and times grew worse
 and worse
For Corinth; and the old woman was at her wits' end.
The child had grown into the girl you saw just now.
She had a lover – that impetuous young man;
So, since he was a Corinthian, she gave the girl,
As if she were giving her own daughter, to this man,
But not in formal marriage. She herself, worn out
With age, remembering that chance might take her off
At any moment, did not hide the truth, but told
The girl how she was found and reared; gave her the
 clothes
She had been wrapped in; also, reflecting how uncertain
All human fortune is, in case the girl should ever
Be in need of help, she told her who her brother was –
Brother by birth, though no one knew it. For she saw,
First, that he was the only relative she had;
And next, she thought it wise to safeguard both of them

154

From unwitting involvement, which might well result
From me – that is, from Ignorance. She knew this boy
Was rich, and always getting drunk; the girl was young
And pretty, and now was being left in a position
That was anything but stable. So the old woman died.
The soldier Polemon, the girl's lover, bought this house
Not long ago; and she, living next door to her brother,
Has breathed no word of what she knows; nor does she
    want
To endanger the distinguished social rank which now
Seems to be his: what Fortune has given him, she feels,
He should enjoy.

            Now, yesterday evening, quite by chance –
I told you he's a lively, aggressive lad, and always
Hanging around the house – he just caught sight of her
When she was sending her servant on some errand. As
    soon
As he saw her there at the door, he ran across and
    began
Kissing and hugging her. She, knowing he was her
    brother,
Did not run away. That moment, up comes Sosias
And sees them. Well, it's easy to guess what happened
    then.
He went off saying he'd ask her at the proper time
What she meant by it. She stood there crying, heart-
    broken that
She was not free to embrace and kiss her own brother.

And all this flared up for the sake of what should follow:
First, to set Polemon in a rage – by nature he's not
That sort of person; it was I leading him on
To set in motion the whole train of discoveries,
And so that both may at last find their families
And be re-united with them. So, if any of you

Were shocked at what happened and thought it terrible,
    think again.
Evil itself, in the very act, swings round to good
Under Heaven's guiding hand. So, ladies and gentlemen,
Good-bye! Be kind; and give the rest of the play success!

SCENE THREE

Enter SOSIAS *from Pataicos' house.*

SOSIAS: Polemon, our violent warrior of an hour ago,
Polemon, who says women are not to keep their hair –
Is sitting at table, crying. I've just left him there
At lunch with the whole household; and his friends have
   come
In a body to persuade him not to take it all
So much to heart. Since he's no way of finding out
What's going on here [*he points to Polemon's house*] he sends
   me to fetch his cloak.
He doesn't want his cloak; it's just his whim to keep
Me on the run.

> [DORIS *appears with* GLYCERA *at the door of Polemon's
> house; when Doris comes out, Glycera disappears in-
> doors.* SOSIAS *stands at one side, and Doris does not see
> him.*]

DORIS: Yes, madam, I'll just go and see.

SOSIAS [*aside*]: That's Doris. How she's grown up! There's a
   lovely wench!
Well! These Corinthian dames live in some style, I see.
Now, in we go.

> [DORIS *goes across to Myrrhine's door;* SOSIAS, *unseen
> by her, slips into Polemon's house.*]

DORIS: I'll knock at Myrrhine's door. There's no one
About out here. [*She knocks.*] I'm sorry for any girl who
   has
A soldier for a husband. They're a lawless lot;
You just can't trust them. The way he's treated Glycera –
It's so outrageous! [*She knocks again.*] Hullo, there!

> [*While Doris is intent on Myrrhine's door,* SOSIAS *slips
> out of Polemon's house.*]

SOSIAS: Polemon will be pleased
  To hear she's crying at this moment – the very thing
  He wanted.

            [SOSIAS *goes into Pataicos' house. A slave-boy opens*
            Myrrhine's door to Doris.]

DORIS: Ask your mistress, sonny, to come out here.

At this point about seventy lines are missing, during which, it would
seem, Myrrhine comes out, and Glycera comes out of Polemon's
house; and it is arranged that Glycera shall move into Myrrhine's
house for the present. Myrrhine's slave Daos, with some others,
carries Glycera's luggage across – only a few belongings, since most
of her dresses, as we find later, are left in Polemon's house. Probably
in this scene Glycera tells Myrrhine that she is Moschion's sister, and
mentions as proof the ornaments which were left with her when she
was exposed. Myrrhine has always pretended, even to her husband,
that Moschion was her own child.

            [*When Glycera has gone indoors with Myrrhine,* DAOS
            sees Polemon's tipsy guests coming out of Pataicos' house,
            and hurries his fellow-slaves into Myrrhine's house.]

DAOS: Come on, hurry up now! There's a great gang of lads
    coming,
  All drunk. [*To the audience*] I give my mistress full marks;
    she's invited
  Glycera in on purpose. There's a mother for you!
  I must fetch my young master; if I'm not mistaken,
  This is the moment for him to come home double-quick!
            [*Exit* DAOS.]

Act 2

SCENE ONE

MOSCHION *and* DAOS *enter from the town.*

MOSCHION: Daos, you rat, many a time you've told me lies.
 You bare-faced crook!
 Are you once more leading me up the garden? Because if
 you are –
DAOS: If I am, just get a rope and hang me now.
MOSCHION: Say that again.
DAOS: Treat me as you would your enemy. But, if what I've
 said is true,
 If you find her there indoors now, Moschion – if you now
 possess
 All you've been pursuing, if *my* endless arguments induced
 Her to come here, and your mother to receive her, and
 provide
 Everything your heart could wish for: what's *my* future, if
 you please?
MOSCHION:[1] What's your future, Daos? Just think – what
 would please you most of all?
 Come, now, what do you really long for? Isn't the tread-
 mill your first choice?
DAOS: Send me to the treadmill, do – if Polemon doesn't get
 here first.
 Then the wooden collar will soon be clapped on someone
 else's neck.
MOSCHION [*coaxing*]: Look here, Daos: I want to make you
 steward-in-chief of my affairs,
 Major-domo, generalissimo, Daos! Now, don't let me
 down!

---

 1. The MS here is badly damaged, and the next twenty lines are largely
conjecture.

DAOS: Well, the blockade's not begun yet; you've still time
to run indoors.

MOSCHION: But – suppose, now, you betrayed me – sold me
out to Polemon?

DAOS: Look – I'll need some gold – say seven talents –

MOSCHION: Is there anything
You wouldn't do for money?

DAOS: Moschion, let's be realistic now.
I've been shopping.

        [*He taps a large bag which he is carrying.*]

        Plenty of food here. The plain truth is, we're at war.

Right – then let *me* plan the strategy. Spend *twelve* talents,
if need be,

Straight off, rather than be made a fool of. Doesn't that
make sense?

MOSCHION: Tell that to the washer-women, corner-boy!

DAOS: Look – there's a chance
Seven talents may buy off Polemon. Shall I try it?

MOSCHION: Name of Zeus!
You're no general – you're a fried-fish cheap-jack. I'll see
you in jail.

DAOS: Is this meant to win my loyal service, master – talk
like this?

Waste no more time; get indoors now.

MOSCHION: I'd best leave it all to you.
Talk them over if you can, then. If you can't, I'll have to
come

Out and fight this goddam feather-crested brigadier.

DAOS: You will.

MOSCHION: Wait, though, Daos – you go in first. Find out
how the land lies there.

See what Glycera's doing; where my mother is; whether
they feel

Welcoming towards me. I don't need to tell you what to
do,

Do I? You've got your head screwed on.

DAOS: I'll go.

MOSCHION: I'll just walk up and down
  Here by the door and wait for you.

      [DAOS *goes into the house.*]

                              Last night when I went up to her
  She showed clearly how she felt towards me; didn't run
    away;
  Put her arms right round me, held me tight. Well, by
    Athene! I'm
  Not bad-looking; quite good company; girls are apt to
    fall for me.
  This is a critical moment; I'd be wise to say a prayer for
    luck.

      [DAOS *comes out again.*]

DAOS: Moschion! She's had her bath. She's sitting down now.

MOSCHION: Darling girl!

DAOS: Your Mamma's just pottering round with this and
  that. The midday meal's
  Ready. From the look of things I'd say they were expect-
    ing you.

MOSCHION: They've been waiting too long. Who says I'm
  not handsome? – Did you say
  I was here?

DAOS: No.

MOSCHION: Go and tell them.

DAOS [*dashing off*]:   I'll be back in just two ticks.

MOSCHION [*alone*]: If she feels too shy to tell me that she
  loves me – well, I'll just
  Question her, call Daos as witness. – Wait: as soon as I go
    in,
  First I'd better kiss my mother, get her firmly on my
    side,
  Be as sweet as possible to her, be her own and only boy.
  After all, she's shown a personal interest in this affair.

I hear someone coming out.

[DAOS *appears, looking glum.*]

           Well, what's wrong, Daos? Why, you seem
Quite reluctant to come near me.

DAOS: So I am, by Zeus – What's wrong?
Everything. When I went in and told your mother you
    were here,
'That's enough of that,' says she; 'now how does Moschion
    know of this?
Did *you* tell him Glycera was frightened and took refuge
    here?
Out of my sight, blast you,' says she, 'crawl away and
    drown yourself.'
That's the truth, then: once they knew that you were
    waiting here to pounce,
Psst! your prize was whisked away.

MOSCHION: You skunk! You dare to laugh at me?

DAOS: Laughing, am I? Ask your mother –!

MOSCHION: What about her? Did she bring
Glycera here against her will, then? Wasn't this plan set on
    foot
Just for my sake? You said you persuaded her to come to
    me!

DAOS: I said I persuaded her? By Apollo, I said no such
    thing!

MOSCHION: Don't think I don't know what lies you're
    telling; since you also said –
Half a minute ago – you'd got my mother to take in
    Glycera
All for my sake!

DAOS: Well – why, yes! I said that. I remember now.

MOSCHION: *And* you said you thought my mother did this in
    my interest.

DAOS: Oh, I can't be sure of that; but I did try persuading
    her.

MOSCHION: Come here. Nearer.

DAOS: How near?

       [MOSCHION *hits him.*]

MOSCHION: Do you still think lying pays, you rat?

DAOS: Well, sir, no, sir. Tell the truth, sir – Yes, you're
    right, sir; I'm a rat.

MOSCHION: You're being funny with me.

DAOS: No, sir! Cross my heart, sir! Listen, sir:
  Probably she doesn't care for doing things in a rush like
    that,
  On the spur of the moment. She'd prefer to get to know
    you first,
  Listen to what you've got to say. Remember, she's not
    here on hire
  Like a flute-girl or some measly prostitute.

MOSCHION: It seems to me,
  Daos, you've got a point there.

DAOS: Have I? Test it, then. I'm pretty sure
  She's for you. She didn't leave her home, and Polemon,
    just for fun.
  Hang on here for three or four days. Stick it out. She'll
    soon come round.
  She, in fact, said just that to me; – may as well tell the
    whole truth now.

MOSCHION: Daos, where can I lock you up meanwhile?
    You say, just hang on here.
  Hang around for three or four days? I'll be hanged to
    death by then.
  And it's barely ninety seconds since you told me your last
    lie!

DAOS: I need time to think, and you keep interrupting. Your
    best way,
  Master, is to change your tactics. Go in quietly to your
    room –

MOSCHION: You'll keep me supplied at meal-times?

DAOS: Look: there's plenty in this bag.
In now, quickly; and lie down. Between us we'll work
something out.

MOSCHION: All right, you can have your way.

[MOSCHION *goes into Myrrhine's house. At the same
time* SOSIAS, *carrying Polemon's cloak and sword, appears
at the door of Pataicos' house just in time to recognize
Moschion. Daos has not yet seen Sosias.*]

DAOS [*mopping his brow*]: A close thing, that, by Heracles!
I'm still trembling; and my tongue's all dry with fright.
I never thought,
When we started, that this kettle of fish would be so hard
to fry.

[SOSIAS *has come downstage to address the audience.*
DAOS *now sees him and stands aside out of sight.*]

SOSIAS: He's sent me back again here with his sword and
cloak;
I'm to find out what Glycera's doing, and bring him
word.
For two pins I'd tell him I found young Moschion
In the house; that'd make him spring to action. But I
won't.
Poor devil, he's had rough luck, and I'm sorry for him.

[*He looks round towards Myrrhine's house.*]

I didn't dream it: that was Moschion all right;
I recognize him from the last time I was here.

[SOSIAS *goes into Polemon's house.* DAOS *comes forward.*]

DAOS: The Foreign Legion's here! This is a pretty mess,
By Apollo, a proper mix-up; and I haven't yet
Thought of the hottest point of all – the flaming row,
The grand bust-up, my master's going to make, if he
Turns up from the country sooner than expected.

[*Polemon's door opens, and* SOSIAS *comes out holding
two slaves by the scruff of the neck.*]

SOSIAS: You!

   You dung-brained oafs, you mules! You've let her go,
     have you?

   You let her through that door, did you? When Polemon

   Gets angry, you'll be lucky if he just cuts your hair!

     [*He turns to the audience.*]

   She's moved across to the neighbour's, to her fancy man;

   And we, says she, can stay here howling till we're hoarse.

     [SOSIAS *walks towards Myrrhine's house.*]

DAOS [*to the audience*]: Listen to Polemon's pet prophet! He's
   not far wrong.

SOSIAS: I'm going to knock at the door. [*He does so.*]

DAOS: Now then, you mangy mongrel, what do you want?
   What's up?

SOSIAS: Are you from that house?

DAOS: Perhaps.

SOSIAS: And you can call *me* names,

   When *you*'re a lot of lunatics! Great gods above!

   You've got some nerve, to take a free-born woman away

   By force from her husband and lock her up.

DAOS: Don't make me sick.

   Whoever you are, you're a blackmailer; sticks out a mile.

SOSIAS: Do you think we in this house have got no guts, no
   fight?

   Are we men, or aren't we?

DAOS: Men? Ha! Twopenny-halfpenny men!

   And when your ninepenny sergeant picks recruits like
     these [*pointing to Sosias' two companions*]

   We'll fight you any minute you like.

SOSIAS: You whipper-snapper!

DAOS: Oh, go to hell! You heard what I said – go to hell.

   You slave of a comic booby! You'll not get hold of her.

SOSIAS: Oh – then you admit you've got her?

DAOS: Do you remember, now –

   Some time ago – oh, I remember! – the way I dealt

With some of your lot?

SOSIAS: Our lot? Who are you talking about?
And who do you think you're being funny with – tell me
that?
You're off your nut. We'll bust your miserable dolls'
house
Wide open in two ticks. Go and help that fancy chap
Buckle his sword on.

DAOS: If this fuss you keep on making
Is all because you think we've got her in *our* house,
You lousy tramp –

SOSIAS: These twopenny-halfpenny men of mine
Will turn you inside out as soon as spit at you.

DAOS: Twopence-halfpenny? I was joking: you're a sewer-
rat,
A dung-worm.

SOSIAS: You be careful, street-boy! I eat flesh.

DAOS: Shog off! [*To the audience*] If he's a man-eater I'm
going indoors.

[DORIS *has come out of Myrrhine's house in answer to
Sosias' knock.* DAOS *dodges in through the open door.*]

SOSIAS:[1] I warn you, Doris, you've got a lot to answer for;
You're more to blame than anyone else, I tell you
straight.

DORIS: Now, Sosias, be a good fellow and just tell Polemon
That Glycera's gone to stay with a woman friend because
She was frightened.

SOSIAS: Oh, yes! Frightened, was she? Gone to stay
With a woman, has she? Not Myrrhine, by any chance?

DORIS: Just listen, Sosias –

SOSIAS: Gone next door to her fancy man;
To this house, here!

DORIS: You ought to be ashamed of yourself.

1. From here to the next gap in the MS the text is largely conjectural.

166

SOSIAS: Get out of my sight; you're playing a double game,
     I know.

After this comes a gap of more than fifty lines, during which it
seems that Polemon plans with Sosias and his other slaves to take
Myrrhine's house by storm; while Pataicos, who has been talking to
Glycera, tries to persuade Polemon to take a more sober and realistic
attitude. With them is the guitar-girl Habrotonon. The following
fragments may belong to this part of the play.

PATAICOS: When it's your body that's diseased, you need a
     doctor;
  If it's your mind or heart that's sick, you need a friend.

POLEMON: The only cure for anger is an honest word
  From a good friend.

PATAICOS: However much upset you are,
  Don't let annoyance drive you to act precipitately.
  When things go wrong, a sensible man must above all
  Control unreasoning anger.

POLEMON: Nothing's more welcome than a sympathetic
  friend.

Pataicos' attempts at conciliation are resented by Sosias, who meanwhile has been drinking. The MS resumes.

SOSIAS: You mark my words, he's come here bribed by them
     indoors,
  Myrrhine and Moschion. He's betraying you and your men.
PATAICOS: Look here, my dear chap, give this battle-drill a
     rest;
  Go in and sleep it off. You're not yourself, you know –
  Yes, I mean you; you're drunk, I'll swear.

SOSIAS: What, me? Me drunk?
One little cup I had, or less. I said to myself,
There's trouble coming, I'll keep my head clear, just in case
I'm needed. There you are; that's my luck.

POLEMON [*to Pataicos*]: You're right. – Sosias,
Now listen to me.

SOSIAS [*at attention*]: At your orders, Captain.

POLEMON: That's the style.
Here are your orders. – Habrotonon, give the word of
command.

PATAICOS [*to Polemon*]: First, do tell Sosias and his army to
clear off.

SOSIAS [*to Pataicos*]: You're handling this campaign all wrong.
[*In despair, to audience*] He's making peace,
When he ought to be storming the ramparts.

POLEMON: All my troubles, then,
Come from Pataicos, do they?

SOSIAS [*sulkily*]: He's not general.

HABROTONON: Come on, now, dear man, do go in.

SOSIAS: All right, I'm going.
[*Sosias and his two men go into Polemon's house.*]

POLEMON: I thought you'd manage something, Habrotonon.
You'd be
Useful at a siege yourself, either for straight assault
Or lying covered. – Where are you off to, sweetie-pie?
– Is that tart blushing? – Hey, are you all upset with me?
[*Exit* HABROTONON.]

PATAICOS: Now, Polemon: if the case were such as you
describe,
If someone had seduced your lawful wife –

POLEMON: Lawful?
You know she's not, man. But what difference does it make?
I've always thought of her as my lawful wife.

PATAICOS: Don't shout.
Who gave her to you?

POLEMON: Who gave her? Why, she gave herself.

PATAICOS: That's fair enough. And for a time you pleased
her. Now
You don't please her any longer; and since you behaved
Improperly towards her, she has left you.

POLEMON: What do you mean,
Improperly? [*Then with a complete change of tone*] In saying
that you've hit me just
Where it hurts most.

PATAICOS: You surely must admit that what
You're doing now is crazy. Just what is your aim?
To drag her back? She has every right to please herself.
The one course left for a discontented lover is
Persuasion.

POLEMON: What of the man who came behind my back
And seduced her? Isn't he in the wrong?

PATAICOS: He is; and that,
Should it ever come to a dispute, gives you the right
To lodge a complaint; but if you take her away by force
You'll lose your case in a court of law. What he has done
Gives you the right to sue him, but not to take the law
Into your own hands.

POLEMON: What? Not even for this?

PATAICOS: Not even
For this.

POLEMON: I don't know what to say, by God I don't.
I might as well hang myself. Pataicos, Glycera's left me.
She's left me, man – Glycera! Look – what do you think?
Would *you*
See what you can do? You know her, you've often talked
with her.
Be my ambassador; go in and have a word –
Before I try. Please, now, I beg you.

PATAICOS: A good idea.
I will.

POLEMON: I suppose you're fairly good at putting a case?

PATAICOS: Fairly.

POLEMON: Oh, but you must be good at it, Pataicos –
The whole business depends on that. Tell her that I –
If ever I did her any sort of wrong whatever –
I swear I love and cherish her every day and hour –
It's true! – I'd like to show you her dresses –

PATAICOS [*with a deprecating gesture*]:   You're too kind.

POLEMON: Just come and look at them, Pataicos, do. You'll feel
All the more sorry for me.

PATAICOS: Poseidon!

POLEMON: Come along.
Marvellous dresses! And then, how marvellous she looks
When she puts one of them on! I dare say you've not seen –

PATAICOS: I have indeed.

POLEMON: For sheer splendour – they're worth
a look.
– Oh, there I go! What's splendour got to do with it?
I'm raving mad, going on like that.

PATAICOS: No, not at all.

POLEMON: Do you think not? Anyhow, you must come and
see. This way.

PATAICOS: Lead on, then. Let's go in.

        [*They go into Polemon's house.* MOSCHION *looks out
        of the door of Myrrhine's house, sees them disappearing,
        and emerges.*]

MOSCHION: Yes, go in and hang yourselves!
To hell with you! 'Mine enemies with levelled spears
Leapt forth upon me.' Scum! They haven't got the guts
To storm a swallow's nest full of chicks.

        [SOSIAS *wanders out, still very drunk, and goes to sleep
        on the ground.*]

                And Daos said
They'd got a squad of mercenaries – why, *that* must be

One of these famous mercenaries. – It's Sosias!
A one-man army!
                              – Of all the swarms of unhappy men
In the world today – and certainly, for whatever cause,
There's a fine crop of misery at this very moment
All over Hellas – I don't believe there's a single one
Of them all that has such wretched luck as I've been having.
When I got in, I did none of the things I usually do;
I didn't go to see my mother; I didn't call
For any of the servants; just went off to my own room
And lay down on my bed. I was perfectly composed.
I sent Daos to tell my mother I'd arrived –
Just that, no more. But Daos gave not a thought to me.
He found the table set for lunch, and sat straight down
And tucked in. Meanwhile I lay there, telling myself,
'Your mother'll be here any moment with a message
From your sweetheart suggesting how things might be
    arranged.'
And I was practising a little speech . . .

At this point about a hundred and fifty lines are missing. It is clear
that in the course of them Myrrhine's husband comes home. What
part he plays in the dénouement, whether he raises the 'flaming row'
Daos expected, we don't know. It can also be gathered that this
passage was largely occupied with Moschion's eavesdropping; first,
while indoors he has overheard a talk between Myrrhine and Glycera;
then he seems to have heard Pataicos soliloquizing after he came out
of Polemon's house; then when Glycera comes out he listens to her
conversation with Pataicos. What he picked up from these various
sources can be pieced together during the progress of the following
scene between Glycera and Pataicos. Glycera is trying to prove to
Pataicos that she is not involved with Moschion; if she had been,
she says, she would have acted differently.

GLYCERA: . . . Think now, Pataicos: suppose I had taken
    refuge here,

Not to be Moschion's wife, mark you – for since I have
No money or family that's impossible – but to be
His mistress; could I ever have won his father and mother
To accept me? No, of course not. I'd have done my best
To keep it secret, and so would he. But instead of that
He went straight up and introduced me to his father.
When I came to this house I chose deliberately
A foolish course, one that would weigh against me, and
Perhaps invite you to suspect the worst of me.

PATAICOS: Wipe that suspicion out, and your good name is
   clear.

GLYCERA: Pataicos, did you think the same as all the others?
Did you come here assuming I was that sort of girl?

PATAICOS: No, no, as I worship Zeus! I do hope you can show
   That the accusations are in fact unjust. Myself,
   I believe they are. Yet, even so – go back to him!

GLYCERA: Polemon can find other girls to insult and bully.

PATAICOS: It was a wrong, but not a deliberate insult.

GLYCERA: No?
   It was unspeakable, what he did to me. Look there!
     [showing her hair]
   Could any slave-girl be a more revolting sight?

A gap here of sixteen lines, in which Glycera assures Pataicos that
she can prove she is free-born. She is telling him of the tokens she
possesses; Moschion is hidden and listening.

GLYCERA: ... The old woman who brought me up gave me
   those things
   As a gift from my own father and mother, telling me
   Always to keep them with me and look after them.

PATAICOS: What do you want me to do?

GLYCERA: Have these things fetched for me.

PATAICOS: Do you mean that you have given up Polemon
   finally?
   My dear girl, what are you planning?

GLYCERA: Just do this for me.
Will you?

PATAICOS: But this is silly. Above everything else
You ought to yield a little.

GLYCERA: I know what's best for me.

PATAICOS: You really mean that? Well; which of the servants knows
Where these things are?

GLYCERA: Doris knows. – Someone call her out.

PATAICOS: Yet all the same, Glycera, I beg you in God's name,
Make up your quarrel with Polemon on the kind of terms
I spoke about just now.

       [*Enter* DORIS.]

DORIS: Here I am, madam. Anything I can do for you?

MOSCHION [*aside*]: Now I'll soon know the worst.

GLYCERA: Yes, Doris. Go and fetch
My little chest, the one where those embroideries
Are kept. I gave it to you to keep carefully;
I'm sure you know the one I mean. Go, hurry now.

       [DORIS *goes*.]

MOSCHION [*aside*]: Great gods in glory! This is a most extraordinary
Experience for me. Glycera, apparently,
Has not the slightest . . .

A gap of seven lines, in which Doris brings out the chest and Pataicos begins looking at the contents.

PATAICOS: . . . This is just like that same embroidered scarf I saw
Then – all those years ago! Look, this now, next to it –
Isn't this a goat, or cow, or some such animal?

GLYCERA: Why, dear Pataicos, that's no goat! Look, it's a stag.

PATAICOS: Well, all I know is, it's got horns.

GLYCERA: What's this third thing?

PATAICOS: A winged horse – yes! These *are* my wife's things –
my poor wife!

MOSCHION [*aside*]: Would you have thought it possible? I
can't believe

That my own mother would do a thing so scandalous
As abandon her own child, the girl she'd borne herself.
If this *can* be believed, and Glycera is my sister,
To lose so sweet a sweetheart's just my rotten luck.

PATAICOS [*to himself*]: I had *two* children. Where's my son?
More sadness yet.

GLYCERA: What is it? There's some question on your mind.
Ask me.

PATAICOS: Where did you get these things?

GLYCERA: Why, I was wearing them
When I was picked up as a baby.

PATAICOS: Glycera,
Stand back a little – there; I want to see your face.

MOSCHION [*aside*]: This moment is the turning-point of my
whole life.

PATAICOS: And when they found you, were you alone? I
want to know.

GLYCERA: No indeed; my brother and I had been exposed
together.

MOSCHION [*aside*]: That answers one of my questions.

PATAICOS: Then how did you come
To be separated?

GLYCERA: I could tell you the whole story;
But – ask what I have a right to tell you – about myself.
The rest I must not speak of; I gave her my oath.

MOSCHION [*aside*]: There! that's a second point – it tallies
perfectly.
She gave her oath to my mother. Oh, my head's going
round!

PATAICOS: I see. Who was it found you, then? Who brought you up?

GLYCERA: A woman who found me lying there took care of me.

PATAICOS: Did she describe the sort of place she found you in?

GLYCERA: It was beside a spring, she said, shaded by trees.

PATAICOS: The man who took my children spoke of such a place.

GLYCERA: But who was he? – if it is proper for me to ask.

PATAICOS: A slave; but it was I who shirked caring for you.

GLYCERA: We were your true-born children, and you exposed us? Why?

PATAICOS: Many things unbelievable are done, my girl.
 Your mother died soon after giving birth to you;
 Also, one day before she died, one day before –

GLYCERA: What happened, father? Something dreadful!

PATAICOS: I became
 Penniless, after living in comfort all my life.

GLYCERA: Could all that happen in one day? How terrible!

PATAICOS: Yes; news came that the ship which earned my livelihood
 Was swallowed in the stormy surge of the Aegean.

GLYCERA: That was a cruel day for me.

PATAICOS: For a bankrupt man,
 To shoulder the extra burden of two mouths to feed
 Seemed to me then the sheerest folly.

GLYCERA:[1] ...
 But were no tokens left with them for recognition?

PATAICOS: Yes, various necklaces were left with them, some clothes –
 Not many; and a little box.

GLYCERA: You're right so far;
 Now tell me what was in it.

                    1. The line is missing.

                         175

PATAICOS: Let me see – why, yes!
  There was a woman's girdle.

GLYCERA: Yes, there was! But, father,
  What figures were embroidered on it? Can you say?

PATAICOS: Yes; there were girls dancing together.

MOSCHION [*aside*]:   I begin
  To see it all.

GLYCERA: You're right; I have it still. What next?

PATAICOS: A golden headband. – Must I go through the
  whole list?

GLYCERA: Dear father, I'll stop doubting. Was I unfair?
  Forgive me!
     [*They embrace each other.*]

Here follows a gap of a hundred lines. It seems that the tokens which
Pataicos has just described are those which Moschion has in his
possession; and that at this point Moschion comes out of hiding and
is united with his father and sister. During the next few scenes
Glycera moves into Pataicos' house, and Polemon learns that she
and Moschion have been recognized as Pataicos' children. This makes
Polemon quite sure that Glycera will never again have anything to
do with him. He is talking with Doris.

POLEMON: . . . I meant to hang myself.

DORIS: No, no! Don't say that!

POLEMON: But what shall I do, Doris?
  How shall I live without her? Life's not worth living.

DORIS: Glycera says now, she'll go back to you – !

POLEMON: She says –
  Good gods!

DORIS: – if you're resolved from now on to have done
  With bad behaviour.

POLEMON: Doris, I give my oath to that.
  I will be faultless. Oh, your news is wonderful!
  Go to her now. Tomorrow, Doris, I'll set you free.
  Now this is what you are to say – listen! – She's gone!

Oh, raging, jealous Love!
You took my heart by storm. It was her brother, then,
And not her lover, that she kissed. I should have asked
For an explanation; instead, curse-ridden with jealousy,
I acted all in a moment like a drunken fool.
That's why I meant to hang myself; – and serve me right.
     [DORIS *reappears.*]
Doris, dear Doris, what's your news?

DORIS: Good news: she'll come!

POLEMON: She said that? She was making fun of me.

DORIS: Oh, no,
She was not, by Aphrodite! She was putting on
Her best gown; and her father stood and looked at her.
You ought to have offered sacrifice to thank the gods
For what they've done for her. This is her day of days,
And a gloomy face like yours is sheer impiety.

POLEMON: By Zeus, you're right. – The very thing – the
    cook's indoors.
He must kill the sow, and we'll have a feast.

DORIS: But what about
The basket, and all the other things?

POLEMON: Basket? Don't worry!
We'll do all that stuff later. Tell the cook to kill
That sow. And better still, I'm going to take a wreath
From the altar here and wear it.

DORIS: That's a good idea;
You'll look much more persuasive.

POLEMON: Go and fetch Glycera,
Quickly!

DORIS: She was just coming, and her father, too.

POLEMON: Her father, too? Then what's in store for me?
       [*He hears the door of Pataicos' house opening, and runs
       into his own house.*]

DORIS [*laughing*]:   Polemon!
Are you running away? What do you expect to see

When a door opens? A man-eating dragon? Well!
I'll go in too, and be of any use I can!

    [DORIS *follows Polemon into his house. Enter* PATAICOS
    and GLYCERA.]

PATAICOS [*to Glycera*]: I'm more than glad to hear you say
  you'll make it up.

When you've enjoyed good fortune, to be ready then
To accept honest amends – that proves you a true Greek.
– Here, boy! Run and call Polemon, quick!

POLEMON [*appearing at his door*]:   I'm coming.
I went in to arrange about a sacrifice
To thank the gods for this great news. I've just been told
Glycera's found her father – all her dreams come true.

PATAICOS: Yes; and I've something more to add: I here give
  you
Glycera, your wedded wife, to bear you lawful sons.

POLEMON: I take her.

PATAICOS: And a dowry of three talents.

POLEMON: Why,
That's marvellous!

PATAICOS: And, my boy, in future just forget
You're a soldier, and be less ferocious to your friends.

POLEMON: Good gods! Do you think, when I've just been
  within an inch
Of destroying my whole life, I'm going to turn ferocious
Ever again, or even dream of it? – Glycera,
Dearest! Only say you forgive me.

GLYCERA: Your crazy act
Has been our beginning of happiness.

POLEMON: Darling, it has.

GLYCERA: And that, of course, is why I forgive you!

POLEMON: Pataicos,
There's a banquet on; come and join us.

PATAICOS: Wait a moment, though.
One wedding's not enough. I've got to find a wife

For my son Moschion. [*He pulls Moschion forward.*]
    Who shall I get for Moschion?
  Why, there's Philinos' daughter –

MOSCHION: Oh, almighty gods
  Preserve me! . . .

THE SAMIAN WOMAN

CHARACTERS

DEMEAS, *a rich Athenian citizen*
PARMENON, *house-slave of Demeas*
CHRYSIS, *a free-born woman from Samos, Demeas' mistress*
NICERATOS, *Demeas' poor neighbour, father of Plangon*
MOSCHION, *adopted son of Demeas*
A COOK
CHORUS *of wedding-guests*
An old Nurse; a number of slaves, male and female

*

Scene: A street in Athens, with Demeas' house on one side, Niceratos' house on the other.

PROLOGUE

The opening five lines are lost; the next sixteen have their first few syllables missing. The gaps in the Prologue probably included the information that Demeas and Niceratos have been travelling together to Asia Minor on business, and are expected back very soon; that Chrysis was pregnant by Demeas when he went away, and that he had instructed her that the child was to be exposed at birth; and that Chrysis had borne a child, but it had died. The translation begins five lines after the gap, with some supplementation. The speaker is Moschion.

MOSCHION: ... and I think the most
Sensible way that I could do this for you would be
To give you a full description of his character.

    He adopted me when I was a small boy. How delighted
I was at the time, I remember clearly; and I won't
Enlarge on it. He conferred these favours on me when
I was still too young to understand. I was thought of
As being in no way different from anyone else;
To use the common phrase, I was one of *hoi polloi* –
Though now, God knows, I've met more difficulties than
      most.
We're a leading family; and I soon became different
By the fact of being *choregos*, holding a position
Of some distinction. My father would keep hounds for me,
And horses; as a cavalry officer I did well.
I was able to give modest assistance to my friends
If they needed it. My father gave me a man's life.
At the same time I repaid my debt with a certain charm;
I was well-behaved.

                  In course of time it happened (for I
Must give you now a complete account of our affairs;
I've plenty of time) that Demeas grew rather keen
On a Samian woman, an *hetaira*; naturally

Enough, he wanted to keep it secret, being a bit
Embarrassed. However, I realized the situation.
I reckoned, if he did not establish an open claim
To her, he would have constant trouble with young rivals;
That, perhaps on my account, he shrank from doing this.

Here nearly 30 lines are missing or defective; they evidently contained the first mention of a romantic acquaintance between Moschion and Plangon.

Now this girl's mother lived on the most friendly terms
With my father's mistress; who was held in high regard
By them, and they in turn by us. Well now, one day,
On hurrying home from the farm, I met them gathered here
All ready to celebrate the Adonis festival
With some other women. The festival, as you'd expect,
Included a lot of fun; I stood with them to watch;
For all the excitement soon dispelled my wish to sleep.
They were bringing people from the garden up to the roof,
They were dancing, everywhere girls were making a night
    of it.

I hesitate to tell you the sequel; and perhaps –
Well, I'm embarrassed; I know that's no help – but I am.
The girl became pregnant – which makes clear the way
    things went
That night. I didn't deny being responsible;
I went, without being asked, to see the girl's mother.
I promised marriage, as soon as my father should return,
And gave my oath. A boy was born quite recently;
And I've acknowledged him.

                    Now, by pure coincidence,
Chrysis happened to bear a child at the same time;
For we call this . . .

Here about 28 lines are missing; they include the opening of Act I.

Act 1

There is first a fragment spoken perhaps by Chrysis:

... And I, waiting to hear what they were saying ...

[*Enter* MOSCHION *from the street and* PARMENON *from Demeas' house.*]

MOSCHION: What, have you actually seen my father, Parmenon?

PARMENON: Why, didn't you hear me? I said so.

MOSCHION: And our neighbour too?

PARMENON: They're both here.

MOSCHION: Good work.

PARMENON: Take your courage in both hands
And open the subject of your marriage immediately.

MOSCHION: But how? Now that the matter's become imminent
I already feel weak at the knees.

PARMENON: What's that? Afraid?

MOSCHION: I'm nervous before my father.

PARMENON: Then what about the girl
You got into trouble? And her mother? Bless my soul,
You're trembling, sissy!

[CHRYSIS *appears at the door of Demeas' house, accompanied by a slave-girl holding the baby.*]

CHRYSIS [*to the baby*]: What are you moaning about, misery?

PARMENON: Here's Chrysis. — Why do you ask me what
I'm moaning about?
Ridiculous question! I want this wedding to happen *now.*
I want Moschion to stop watering this door-post
With tears, and remember certain things he swore to do:
To sacrifice, put on a garland, stand forward
And make sesame-pie himself. Don't you agree
I've got reasons enough?

MOSCHION: I'll do all that. Why make
A fuss?

CHRYSIS: I think, myself –

PARMENON: We'd better leave the baby
Where it is now, for Chrysis to bring up, and say
That it's her own child.

CHRYSIS: Yes, why not?

MOSCHION: My father will
Resent it.

CHRYSIS: At first, perhaps; but then he'll stop. Dear boy,
Your father's just as badly in love as you are. Love
Brings a man round in no time, however irritable
He may be. I think I would put up with anything
Sooner than let this baby go to a hired nurse
Out in some village. . .

Here about 25 lines are missing.

MOSCHION: . . . a pitiable wretch. Hadn't I better hang
    myself?
Courage is the only friendly advocate; and I
Am somewhat cowardly in this kind of argument.
Why don't I slink away to some secluded place
And practise? This ordeal will be no easy one.

        [*Exit* MOSCHION. *Enter* DEMEAS *and* NICERATOS
        from Demeas' house.]

DEMEAS: Well, now we've come home, don't you feel the
    change of scene?
What a difference between here and further east! Pontus!
Thick-witted, gross old men; millions of fish; a kind
Of unpleasantness in business. Then Byzantium – ugh!
Wormwood in every dish – Apollo! Ah, but here –
The untainted blessings of the poor! Dear, dear Athens!
May you attain the wealth that you deserve! May we,
Who love our city, be blessed with every happiness!

— Indoors, now, everybody! [*To Niceratos*] You stand
  staring at me
As if you'd had a stroke.

NICERATOS: The thing that struck me most,
  Demeas, of the strange things we met abroad, was this:
  The sun, sometimes for days on end, was invisible;
  A kind of thick fog, so it seemed, would cloud it over.

DEMEAS: Not at all. The sun saw nothing there worth
  looking at;
  He was doing his duty to those people, and no more.

NICERATOS: You're right, by Dionysos!

DEMEAS: However, let's leave that
  For others to argue, and return to our discussion.
  What do you mean to do?

NICERATOS: About your young man's marriage?

DEMEAS: Of course; that's what I'm always talking about.
  Let's act;
  Fix on a day, and hope for the best.

NICERATOS: Yes, I've made up
  My mind to that.

DEMEAS: I made mine up before you did.

NICERATOS: Call on me when you're going out.

Here there is a gap of about 15 lines; it includes the opening of Act II.

Act 2

The MS resumes with seven defective lines in which Moschion describes how he carried out his resolve to go to some secluded place and practise his part in the wedding ceremony.

MOSCHION: I, after attending to ... when I got outside ...
I was sacrificing ... to the banquet ... I was escorting
the ladies to the ceremony of purification ... I was
distributing the sesame-cake ...
[I was singing] the wedding-hymn, whistling; I was a
complete fool at it.

Well, when I'd had all I wanted – but, by Apollo, here's
My father, I'm sure I heard him. — Father, good-day to
you.

DEMEAS: Good-day to you too, son.

MOSCHION: But why are you scowling?

DEMEAS: Why?
It seems that, though I wasn't aware of it, I have
A wedded wife for a mistress.

MOSCHION: A wife? How do you mean?
I don't understand.

DEMEAS: I've been presented, apparently,
With a son that I know nothing about. Well, he shall go,
Plague take him! To hell with him! Out of my house!

MOSCHION: Oh! No!

DEMEAS: Why, 'Oh, no'? Do you expect me to bring up,
here in my house,
A bastard? That's not my way – not that sort of folly.

MOSCHION: A bastard – for God's sake! What's that? And
which of us
Can truly claim to be legitimate?

DEMEAS: I think
You're joking.

MOSCHION: By Dionysos, I'm dead serious.
To my mind, one heredity or another makes
Not an atom of difference. If you examine the matter
Justly, the good man is legitimate, and the bad
A bastard.

Here about 29 lines are missing, and seven more are fragmentary. The
passage probably contained the following elements:
1. Moschion succeeds in persuading Demeas to allow Chrysis to keep
   the baby.
2. Demeas tells Moschion that he wishes him to marry Plangon.
3. Moschion happily consents.
4. Demeas says, 'Then let's have the wedding today, if Niceratos will
   agree.'
5. 'The whole affair' which Moschion refers to in 151 would seem
   to be some incident related by Moschion to prove the seriousness
   of his intention.

MOSCHION: But if you'd been told nothing about the
      whole affair,
   How could you know I was serious, and back me up?
DEMEAS: If I'd not known that you were in earnest?
      Moschion,
   I've grasped the whole thing; and I'm off this moment,
      to tell
   Niceratos to get the wedding organized.
   The backing-up you speak of shall be forthcoming.
   I'll go and get purified, and offer a libation,
   And put some incense on; and I'll be here again.
MOSCHION: And I'll go and fetch Plangon.
DEMEAS: Don't go yet, before
   I learn whether her father'll fall in with our plan.
MOSCHION: He won't oppose you. But it would be
      unsuitable
   For me to obtrude my presence on your interview.
   So, father, I'm going.
         [*Exit* MOSCHION.]

DEMEAS: Somehow or other, Providence, of its own accord,
Seems to take care of matters beyond our cognizance.
I had no idea that Moschion was in love; and now . . .

Here 27 lines are missing, followed by 27 mutilated lines, from which
the following scraps are comprehensible:

DEMEAS [*alone*]: I want [to persuade] him [to have the
wedding today.]
[*He knocks at Niceratos' door.*]
[Good-day, Niceratos.] Come out here. [I want to talk to
you.]

NICERATOS: What about? Good-day to you too.

DEMEAS: . . . Tell me, you remember . . . we fixed a day?

NICERATOS: Yes, I remember.

DEMEAS: [Well, I want the wedding to take place now,] this
very day. . . . you are fully aware.

NICERATOS: Where? When?

DEMEAS: [I wish it] to take place quickly . . .

NICERATOS: . . . But it is impossible.

DEMEAS: [The expense can be put down to me,] not to you
at all.

NICERATOS: Oh, Heracles!

DEMEAS: . . . to explain to you in this way . . . before
telling our friends. Niceratos, [we shall be] grateful.

NICERATOS: . . . if I consent to your suggestion . . .

DEMEAS: . . . it will be an advantage to you . . .
Here, Parmenon! Boy! Parmenon!
[*Enter* PARMENON.]
Fetch garlands, quick;
And get a sheep for sacrifice; and sesame-cake.
Run to the market, buy simply everything they've got,
And come back.

PARMENON: Everything? You leave it all to me?

DEMEAS: Yes, and be quick, I tell you. — Oh, and hire a
cook.

PARMENON: And hire a cook – after I've bought the
   market?

DEMEAS: Yes,
   After you've bought it.

PARMENON: Give me the money, and I'm off.

DEMEAS: Aren't *you* off yet, Niceratos?

NICERATOS: I'll just nip in
   And warn my wife to get everything ready indoors, and
      then
   I'll be on Parmenon's tracks in no time.

         [NICERATOS *goes into his house*.]

PARMENON: I don't know
   A single thing, except that I've been given these orders,
   And off I go, full speed.

         [*He still hesitates at the exit*.]

DEMEAS [*to audience*]:   Persuading his wife will cause
   Niceratos some trouble. Well, it's no use letting
   Anyone argue or dilly-dally. [*To Parmenon*] You still
      there?
   Get running!

         [*Exit* PARMENON.]

Here there is a gap of ten lines, during which Act III begins.

Act 3

DEMEAS: ... It sometimes happens at sea,
That when a man's enjoying calm water and fair wind
He is overtaken by a sudden hurricane which
Comes crashing down when least expected; and this
    storm
Soon shatters and capsizes those who before were running
Smoothly before the breeze. That's *my* position now.
Here am I – a man organizing a wedding, a man
Sacrificing to the gods; for whom, an hour ago,
Everything was working out just as he wished; and now,
By Athena, I don't even know if I'm seeing straight.
No, I do not. I come out here in front of my house
Seized with a sudden pain that's worse than anything
    else.
Is it credible? Please, judge whether I'm in my right
    mind
Or mad. Did I entirely misunderstand the thing
That happened just now? Am I inventing for myself
A great misfortune out of nothing?
                                    I'd just gone in
To hurry on preparations for my son's wedding.
I was telling them all, 'Moschion's to be married today;
So now, get everything ready, clean the whole place up,
Make cakes, and fill the basket for the ceremony.'
Well, things were going smoothly enough; though
    naturally
The sudden hurry put them all in a bit of a stew; —
And there, lying on a bed, just shoved down out of the
    way,
Was the baby, howling. The maids were shouting,
    'Where's the flour?
Fetch in some water; hand me the oil; put on more coal!'

Well, I was issuing stores, and helping; and I'd just
Gone into the store-room, where I was busy choosing out
Still more stuff, keeping an eye on everything; and so
I didn't come out at once; and while I was still in there
A woman came down the stairs into the room that's just
Opposite the store-room door. It's a sort of
    weaving-room;
The way upstairs is through it; and I go through it too
To get to the store-room. Now, this woman was once
    nurse
To Moschion; she's free now, but I keep her on
As a servant; she's quite elderly. Well, she saw the baby
Left there alone and crying. She had no idea
I was in the store-room; for all she knew, she was safe in
    saying
Whatever she pleased. She went up to the kid, and began
The usual baby-talk – 'Duckie, sweetie-pie,' says she,
And 'Aren't you a beautiful boy?' and 'Where's your
    mummy gone?'
She kissed it, carried it up and down; and when it
    stopped
Crying, 'Oh, dear,' says she, 'it seems only yesterday
I was nursing Moschion, a darling little mite like this.
Now Moschion's got a son of his own; and someone else
Will nurse it, and . . .

About four lines are missing here.

Some little maid came running in, and the old woman
Called to her, 'Give the baby his bath, lazybones!
This is a fine way to go on,' says she, 'to leave
The baby uncared-for on his father's wedding-day!'
Then straight away the little maid said, 'Hush, you fool –
Talking like that! Master's in the house.' — 'No! Is he?
    Where?'

'He's in the store-room.' Then she changed her voice a
  bit;
'Nurse, the mistress is calling you; go on, be quick. –
He hasn't heard a thing; that's a bit of luck.' So then
The old woman went off, muttering, 'Dear, oh dear,
My tongue again!' – and disappeared. Then I stepped out,
Quite quiet and calm – the way I came out here just
  now,
Exactly as if I'd seen nothing, heard nothing; – and there
I saw Chrysis herself in the courtyard holding the child;
And as I went past she was putting it to her breast.
So this at least is certain, that the baby's hers;
But who's the father? Me? Or — ? Friends, I'd rather not
Say anything, or even guess; but I put to you
The plain facts, and the words I heard with my own ears.
No, I'm not angry – yet. And as for the young man,
His behaviour up to now has been exemplary,
I'll take my oath on that; and his attitude to me
Could not have been more proper or more honourable.
But then again, when I realize that this woman
Who said those words was Moschion's nurse, and never
  dreamt
She was speaking in my hearing; and when I reflect
That it was Chrysis who so doted on the child,
And – against my will – insisted we should bring it up,
I fly right off the handle. — Oh, here's Parmenon
Back from the market; just at the right moment too.
I'll just wait while he takes the Cook and his crew
  indoors.

> [DEMEAS *stands aside. Enter* PARMENON *bringing the*
> COOK *and his assistants.*]

PARMENON: Here, Cook, for the gods' sake hurry, now! I
  can't think why
  You carry that chopper round with you; your tongue's
  enough

To make mincemeat of anything.

COOK: You ignorant
Amateur.

PARMENON: What, me?

COOK: By all the gods, I reckon so.
Why grumble at me, simply because I want to know
How many tables you intend to serve, how many
Ladies are coming, what time you want dinner ready,
Whether I'll need to get a butler, whether you've got
Crockery enough of your own, whether your bakery's
Indoors or out, whether you're adequately equipped
With all the other –

PARMENON: Look here, mate, if you didn't know,
You're mashing me into hash, you are, I tell you straight.
You beat all, you do.

COOK: Boil your head.

PARMENON: And the same to you,
And many of 'em. Go on in now.

[*The* COOK *with his assistants enters the house.*
PARMENON *is about to follow him, when* DEMEAS
speaks.]

DEMEAS: Parmenon!

PARMENON [*turning*]: Someone called me?

DEMEAS: Yes, I did.

PARMENON: Oh – good morning, sir.

DEMEAS [*sternly*]: Just put that hamper indoors; then come
back here.

PARMENON [*alarmed*]: Yes, sir –
God bless you, sir!

[*He goes indoors.*]

DEMEAS: He doesn't miss much. If anything
Of this sort's going on, I'm certain Parmenon knows.
He's a busybody, if ever there was one. – Here he comes.

[*As* PARMENON *enters, he calls back to Chrysis
inside.*]

PARMENON: Chrysis, see that the Cook gets everything he
  wants;
  And, for the gods' sake, keep that old crone's fingers out
  Of the pie-dishes. – Here I am, sir. What do you wish
  me to do?
DEMEAS: Wish you to do? Come here, away from the
  door. Further.
PARMENON: Yes, sir.
DEMEAS: Now listen, Parmenon. I swear to you
  By the gods, I've not the slightest wish – for many
  reasons –
  To give you a flogging.
PARMENON: A flogging, sir? Why, what have I done?
DEMEAS: You're hiding something from me, I've discovered.
PARMENON: No, sir!
  By Dionysos, by Apollo and Saviour Zeus,
  By Asclepios –
DEMEAS: Stop that, now! What I've said isn't just
  A guess.
PARMENON: Why, strike me dead, sir –
DEMEAS: Look me in the eyes.
PARMENON: I'm looking.
DEMEAS: Tell me, whose child is it?
PARMENON [playing for time]:   I'm looking, sir.
DEMEAS: I asked you, Whose child is it?
PARMENON: Why, it's Chrysis' child.
DEMEAS: And who is the father?
PARMENON: You, she says.
DEMEAS: That's done for you.
  I'm well aware of the whole business: that this child
  Is Moschion's; that you know it is; and that Chrysis
  Is rearing him for Moschion.
PARMENON: And who says this?
DEMEAS: Everyone. Still, just answer me: is all this true?
PARMENON: It's true, master; but nobody need know –

DEMEAS: Nobody
  Need know? [*To a slave*] You there – a whip for this
    damned criminal!
PARMENON: No, don't, sir, don't for God's sake.
DEMEAS [*taking the whip*]:   I'll tattoo your hide.
PARMENON: Tattoo my –
DEMEAS: Yes, I'll do it now.
PARMENON [*breaking free and running for it*]: Help, help!
DEMEAS: Here, you!
  Come here, you devil! Hold him, there! Oh, oh, oh, oh!
  O all you host of heaven! O earth! What else?
  And shall I couple hell? – Come off it, Demeas!
  Why shout like a fool? Steady now – take a grip of
    yourself.
  Moschion hasn't wronged you! [*To audience*] To say
    that, my friends,
  May seem surprising; but it's true. Supposing, now,
  He had done this thing deliberately, or in the throes
  Of passionate love, or simply because he hated me,
  His behaviour to me now would be what it was then –
  Hostile. Instead, he has cleared himself by welcoming
  This marriage I've provided. Yes: what drove him on
  Was not love, as I at first imagined, but the wish
  To escape at all costs from that Helen of mine indoors!
  Yes, she is the one responsible. It's obvious:
  She found him drunk, perhaps, or not himself. Strong wine
  And young blood, when they find an accomplice close at
    hand
  To help their plotting, can lead to any reckless act.
  I find it in every way incredible, that one
  Who is well-behaved and decent to all and sundry,
    should
  Behave like this – to *me*! If he were twenty times
  An adopted son, not mine by birth, I'd still judge him
  By his known character, not by his origin.

But she – the dirty slut! The whore, the – why go on?
It'll do no good; so be a man, Demeas; forget
What you would like to remember. Stop longing for her.
What has happened is bad luck; well, then, for the boy's
    sake
Hide it as best you can – but throw that handsome
    Samian
Out on her ear! To hell with her! You've got an
    excuse –
She kept the child. So, no more words; explain nothing.
Keep a stiff lip; have pride enough to take the blow.
       [*The* COOK *appears at Demeas' door.*]
COOK: He must be out here somewhere. [*Bawling*] Hi,
    there! Parmenon!
Run out on me, he has; done not a stroke of work!
     [DEMEAS, *reminded of the wedding, turns to go indoors.*]
DEMEAS: You get to hell out of my way!
       [*Exit* DEMEAS *into his house.*]
COOK [*staggering*]:   Whew! Heracles!
What's going on? – Parmenon! – Some aged lunatic
Has just pelted indoors! What's happening? –
    Parmenon! –
I'll swear he's raving mad. What an almighty bellow!
– Oh, help! I've left my dishes lying all over the place –
A nice thing if he smashes the lot to little bits!
There – that's him at the door again. Oh, Parmenon,
I hope you roast in hell for hiring me on this job!
– I'll stand here out of his way.
     [CHRYSIS *runs out of the house,* DEMEAS *following.*]
DEMEAS: Well, didn't you hear me? Go!
CHRYSIS: Go where, for pity's sake?
DEMEAS: To hell, and lose no time.
CHRYSIS: Oh, cruel! [*She bursts into tears.*]
DEMEAS: Yes, cruel – that's it: a flood of tears to make
Me sorry for you. But I'll stop your goings-on –

CHRYSIS: What goings-on?

DEMEAS: Nothing. You've got your baby now;
You've got the nurse. All right – clear out.

CHRYSIS: Is this because
I kept the baby?

DEMEAS: Because of that, yes; and –

CHRYSIS: And what?

DEMEAS: Just that.

COOK [to audience]: I'll bet the trouble was something of
that sort.

DEMEAS: You had no notion how to live in style.

CHRYSIS: In style?
What *are* you talking about?

DEMEAS: When you first came to me,
Remember, you wore a cotton dress, a cheap one too.

CHRYSIS: Well, what of that?

DEMEAS: Then I was everything to you,
When you were poor.

CHRYSIS: Well, who is now?

DEMEAS: Don't talk to me.
You've got all your own things. I'm giving you as well
Your maids, and all your jewellery. Now leave my
house.

COOK: This is a fit of anger. I'll have a word with him.
Look here, my good sir –

DEMEAS: What have *you* got to say?

COOK: Don't bite.

DEMEAS [ignoring him]: From now on, Chrysis, someone
else'll enjoy my home,
And think herself lucky.

COOK: And who is she?

DEMEAS: You've borne a son;
You've got everything you wanted.

COOK: He's not biting yet.
All the same–

DEMEAS [*to Cook*]: I'll break your head, fellow, if you talk
   to me.

COOK: Quite right, sir. Look, I'm going now.

DEMEAS: Thank heaven for that.

  [*To Chrysis*] Up in the city, you'll soon find out your
   natural bent.

  Your type, my girl, can only earn ten drachmas a time;
  They trot round all the dinner-parties and drink
   themselves
  To death with neat wine; or if they can't manage that,
  They live and starve. You'll be as good as any of them,
  I'll bet, at learning how it's done. And then you'll know
  Just what you did when you behaved like that to me.
  [*As Chrysis moves towards him*] Stay where you are!
      [DEMEAS *goes into his house.*]

CHRYSIS: What shall I do? What shall I do?
      [*Enter* NICERATOS *with a slave bringing a live sheep.*]

NICERATOS: This sheep I've got, when sacrificed, will
   satisfy
  All due requirements for the gods and goddesses.
  It's got some blood; sufficient gall; some lovely bones;
  Large spleen – all things essential to Olympians.
  When those are offered, I'll cut up and give away
  As tit-bits to my friends all I'll have left – the skin!
     [*The slave takes the sheep into the house.*]
  Why, Heracles! What's going on? That can't be Chrysis
  Standing out on the doorstep weeping? Yes, it is! –
  What on earth's happened?

CHRYSIS: What do you think? Your worthy friend
  Has turned me out.

NICERATOS: Good heavens above! Who? Demeas?

CHRYSIS: Yes, Demeas.

NICERATOS: What for?

CHRYSIS: Because of the child.

NICERATOS: Why, yes;

My women-folk were telling me you'd taken on
A child, and meant to bring it up. A mad idea –
Still, Demeas is soft-hearted.

CHRYSIS: He wasn't angry at all
At first, but only later on; in fact, just now
He told me himself to get ready everything indoors
For the wedding today; then while I'm in the middle of it
He bursts in, charges at me like a lunatic;
And now he's locked me out.

NICERATOS: Demeas is bilious.
The Black Sea coast's a very unhealthy place. Listen:
Just come indoors with me and see my wife. Cheer up.
Demeas will get over this insanity,
When once he takes a steady look at what he's doing.

CHORAL INTERLUDE

Act 4

As NICERATOS *enters from his house, he turns back to speak to his wife indoors.*

NICERATOS: I'll be back soon, dear; I'm going now to tackle
  Demeas.
  [*To audience*] Holy gods! A load of gold would not have
  persuaded me that this
  Could ever happen. Right in the middle of wedding
  festivities, if you please,
  Comes this bolt from the blue – a woman's thrown out;
  and now, here she is,
  Baby and all, in our house. Everywhere tears flowing,
  women upset.
  Demeas is a swine; and he'll be sorry he made a fool of
  himself.
    [*Enter* MOSCHION *from the town.*]
MOSCHION: Oh! The sun will never set! How can I
  describe it? Afternoon's
  Endless. Night's grown absent-minded. I'll go and wash –
  for the third time.
  Well, what else is there to do?
NICERATOS:　　　　　　　　　　Oh! Glad to see you,
  Moschion.
MOSCHION: Are we having the wedding now? A minute
  ago that Parmenon
  Met me in the street and asked me, 'Why don't you go
  straight away,
  Now, to fetch your bride? What stops you?'
NICERATOS:　　　　　　　　　Don't you know what's
  happened here?
MOSCHION: Happened? Why, what?
NICERATOS: Something most unpleasant, quite extraordinary.

MOSCHION: Heracles! What is it? I know nothing.

NICERATOS: My dear boy, it's this:
   Your own father's just turned Chrysis out of doors.

MOSCHION: You can't mean that!

NICERATOS: That's what's happened.

MOSCHION: Why?

NICERATOS: Because of the baby.

MOSCHION: Oh; where is she now?

NICERATOS: In our house.

MOSCHION: This is a terrible business. It's astonishing.

NICERATOS: If you call this terrible, just —
         [DEMEAS, *as he enters, turns round and speaks his first
         four lines to slaves inside his house.*]

DEMEAS: Wait till I get hold of a stick,
   I'll wipe up your tears, and no mistake. What's all this
      drivelling?
   Do what the cook orders, will you? Yes, by God, you've
      really got
   Something to cry about: she's gone! This house has lost a
      valuable
   Treasure! Her actions show it, don't they?
         [*He slams the door, and turns to the statue of Apollo
         which stands beside it.*]
                          Dear Apollo, I greet you. Grant
   That this marriage, which we are now about to celebrate,
      may bring
   Blessing to everyone. [*To audience*] My mind's made up;
      I'll swallow all my gall,
   And this wedding shall go through. [*He turns to Apollo
   again.*]
                          So, Master, take good care that I
   Don't betray my feelings to another soul; compel me to
   Sing the wedding-hymn! [*To audience*] As things are, you
      won't hear me at my best.
   So what? She shall not come back.

NICERATOS: You tackle him first, Moschion.

MOSCHION: All right. – Father, what is this you've done?

DEMEAS: Your meaning, Moschion?

MOSCHION: Can you ask that? Why has Chrysis left our house? Explain this, please.

DEMEAS: Heracles! This is a deputation! Hell! – In Apollo's name,

This affair is not your business; it is mine exclusively.

What is all this nonsense? Damn it! Now *he* comes to back you up

In attacking me.

MOSCHION: What do you mean?

DEMEAS: Isn't it obvious?

He's come here to argue with me on her behalf – that's it, of course!

MOSCHION: Now we know what's happened, father, as your friends, what do you expect

We would say?

DEMEAS: You'll kindly allow *me*, Moschion, to decide who are

My friends.

MOSCHION: If I let you act like this I'd be ashamed of myself.

DEMEAS: So, you'll stop me, will you?

MOSCHION: Yes, I will.

DEMEAS: This puts the cap on it;

Your first act was bad enough – this is worse.

MOSCHION: It's not advisable

To let anger rule you in everything.

NICERATOS: He's quite right, Demeas.

MOSCHION: You go in, Niceratos, and tell Chrysis to run out here.

[NICERATOS *goes into his house.*]

DEMEAS: Moschion, just you let me alone – do you hear me? Let me alone, let me

204

Alone, I tell you! I know everything.

MOSCHION: What do you mean – everything?

DEMEAS: That will do.

MOSCHION: But, father, I must know.

DEMEAS: You *must* know? Am I not
Master of my own affairs?

MOSCHION: I ask it as a favour, then.

DEMEAS: Favour – hear that! And there's another favour
you'd like me to grant,
Doubtless – walk out of my own house leaving you two
snug at home!
Just let's get this wedding settled, if you have one grain of
sense –
Let me just get through this wedding –

MOSCHION: Why, of course I'm letting you!
But let Chrysis be there with us.

DEMEAS: Chrysis?

MOSCHION: Yes; it's for your sake,
Chiefly, that I want this –

DEMEAS: There! It's evident, it's clear as day!
Witness, Apollo! Isn't this conspiracy with my enemies?
It's an outrage! I shall burst a blood-vessel!

MOSCHION: What *do* you mean?

DEMEAS: Shall I tell you?

MOSCHION: Yes.

DEMEAS: Come here, then.

MOSCHION: Tell me.

DEMEAS: Yes, I will. This child
Is your child, I know it. Parmenon knows your secrets.
He told me.
So now, don't you try to fool me.

MOSCHION: What if it is mine? Does that make
Chrysis guilty?

[*Enter* NICERATOS *alone.*]

DEMEAS: Well, who *is*? You –

MOSCHION: How is *she* responsible?

DEMEAS: What are you saying? Don't you realize
  anything, you two?

MOSCHION: Why this fuss?

DEMEAS: Why this fuss? You scum, you ask that? Say
  then, do you accept the blame
  On yourself, and still dare look me in the face and speak
  such words?
  Then I utterly disown you, as you have me.

MOSCHION: Disowned you? Why?

DEMEAS: You ask why? You dare to ask?

MOSCHION: It's not so terrible a crime;
  Thousands, father, have done the same thing, surely!

DEMEAS: Gods! The effrontery!
  Look – I'm asking you before these witnesses: from what
  woman
  Did you breed this child? Now give your answer to
  Niceratos,
  Since you call it 'nothing terrible'.

MOSCHION: Oh! – but it *is* terrible,
  Now, for me to tell the whole truth to Niceratos. He'll
  be
  Outraged.

NICERATOS: Oh, you most depraved of all men! I at last
  begin
  To perceive the whole disgraceful story.

MOSCHION [*aside*]:   This puts 'paid' to me.

DEMEAS: Now you see, Niceratos.

NICERATOS: See? I should think so! This
  outdoes
  All the fabled crimes – Thyestes, Tereus, Oedipus and the
  rest,
  Lechers, liars, murderers – *you* make them look like
  harmless babes!

MOSCHION: *I* do?

NICERATOS: You could have the face, the heart, to do that? –
  Demeas,

  Take Amyntor for your pattern: rage at him – put out
    his eyes!

DEMEAS: It's through you that the whole truth has come to
    light.

NICERATOS: What crime would be
  Too abominable for you? What would you not
    perpetrate?

  After this, am I to give you my own daughter for your
    wife?

  [1]Heaven protect us! Why, I'd sooner sell her to a
    bawdy-house.

  Demeas, your Samian and your son are well matched,
    are they not?

DEMEAS: I would explode, if I restrained myself under such
    injury.

NICERATOS: I say, sell her as a slave. If it were *me* he'd
    cuckolded,

  He'd not play that game a second time – nor would the
    woman who

  Went to bed with him. [2]I'd have her up for sale – the
    whore! I'd be

  First man there when market opened; and I'd sell the
    brat with her.

  Every portico, I tell you, every barber's shop would be

  Crowded out from sunrise on, they'd sit round, talking
    about *me*:

  'See there, how Niceratos,' they'd say, 'has shown
    himself a man;

  He insists on justice, *he* won't stand for murder!'

---

1. The text is defective here; this line and the next are partly conjectural.

2. The meaning of these two lines seems to be ambiguous. An alternative version is:
    ... with him. She's not his wife – I'd sell her; I'd be there
    When the market opened; what's more, I'd disown my son as well.

MOSCHION: What do you mean –
'Murder'?

NICERATOS: Yes, I call it murder when some rebel acts like
this.

MOSCHION: By the gods, I'm dumb, I'm thunderstruck at
this enormity!

NICERATOS: Now, to crown all, look what I've done –
welcomed to my hearth and home
This disgrace, this criminal!

DEMEAS: Niceratos, I beg of you,
Throw her out! You're wronged as much as I am; show
yourself a true
Friend!

NICERATOS [to Moschion]: The very sight of you revolts
me. You barbarian,
Thracian, aboriginal! I'm going – get out of my way.
         [NICERATOS rushes into his house.]

MOSCHION: Father, in the gods' name, listen –

DEMEAS: I'll not listen to one word.

MOSCHION: Not a thing that you think happened,
happened! I've just tumbled to it.

DEMEAS: Not a thing? How's that?

MOSCHION: Chrysis is not the mother of that child.
She just calls it hers because I asked her to.

DEMEAS: What are you saying?

MOSCHION: The plain truth.

DEMEAS: Why does she call it hers because you asked her to?

MOSCHION: I'm reluctant to tell this; yet, if you have the
simple facts,
I escape the weightier charge by shouldering the lighter
one.

DEMEAS: Oh! . . . Before you speak you kill me.

MOSCHION: That child is Niceratos'
Daughter's child and mine. That's what I wanted to
remain unknown.

DEMEAS: So that's . . .?

MOSCHION: Those are the plain facts.

DEMEAS: Don't lead me down the garden path.

MOSCHION: You can prove it.

DEMEAS: Well, how would that help?

MOSCHION: It wouldn't help. But wait –
  Someone's coming out now.

  [NICERATOS *rushes out.*]

NICERATOS: Oh! But this is ruin! What do you think
  I've just seen, with my own eyes? I shall go mad! I
    never thought
  I should suffer such a blow, straight to the heart! This is
    the end!

DEMEAS: What is he going to say?

NICERATOS: Just now, indoors, I saw my own daughter
  Put that infant to her breast.

MOSCHION: Quite natural. You hear, father?

DEMEAS: Moschion, it's not you who've done wrong; *I*
  have, in suspecting you.

NICERATOS: Demeas, I turn to you now.

MOSCHION: I'll be going.

DEMEAS: Moschion,
  Don't be downcast, now.

MOSCHION [*looking at Niceratos*]: He looks like murder.

DEMEAS [*to Niceratos*]: What's tormenting you?

NICERATOS: Just now – there, indoors, I saw her with that
    infant at her breast –
  My own daughter!

DEMEAS: Maybe she was playing.

NICERATOS: She was not playing!
  When she saw me coming in, she crumpled up
    immediately.

DEMEAS: Maybe you just thought you saw her –

NICERATOS: Are you going to keep on saying
  'Maybe' all day long?

MENANDER

MOSCHION [*aside*]:   All this is *my* fault. [*He goes out.*]

NICERATOS: What's that?

DEMEAS: This story of yours

Strikes me as improbable.

NICERATOS: I tell you I saw –

DEMEAS: You're drivelling.

NICERATOS: That's no way to argue. Right – I'm going in.
      [*He goes into his house again.*]

DEMEAS: Buzz, buzz! – Hold on

Half a moment, friend! – He's gone. Now everything's
    turned upside down.

It's the end, by Zeus! He'll get the truth from her –
    he'll roar with rage.

He's a rough type, a real swine, stubborn as a mule. –
    Yet, look at me:

I'm a swine too! Why should I suspect my son of such a
    crime?

I, of all men! Damn it, I don't deserve to live.
      [*An uproar is heard from Niceratos' house.*]
                    Now what in hell

Can that row be?
      [*He goes to the door to listen.*]
        Yes, it is! He's bellowing, 'Make up the fire!'
Says he'll kill the baby and burn it. That's the next thing
    we shall see –

Roasting grandson! – Gods! he's coming. What a man!
    He's much more like

A tornado or a thunderbolt.
      [*Enter* NICERATOS.]

NICERATOS: Demeas, it's scandalous!

Chrysis there – she's plotting against me.

DEMEAS: What?

NICERATOS: Yes! She's induced my wife

And the girl to back her up in not confessing a single
    thing;

210

Holds on to the brat by main force, swears she'll never
  let it go.
Don't let it surprise you if I kill that woman.

DEMEAS: Kill Chrysis?

NICERATOS: She knows all about the whole thing!

DEMEAS: You'll do nothing of the sort!

NICERATOS: I just thought I'd give you warning, that's all.
    [*He rushes back into his house.*]

DEMEAS: The man's raving mad.
He's whipped in again. Everything's going wrong. What
  is a man to do?
All I know is, never before was I in such an unholy mess.
Should I now tell him the whole truth? That would,
  after all, be best –
Help, Apollo! Someone's coming out again!
    [*From Niceratos' house* CHRYSIS *enters holding the baby
    and pursued by* NICERATOS.]

CHRYSIS: What shall I do?
Where can I go? He's going to take my baby!

DEMEAS [*pointing to his own door*]:   Chrysis, come this way!

CHRYSIS [*who does not at first see Demeas*]: Who's that?

DEMEAS: Run inside here.

NICERATOS: Here, you! Where are you off to?

DEMEAS [*to audience*]:   Watch me now –
Heavyweight champion! [*To Niceratos*] What's this?
  Who are you chasing round?

NICERATOS: Now, Demeas,
You keep out of this. I mean to get that baby. Then I'll
  hear
What these women have got to say about the business.

DEMEAS [*to audience, indicating Niceratos*]:   Mental case.
– Oh, you'll hit me, will you?

NICERATOS [*hitting him*]:   Yes, I will.

DEMEAS [*to Chrysis*]:   You get indoors, damn it!
– All right, here's for you, then. [*He hits Niceratos.*]

[*To Chrysis*] Run in; he's a stronger man than me.
[CHRYSIS *runs into Demeas' house.*]

NICERATOS: There now – you laid hands on me first. I'll
swear that in court.

DEMEAS: And you
Take a stick to a free-born woman and chase her, do you?

NICERATOS: Blackmailer!

DEMEAS: So are you, then.

NICERATOS: You won't let me have that child?

DEMEAS: Don't make me laugh!
When it's mine?

NICERATOS: It isn't yours.
[*He pushes Demeas aside and goes towards Demeas'
door.*]

DEMEAS: Help, friends! I'm being attacked!

NICERATOS: Go on,
Bawl your head off! I'm going in to kill that woman.

DEMEAS: What shall I do?
This is frightful. I won't let him. – Where are you
going? You stay here!

NICERATOS: Don't you lay a finger on me.

DEMEAS: Just control yourself.

NICERATOS: Look here,
Demeas, you're pulling a fast one on me – why, it's
obvious:
You know all about this business.

DEMEAS: Listen while I tell you, then;
And – you keep your hands off Chrysis.

NICERATOS: Your son Moschion – hasn't he
Simply fooled me over Plangon?

DEMEAS: Rubbish! First, he'll marry her.
Next, things aren't as you imagine. Come now, let's
walk up and down
Here and talk it over.

NICERATOS: Walk up and . . .?

DEMEAS: Why not? Take yourself in hand.
   [*They walk up and down together.*]
  Tell me now, Niceratos: you've often heard, in tragic
    plays,
  Stories of how Zeus once turned himself to gold, and
    trickled down
  Through the roof, and went to bed with a young girl
    imprisoned there?

NICERATOS: What of it?

DEMEAS: Just this: one's got to be prepared for anything!
  Has your roof, I wonder, got a leak or two?

NICERATOS: My whole roof leaks!
  What has that to do with it?

DEMEAS: Why, Zeus sometimes comes down as rain,
  Sometimes gold. Well, don't you see? It's Zeus's doing!
    Question solved
  In a moment.[1]

NICERATOS: What's all this? Is it bran-mash you're feeding
    me?

DEMEAS: No, by Apollo I'm not. In fact, you aren't one
    little bit worse off
  Than Danaë's father. Look: if Zeus was pleased to lie
    with Danaë,
  Why should not your daughter –

NICERATOS: But this is outrageous. Moschion's
  Made a stuffed owl of me.

DEMEAS: Moschion will marry her, never fear.
  This is a miracle-child, you take my word for it. Why, I
    could name
    [*his eye wanders over the audience*]
  Thousands walking round in Athens – born from gods!

   1. Perhaps Demeas means: Your leaky roof lets in rain-water; but when it
let Zeus, i.e. Moschion, in, it allied you, a poor man, with me, your rich
neighbour, and was thus a shower of gold like Danaë's – a tactful and humorous
way of pointing out one advantage that will come of the marriage.

And do you cry

Stinking fish because your daughter's had a little accident?

Look, to begin with [*he points to a member of the audience*] – there!

The universal sponger, Chairophon!

Wouldn't you say *he's* immortal?

NICERATOS: Probably. What do *I* care?

I'm not going to argue over nothing.

DEMEAS: Well, you're very wise.

Look at Androcles, now, living all these years! Trotting about;

Lots of boy friends; walks along with grey hair dyed a lovely black;

He won't die, even if you cut his throat. Then isn't he a god?

Come, now, make your offerings; pray that all will turn out happily.

You and I will be 'in-laws' now – and a very good thing too.

As for my son, he'll get married – and he'd better!

NICERATOS: Yes, you're right.

But [*bridling up again*] if I'd just caught him when he –

DEMEAS: Tut, tut! Don't get blood-pressure!

Are things ready in your house yet?

NICERATOS: Yes, oh yes – Belshazzar's feast!

DEMEAS: You're a wit!

       [*Exit* NICERATOS *into his house.*]

[*To himself*] Well! All those miserable suspicions I endured!

Thank the gods I've found there's no truth in them – thank the blessed gods!

       [*Exit* DEMEAS *into his house. A* CHORUS *of wedding-guests enters and gives a performance of music and dancing.*]

Act 5

Enter MOSCHION *from Demeas' house.*

MOSCHION: A little while ago I was extremely pleased
  To have cleared myself – with difficulty – on all counts;
  I reckoned that was quite a piece of well-earned luck.
  But now that I'm somewhat more in my right mind, and set
  One thing against another, I feel furious –
  Yes, absolutely livid, to think what my father
  Suspected me of doing. Hell! If Plangon now
  Were in a happier situation, and if I
  Weren't hampered by so much that makes a slave of me –
  By vows, affection, long acquaintance, and desire –
  I'd not give the old man a second chance to make
  Such accusations to my face; I'd get to hell
  Out of this city, away to Bactria, Caria –
  Somewhere out East, and do a spell of soldiering.
  As it is – for your sake, Plangon darling, I'll refrain
  From heroism; in fact, it's quite unthinkable –
  Forbidden by the new master of my purpose, Love.
  Still, I don't feel like overlooking the whole affair
  And showing myself submissive and degenerate.
  If nothing else, I'll drop a word about taking off,
  And give the old man a fright; so that another time
  He'll take care not to ignore my sensibilities
  When once he sees that I don't laugh off this incident.
      [*He sees Parmenon approaching.*]
  Why, here's the very man I want, and just in time.
      [MOSCHION *stands aside as* PARMENON *soliloquizes.*]

PARMENON: By Zeus Almighty, what an utter fool I've been!
  A contemptible fool. I just took fright and ran away

From my master, though I'd done nothing wrong. What
   had I done,
To run away? Let's look at everything, point by point.
First, my young master went to bed with a free-born
   girl;
No blame for that, surely, on Parmenon. The girl
Got pregnant – that's not Parmenon's fault. The baby
   then
Came to our house – young master brought it, *I* didn't.
One of the slaves indoors told Master about it – well,
Has Parmenon done anything wrong there? Nothing.
Then why on earth do you run away, you blundering
   fool?
He frightened me. – Ridiculous! – He threatened he'd
Mark me for life. – What reason could he have had for
   that?
– It makes not a jot of difference, when you're marked
   for life,
Whether you've deserved it or not deserved it. In either
   case
It's just not nice.

MOSCHION: Hey, there!
PARMENON: Good-day, sir.
MOSCHION: Cut that talk
And get indoors, quick.
PARMENON: Yes, and do what, sir?
MOSCHION: Bring me out
A cloak and sword.
PARMENON: A sword? For *you*, sir?
MOSCHION: Yes, and quick.
PARMENON: What for?
MOSCHION: Get going; do as I tell you; and say nothing.
PARMENON: But what is it all about?
MOSCHION: If I get hold of a strap –
PARMENON: No, no! I'm going.

MOSCHION: Go, then.

[*Exit* PARMENON.]

Now my father'll come.

He'll beg me to stay on here; and he'll beg in vain –

For a while; he must. Then, when I judge the moment's
come,

I'll yield to him. If I can only act it plausibly! –

And that, Dionysos knows, is not my strongest point.

Well, this is it; he's coming.

[*Enter* PARMENON.]

PARMENON: Sir, you're out of date entirely with what's
going on indoors!

You know nothing, you've heard nothing; so you've got
into a state

All for nothing. Drop all this and join the party.

MOSCHION: Haven't you brought –

PARMENON: They're all busy with your wedding – filling
high the sparkling bowl –

Flame of incense leaps to heaven –

MOSCHION: You rat, where's my cloak and sword?

PARMENON: Oh, forget it! All your friends are waiting for
you this half-hour.

Go and fetch your bride; lose no more time, this is your
lucky day!

You've got nothing to look glum at. Cheer up! Well,
what more d'you want?

MOSCHION: Are you lecturing me, you horse-thief? [*He
hits him.*]

PARMENON: What's that for, sir?

MOSCHION: You run in

Quick and bring me what I told you.

PARMENON: Look, my lip's cut open, sir.

MOSCHION: You still talking?

PARMENON: No, I'm going. Look at the reward I get!

MOSCHION: Still here?

PARMENON [*opening the door*]: See for yourself now –
  there's your wedding in full swing.

MOSCHION: Again?

      [PARMENON *goes in and shuts the door quietly.*]

  Wait, just tell me – [*But Parmenon is not there.*]

      Now my father's bound to come. One further point
  I'd forgotten, friends, is this: suppose, instead of begging me
  To stay here, he flies into a rage and says, All right, then,
      go!
  What'll I do then? He's not likely to say that; but
    anything's
  Possible. I'd look ridiculous if I had to eat my words.

      [PARMENON *returns.*]

PARMENON: Here you are – this cloak; a sword.

MOSCHION: Come, give me them.

PARMENON: Now put them on.

MOSCHION: No one saw you fetch them?

PARMENON: No one.

MOSCHION: Not a soul?

PARMENON: That's what I said.

MOSCHION: Are you telling the truth? – God rot you!

PARMENON: If you're going, go; and stop
  Drivelling.

      [*Enter* DEMEAS, *turning back to speak to someone
    indoors.*]

DEMEAS: Well, just tell me then, where is he?

      [*He shuts the door, and now sees Moschion.*]

                         Why, whatever's this?

PARMENON [*to Moschion*]: Quick, get going!

DEMEAS: What's the fancy dress for? What's the matter with
  you?
  Are you leaving, Moschion? Tell me.

PARMENON: As you see, he's on his way
  Now, just going. He's asked *me* to say good-bye to all at
  home.

I'll do that now.

    [PARMENON *goes into Demeas' house.*]

DEMEAS: Moschion, you're angry; and I love you for it.

I've no right to blame you. If you've been unjustly
    charged, the blame

Is all mine. Yet think of this too: Who is it you want to
    hurt?

I'm your father; I received you as an infant; brought you
    up.

If there's any point in which you've found your life
    agreeable,

That was my gift. This provides some reason, surely, why
    you should

Show forbearance for the offence I gave you, put up with
    my ways

As a true son would. My accusation, I admit, was
    unjust;

I was ignorant, mistaken, mad. Yet think of this as well:

At the cost of being unfair to others, I took thought for
    you,

Tried to seal up in my own heart this surmise I could not
    prove;

I did not display it for the delight of those who wish us
    ill.

But you now are publishing my error, calling witnesses

To my folly. Moschion, I beg you not to. Don't forget

All those earlier years, remembering the one day of my
    whole life

When I was an utter fool. Well, there's a lot more I
    could say;

But I'd rather not. You mark my words, a son who
    gives consent

Grudgingly earns little credit; willingness is everything.

    [*Enter* NICERATOS.]

NICERATOS [*to his wife indoors*]: You stop nagging. [*To*

Demeas] Everything's done – holy water, sacrifice –
It's a wedding! As soon as *he* turns up, he can take the
girl away.

Why, what's all this?

DEMEAS: I don't know, and that's the truth.

NICERATOS: What? You don't know?

Why this cloak? The rascal's setting off somewhere.

DEMEAS: He says he is.

NICERATOS: *He* says? Well, who's going to let him?
Caught in the act of lechery –

Even admits it! Why waste time, then? Young man, I
arrest you, now.

MOSCHION: Yes, arrest me, please!

NICERATOS [*put out by Moschion's smile*]: Will you stop
taking the micky out of me?

Throw that sword down, quickly.

DEMEAS: Moschion, throw it down, for the gods' sake!
Don't exasperate him.

MOSCHION [*dropping the sword*]: Let it go. Your entreaties
have prevailed.

NICERATOS [*outraged*]: Our entreaties? Just you come here.

MOSCHION: You'll arrest me now,
perhaps?

DEMEAS [*to Niceratos*]: Not at all. – Moschion, you bring
the bride out here.

NICERATOS: So, you agree?

DEMEAS: Of course.

MOSCHION: Father, if you'd done that at once, you'd
have saved yourself the trouble

Of that impressive lecture.

[PLANGON *appears at the door;* MOSCHION *leads her
forward.*]

NICERATOS: Come here, girl. – Before these witnesses
I give her to be your wedded wife, to bear you lawful
sons,

And my whole estate as dowry when I die – which God
  forbid!

May I live for ever!

MOSCHION: I take, I have, I love her as my wife.

DEMEAS: Now it remains to fetch the holy water from
  Callirrhoe.

Chrysis, give the women their places – water-bearer,
  flute-player.

Come on! Someone, bring out torches, garlands, so that
  we can all

Join the procession.

MOSCHION: Here they are – he's bringing them.

DEMEAS: Now, Moschion,

Put your garland on, and make yourself look decent.

MOSCHION: There – how's that?

DEMEAS [*to audience*]: All you pretty children, young men,
  old men, citizens, be kind!

Raise a thunderous clapping, to show Bacchus that you
  wish us well.

And may the immortal goddess Victory, as President

Of all noble contests, grant perpetual favour to my plays!

THE SHIELD

CHARACTERS

DAOS, *a slave, tutor of Cleostratos*

SMICRINES, *an old miser, elder brother of Chairestratos, and uncle of Cleostratos*

CHANCE, *a goddess, who speaks the Prologue*

A COOK *hired by Chairestratos*

A BUTLER

CHAIRESTRATOS, *a rich old man, younger brother of Smicrines, uncle of Cleostratos, stepfather of Chaireas*

CHAIREAS, *a young man, in love with Cleostratos' sister*

A DOCTOR, *a friend of Chaireas in disguise*

CLEOSTRATOS, *a young soldier, son of the deceased brother of Smicrines and Chairestratos*

Also: A group of Lycian prisoners-of-war; a Chorus of tipsy people; an old female slave of Smicrines; the Cook's boy, SPINTHER; *Chairestratos' wife, mother of Chaireas; the daughter of Chairestratos; the sister of Cleostratos*

*

The place is Athens; the scene shows two houses, belonging respectively to Smicrines and Chairestratos.

The plot of this play partly depends on a peculiar provision in the Athenian law of inheritance. If an unmarried girl was left as heiress to an estate, her nearest male relative was entitled to marry her. If the inheritance was small he was bound by law either to marry her or to endow her from his own estate; and in order to do this he was even allowed to divorce his existing wife. The play shows that public opinion demanded reasonable consideration in the use of this law; but if the demands of public opinion were enough, no laws would be needed.

Apart from this, the piece speaks for itself. It is the only one of the five major surviving plays to present a figure often met with in the shorter fragments – the honest slave who is guide, philosopher and friend to everyone else. The first half of the play is fairly sombre in tone, though lightened by the Prologue; Act 3 seems to be dedicated to hilarious farce; Act 4 to the return of Cleostratos. How Menander completed the pattern in Act 5 is impossible to guess, except that the ending is a happy one. The characters, being simply good or bad, do not offer, as far as we can tell, the human interest which we find in *The Samian Woman*; but even this cannot be firmly asserted when half of the text is missing.

Act 1

Enter DAOS. *He carries a battered shield, and is leading a group of prisoners-of-war, some of whom are carrying boxes and bales of various articles.*

DAOS: My dear young master! This in truth is my black day.
   With what high hopes I set out – and how different now
   Is every prospect! I thought then you would come home
   Covered with glory, safe, to live the rest of your years
   Enjoying the life of a distinguished citizen,
   With the title of a general or a councillor;
   And that your sister, for whose sake you enlisted then,
   Would clasp you to her heart on your return, and you
   Would settle her with a husband worthy of yourself;
   While I, after long months of hardship and of loyal
   Service, could then look forward to a quiet old age.
   Now you are gone, cut off in mockery of our hopes;
   And I, Cleostratos, your childhood's slave and friend,
   Bring home this shield, which many times you carried
     back
   Safe out of battle, but which did not save you. For you
   Were a brave man, if ever there was one.

SMICRINES: Oh, Daos!
   We little thought it would end this way.

DAOS: It's terrible.

SMICRINES: What happened? How did he die?

DAOS: For a soldier, Smicrines,
   Dying's no problem; only staying alive.

SMICRINES: Still, Daos,
   Tell me what happened – the whole story.

DAOS: Well, there's a river
   Called Xanthos, in the country of Lycia; and we
   Had been pretty fortunate in a number of battles there,

And the enemy had all fled and abandoned the open
    plain.
And perhaps it would have been well to be less
    fortunate –
When you've once come a cropper you go more
    carefully.
Well, we went unprepared against emergencies,
And thought nothing of it. The men would leave the
    palisade
And go plundering villages and cutting crops
And selling prisoners; everyone made a tidy sum
For himself.

SMICRINES: How splendid!

DAOS: Then my master got together
    Six hundred gold coins, and a sizeable collection
    Of silver wine-cups, and that bunch of prisoners
    You see over there, and sent me off to the city of
        Rhodes
    With instructions to leave everything with a friend of his
    And go straight back to him.

SMICRINES: What happened then?

DAOS: Well, I
    Set out at dawn; and on the very day I left,
    An enemy force slipped past our scouts and occupied
    A hill directly in front of us; and there they stayed,
    Having learnt from some deserters that our troops were
        all
    Scattered. When evening came, the men were in their
        tents;
    And, since the country offered plunder unlimited,
    Most of them were gorging themselves, as you'd expect.

SMICRINES: That's inexcusable.

DAOS: It was; for suddenly
    They were attacked by something like –

Three lines here are fragmentary, and are supplied by conjecture.

SMICRINES [*interrupting*]: But if you'd gone,
How did you know all this?

DAOS: I'll tell you, if you'll only
Give me a chance. We didn't get far on the first day –
In fact, a mile or so. Well, it was about midnight;
I was on guard in front of my tent, walking about
And keeping an eye on the money and the prisoners,
When I heard an uproar – shrieking, wailing, rushing about;
I could hear men calling aloud to one another by name;
That's how I learnt what happened. Fortunately, quite close
There was a small defensible hill; we climbed up there
In a body; and as we went, a stream of wounded men
From the camp came up to join us – horsemen, shield-bearers,
Spearmen –

SMICRINES: How lucky that you set off when you did!

DAOS: Well, we stayed there; and in the morning we knocked up
Some kind of palisade. Those who at the time of the attack
Had been dispersed, as I mentioned, on their plundering raids –
Those were the ones we blamed. On the fourth day we went
Back to the camp, having learnt that the Lycians were away
To the highland villages with the prisoners they had taken.

SMICRINES: I suppose you found Cleostratos lying among the dead?

DAOS: They'd been left there four days; it wasn't possible
To identify him for certain – the faces were all swollen.

SMICRINES: Then how do you know?

DAOS: He lay there with this shield – all
   smashed;
  I reckon that's why none of the enemy picked it up.
  Our noble captain wouldn't allow us to carry out
  The burial rites individually, in view of the time
  It would take to separate the remains; he collected them
  On to one pyre and burnt them. Then after hastily
  Burying the ashes, he moved on; while we took ship
  To Rhodes first, where we stayed some days; and finally
  We sailed back here to Athens. That's my whole story.

SMICRINES: You say you've brought six hundred gold
   pieces?

DAOS: I have.

SMICRINES: And wine-cups?

DAOS: Perhaps forty pounds by weight.

SMICRINES: No more?

DAOS: The legatee asks!

SMICRINES: What? Do you suppose that was my reason
  For asking? Good God! – The enemy got all the rest?

DAOS: The bulk of it, except what I originally
  Took charge of. There are some gowns here; cloaks; and
   all those slaves
  Belong to the family.

SMICRINES: They are of no interest
  To me. I wish Cleostratos were alive.

DAOS: I too.
  Come, let's bring our unhappy news indoors, to greet
  Those least prepared to hear it.

SMICRINES: Daos, I would like,
  When there's more time, to have a talk with you. Just
   now
  I'd rather go indoors, and try to think out what's
  The most considerate line to take with the family.

     [SMICRINES *goes into his own house,* DAOS *into*
     Chairestratos' *house. Enter* CHANCE *as* PROLOGUE.]

CHANCE: Well! If this news meant ruin for the family,
Since I'm divine, the next on stage would not be *me*.
As it is, they are ignorant and mistaken, as every one
Of you who gives me his kind attention will perceive.

Cleostratos and his band of mercenaries were there
In camp, when this attack was made by the enemy.
Without a second's delay he gave the word. Each man
Arming himself with what lay handiest, they all
Charged. So it was that the man who chanced to be
  standing next
To Cleostratos went into battle with this shield,
And was cut down at once. When Daos saw the shield
Lying among the bodies, the disfigured face
Led him to his mistake. Cleostratos, with other
Weapons, joined in the charge, and was made prisoner.
He lives, and will at any moment come safe home.
That's all you need be told about Cleostratos.

The old man who just now was asking all those questions
Is his father's brother, and so his uncle; but for sheer
Wickedness he's unrivalled in the human race.
Kinsman, or friend – the words mean nothing to him.
  Disgrace
In whatever form causes him no uneasiness.
Getting is his whole life: he must get everything.
He lives alone, looked after by one aged woman.
The man whose house the slave went into is younger
  brother
To this old miser, and lives next door. He too is uncle
To the young man, but a truly honourable character;
He is also rich. He has a wife, and one unmarried
Daughter; and when Cleostratos went abroad he left
His sister in this uncle's charge, and these two girls
Have been brought up together. Now this man, as I said,

Is honourable; so, finding that Cleostratos
Was likely to be abroad for some time, and aware
That she had little money in her own right, he resolved
To marry the girl to Chaireas, his own wife's son
By her first husband, and as dowry settled on her
Two talents; and just now he was on the very point
Of celebrating the wedding. But the arrival of
This news will upset everything. The old scoundrel
Smicrines, who has just learnt about those six hundred
Gold coins, and caught a glimpse of Lycian
   house-servants,
Pack-mules, and slave-girls – since his niece is heiress to
Her brother, he'll be keen to possess her for himself,
Claiming the bride through right of seniority.
Well, he shall sweat himself to death, and all for nothing;
What's more, he'll show the world what sort of man he is
Plainer than ever, and then crawl back to Square One.

Lastly, I must introduce myself by name: of all
These matters the sole arbiter and disposer, Chance!
   [*Exit* CHANCE. *Enter* SMICRINES.]
SMICRINES: So that no one should remark I was too fond
   of money,
I didn't question him closely about the amount of gold
Or the number of silver objects he's brought home. I made
No reckoning of any item; I was cordial,
Just let him bring it all in. – For everything I do
They slander me. Well, the true count will be confirmed,
So long as those who carry it are our own servants.
I think, now, they'll be willing enough to keep the law
And do what's right; if they should not, they'll be
   opposed
By everyone. As for this wedding now in train,
I mean to warn them to let it drop. It may indeed
Be irrelevant even to mention this; when such bad news

Has just arrived, it's not the day for a wedding-feast.
I'll knock at the door, for all that, and call Daos out,
Since he's the only man here who'll pay heed to me.

[*He knocks.* DAOS *appears, addressing his first remarks
to those inside the house.*]

DAOS: Yes, what you're doing is perfectly
  understandable;
We should confront what's happened in as humane a spirit
As circumstances render possible.

SMICRINES: Daos, it's you
I've come to see.

DAOS: To see me?

SMICRINES: Certainly. If only
Cleostratos were alive, as he should be by rights,
To deal with all this, and when I pass on, become
The lawful heir to all I have!

DAOS: I wish the same.
What then?

SMICRINES: Do you ask? I'm the eldest of this family;
Yet I accept slights; here's my brother – he always finds
New ways to overreach me. I see him do it; and I
Put up with it.

DAOS: You're wise.

SMICRINES: But, friend, there's no limit!
He treats me as some slave, or bastard – nothing else!
This wedding, now – he plans it, gives away the girl
To God knows who; no consultation, doesn't ask
My advice, though I'm – no less than he – the girl's
  uncle.

DAOS: What of it?

SMICRINES: It makes me angry to see all this. My brother
Adopts a hostile attitude – well, then, I'll do
The same to him: I'll leave my fortune – not for his
Family to tear in pieces; no, I'll take the advice
Of certain friends, and I shall marry the girl myself.

The law, as I understand it, Daos, more or less
Enjoins this. So now, you too put your wits to work
On my behalf, to find how this can best be done.

DAOS: Oh, Smicrines! I think that proverb, 'Know
    yourself',
Holds a profound wisdom. Let me abide by that.
Consult me on any matter on which it's suitable
To consult an honest slave; on all such matters you
Shall have my opinion. [1]But remember: you are free,
I am a slave; and, since my master's death, I'm yours.
I'll do slave's work for you. As for this girl indoors,
On going abroad my master signed a deed of trust
With certain persons. If instructed, I can reveal
The provisions of this deed in detail, and say where,
How, and before what witness it was made. But if
You're talking of an estate – still more, an heiress – or
If it's a matter of marriage, family, or disputes
Between relations, don't ask Daos to get involved.
Free men's affairs belong to free men; you yourselves
Must manage them.

SMICRINES: So *you* think I am in the wrong?

DAOS: I come from Phrygia; many things that you in
    Athens
Call right seem scandalous to me; the contrary
Is no less true. Why listen to me? You probably
Have a better brain than I have.

SMICRINES: All the same I think
You have a point there. What you're saying is, in effect,
'Don't get me into trouble.' I understand. – I'll have
To go to the town and see my brother, or someone, if
Nobody's at home.

DAOS: No, no one.
    [*Exit* SMICRINES.]

                    O cruel goddess, Chance!

1. The text is defective here; the next two lines are partly conjecture.

You'd take me from my dear young master and hand me
  on
To this old scoundrel? What harm have I done to you?
      [*Enter* COOK *from Chairestratos' house, followed by his
      boy.*]

COOK: I always have the same luck. When I get a job
  At last, what happens? Someone's died! Nothing to do
  But shog off home without my wages. Or there's been
  A baby born, that no one knew was on the way;
  So, suddenly the party's off, and I must be
  Off too.

DAOS: For the gods' sake, Cook, be off!

COOK: Well, what do you think
  I *am* doing? Boy, pick up those carving-knives, quick
   now! –
  Three drachmas a day for ten days – that was to be my
   price
  When I got the job. I reckoned I had those thirty drachs
  Safe! Then some corpse comes home from Lycia; nicks
   the lot.
  [*To the boy*] You steaming blackguard! When the whole
   household's shattered by
  Bereavement, when you see the women in floods of tears,
  Tearing their hair – you come out with my oil-bottle
  Empty? [*Hits him.*] That'll teach you what an opportunity
  You wasted. – Look at my cook-boy: Aristeides the Just
  His real name is, not Spinther! – You go supperless,
  I'll see to that.
        [*Enter the* BUTLER.]
                Oh, here's the Butler; perhaps he'll stay
  For the funeral feast.

BUTLER: [1]If I'm to lose my drachma, I'll get

---

1. It seems that the Butler has been sub-contracted by the Cook, from
another master. Just below, Daos' question and the Butler's reply are con-
jecturally supplied to fill a gap in the MS.

A beating, and be no better off than either of you.

DAOS: Come on, now; can't you see he wants to be off?

BUTLER: Are you

The man who's just come home with news of
Cleostratos?

DAOS: I am.

BUTLER: The red plague rot you, then! What a thing to do!
You lunatic, when you had your fingers on all that gold,
Those slaves – you could have swiped the lot and
escaped; instead
You bring them all safe home to Master! Who are you?
Where
Do you come from?

DAOS: I'm a Phrygian.

BUTLER: Ha! A lump of offal,
Half man, half woman! I tell you, *we* are the only men,
We Thracians, and the Getai especially. Apollo!
There's manhood for you! That's why the mines are full
of us.

DAOS: You take yourself off from our doorstep! – Why,
who's coming?
A crowd of tipsies! [*Addressing them*] Well, you're very
sensible;
Since Chance can play tricks, take your pleasures while
you can.

CHORAL INTERLUDE

Act 2

Enter SMICRINES, CHAIRESTRATOS, CHAIREAS.

SMICRINES: Well now, what have you to say to me,
    Chairestratos?
CHAIRESTRATOS: First, my dear man, proper arrangements
    must be made
For the funeral.
SMICRINES: They shall be. I'm concerned with what
    Comes next. That girl – don't promise her to anyone.
    Her future's *my* business, not yours. I'm senior
    To you. You *have* a wife – a daughter too, in fact;
    And I *need* one.
CHAIREAS: But, Smicrines! Have you no care
    For – decency?
SMICRINES: Why do you ask that, boy?
CHAIREAS: At your age
    You mean to marry a child?
SMICRINES: My age? What age?
CHAIREAS: To me
    You seem utterly old.
SMICRINES: Am I the only man
    Who has married in middle life?
CHAIRESTRATOS: For the gods' sake, Smicrines,
    Be human. Chaireas here was brought up with this girl;
    He intends to marry her. What more is there to say?
    You shall not be the loser; what Cleostratos
    Left, the entire estate, is yours; take everything
    As legal owner, it's our gift; but let the girl
    Enjoy a husband of her own age. I will give,
    From my own pocket, an extra dowry of two talents.
SMICRINES: Just listen to that! Why, gods above, man, do
    you take me

For Simple Simon? I'm to accept the property,
And hand the girl over to marry Chaireas,
And then, when there's a son, I'll find myself in court
For filching his inheritance?

CHAIRESTRATOS: You imagine we'd
Do that? Come off it!

SMICRINES: 'Imagine', you say? Just tell Daos
To fetch me a full list of the goods that he brought home.

CHAIRESTRATOS: And why should that be needed? What
    ought I to have done?

Two lines are missing here.

CHAIRESTRATOS: I thought *you*, Chaireas, were going to
    marry her,
And Cleostratos should have my daughter, so that I
Could leave my whole estate between the two of you.
Must all my hopes give way to this? Why should I live
To see such a thing happen? I'd sooner die today.

            [SMICRINES *and* CHAIRESTRATOS *go into their res-
            pective houses, leaving Chaireas alone.*]

CHAIREAS: Cleostratos! Your sad fate doubtless has first
    claim –
And rightly – on our pity and our tears; but mine
Comes second. No one here has suffered such a blow
As I have. You were my best friend. I fell in love,
Helplessly, with your sister. I did nothing rash,
Nothing unworthy or unfair. I went to see
Your uncle, whom you made your sister's guardian,
And my own mother, who had brought her up, and asked
To have her as my lawful wife. I thought I was
The happiest of all men; and now, when I was sure
I had reached my goal, fulfilment was within my grasp –
I cannot even see her ever again. The law
Demolishes my claim, and lets another man
Possess her.

[DAOS *appears at the door, sees Chaireas, and turns to speak to Chairestratos inside.*]

DAOS: No, Chairestratos, this is not right.
Stand up. Now is no time for grovelling in despair. –
Speak to him, Chaireas. – Don't give in; we are all
In the same boat together. Instead of this, you ought
To open your doors and show your face. Chairestratos,
Will you betray your friends in this ignoble manner?

          [CHAIRESTRATOS *rises, comes to the door as he speaks, and eventually emerges.*]

CHAIRESTRATOS: Daos, my boy, I'm in a bad way. This business
Has made me sick. I'll swear I'm not in my right mind,
I'm simply stark mad. This good brother of mine – his sheer
Wickedness leaves me reeling. He actually intends
To marry her himself!

DAOS: 'Marry', you say: tell me,
Can he?

CHAIRESTRATOS: This soul of honour says he can; and *that*
After I'd offered him everything Cleostratos
Sent home.

DAOS: The dirty old devil!

CHAIRESTRATOS: Dirty from top to toe.
If ever I see this happen, it'll kill me, I swear.

DAOS: Well, now: what shall we do to defeat this criminal?

CHAIRESTRATOS: The hardest thing in the world.

DAOS: Hard, but still possible.

CHAIRESTRATOS: Is it? Defeating him, let me tell you, is going to take
Every ounce of fight you've got.

About 5 lines are missing here.

DAOS: When a headstrong man's committed an error, you will find

238

That he gets in a panic. You can easily deal with him;
He sees nothing, anticipates nothing, but what he wants;
Therefore, as a judge of reality, he's irrational.
CHAIRESTRATOS: Then what's your advice? I'm ready to
   do anything
You wish.
DAOS: You must put on an act; dress up your grief
  As something worse. Make out you've fallen into a
    depression
  (As you said just now) due partly to your nephew's
    death,
  Partly to your niece's marriage; further, when you see
  The deep despair of one you regard as your own son,
  You've been attacked by one of these sudden sicknesses
  (It's a fact of life that most diseases spring from grief);
  Your brother knows you suffer from melancholia
  And jaundice. Then we'll bring in a doctor, to reel off
  Scientific terms, and diagnose pleuritis or
  Phrenitis – something that kills you off in half an hour.
CHAIRESTRATOS: And what then?
DAOS: Suddenly – you're dead. We wail aloud,
  'Farewell, Chairestratos!' then come out here to mourn
  In front of the door. You'll be locked in your room;
    down here
  A dummy corpse will lie in state, all muffled up,
  To represent you.
CHAIRESTRATOS [to Chaireas]: Do you follow him?
CHAIREAS: No, I don't,
  By Dionysos.
CHAIRESTRATOS: Nor do I.
DAOS: Now, on your demise,
  Your daughter in turn becomes an heiress, exactly like
  The present heiress – that's your niece; with this
    difference:
  Your daughter has some sixty talents, your niece – four.

This greedy old man is uncle equally to both –

CHAIRESTRATOS: I see it!

DAOS: I hope so, if you're not stuffed with sawdust. So,
He'll gladly give her, before three thousand witnesses,
To the first man who asks for her, and take instead
Your daughter –

CHAIRESTRATOS: Oh, won't he be livid!

DAOS: – at least he'll think
He takes her. He'll walk round the house with a bunch
  of keys,
Re-arranging things, putting seals on all the doors,
  dreaming
Of wealth!

CHAIRESTRATOS: And what about my dummy?

DAOS: It will lie
Still, while we all sit round it in a ring, and [1][call
To Smicrines to come up closer . . .
He'll be keeping a watchful eye on all our friends . . .
Ready to put each visitor to the test . . .
In what manner . . ., how he came to the house . . .,
If anyone owes money to the deceased; if anyone . . .,
He exacts fully twice the amount of the debt.]

CHAIRESTRATOS: Daos, your project must go forward;
  it's exactly
To my mind. Could anyone wish for a more effective
  way
To punish the old villain?

DAOS: I swear I'll make him pay
In full for every time he has ever made you writhe.
'The gaping wolf goes hungry' – that's a true proverb.
– We must get busy. Chaireas, do you know a doctor –
Not an Athenian, clever, fond of practical jokes?

CHAIREAS: Well, no, I don't.

DAOS: We ought to have one.

1. The text here is defective for about eight lines.

CHAIREAS: Why? I'll fetch
    One of my friends. We'll borrow a wig, and a fancy
       cloak,
    And a cane; and he can put on any accent he knows.
DAOS: Well, lose no time.
CHAIRESTRATOS: And what shall *I* do?
DAOS: What we planned:
    Die – and the best of luck!
CHAIRESTRATOS: I'll do it.
DAOS: Don't let a soul
    Go outdoors. Keep alert; and carry the plot through.
CHAIREAS: Who else will know?
CHAIRESTRATOS: I'll tell my wife, and the two girls,
    To save them weeping; but the rest can sit in the house
    All wailing in wild grief over my dummy corpse.
CHAIREAS: That's fine. Now, someone, take my father
       indoors. He's going
    To enjoy a richly rhythmical experience,
    With its agonizing moments, once his disease sets in –
    If only our doctor plays his part convincingly.
       [*Exeunt.*]

CHORAL INTERLUDE

Act 3

SMICRINES *enters from his house.*

SMICRINES: Well, Daos takes his time in bringing me that
  list
  Of the property. That's all the heed he pays to *me*.
  Daos is on their side. All right, then; this suits me
  Better – it gives me the welcome opportunity,
  In examining his list, to quit being generous
  And study my own profit. – Anything not shown
  Will be worth double what he makes out. The slippery
  rogue!
  I know his tricks.
      [*Enter* DAOS.]
DAOS: O gods! A terrible thing has happened. Holy Sun!
  I'd never have thought a man could fall so suddenly
  Into such a terrible sickness – like a thunderbolt
  Bringing destruction on the house.
SMICRINES: What *does* he mean?

Several lines are missing here.

DAOS: ... 'No mortal finds
  Unbroken happiness' – another marvellous line.
SMICRINES: Daos, you wretch, where are you off to in
  such a hurry?
DAOS: And this too he says somewhere: 'All our human life
  Is ruled by Chance, not Counsel' – a superlative line.
  'For God plants guilt in men, when he would overthrow
  A great house utterly' – the mighty Aeschylus.
SMICRINES: Why all these quotations?
DAOS: 'O horrible, O horrible, most horrible!'
SMICRINES: Will he never stop?
DAOS: 'In human woe nothing is unbelievable',

Says Carcinos, 'for heaven in a single day
Casts down the prosperous man to abject misery!'
All these are splendid utterances, Smicrines.

SMICRINES: What *are* you talking about?

DAOS: Your brother – holy Zeus!
How shall I find the words? – is at the point of death.

SMICRINES: But he was talking to me just now! What's
happened to him?

DAOS: The gall-bladder – some pain – a wandering in the
mind –
And suffocation.

SMICRINES: Gods above! How terrible!

DAOS: 'There is no fate so terrifying to describe,
No bodily pain –'

SMICRINES: You'll wear me out.

DAOS: 'Calamities
That men look not for are dispensed by heaven's hand' –
One from Euripides, and one from Chairemon,
The sort of poets that you don't meet every day.

SMICRINES: Has a doctor been to see him?

DAOS: No, Chaireas has gone
To fetch one.

SMICRINES: Well, which one?

DAOS: Why, here he comes, by Zeus –
Or so it seems. – My good friend, come as quick as you
can.
'The sick are restless, and despair drives patience out.'

SMICRINES [*aside*]: If they see *me* walk in, they'll say I
couldn't wait,
Being so delighted at the news; I'm sure they will.
My brother wouldn't be pleased to see me either . . .

About sixteen lines are missing here. The MS resumes with a number
of defective lines in which the doctor is telling Smicrines about the
patient's condition:

DOCTOR: I think his mind is affected ... we call this *phrenitis*.

SMICRINES: I understand. What follows?
Is there no hope whatever of recovery?

DOCTOR: It is well that no one should offer false comfort in such matters.

SMICRINES: Do not deceive me; tell the truth.

DOCTOR: It is quite impossible that he should live. He is vomiting bile; his sight is growing dim ... he is foaming at the mouth ... he looks like a funeral ... Come over here for a moment, away from the door. You yourself might perhaps not have so long to live.

SMICRINES: Don't worry; just pray to have a constitution like mine.

DOCTOR: Many unexpected things happen. I warn you not to laugh at my skill. I can see you're not in the best of health; some wasting disease is creeping over you. There is no doubt of it, you look like death.

Here comes a gap of over 200 lines, in the course of which Act 4 begins. Some fragmentary lines indicate a scene of ritual mourning: 'Chairestratos is dead; a good man is lost to us', etc. After this, suddenly Cleostratos appears: 'O dearest home ... I thank the gods ... I am here, and see you in answer to my prayers ... May the gods bless Daos ... I must knock at the door.'

[DAOS *comes out, and at first does not recognize his master.*]

DAOS: Who's there?

CLEOSTRATOS: I am.

DAOS: Who are you looking for? The master of this house has just died.

CLEOSTRATOS: He has died? Oh, how terrible!

DAOS: Be quiet; don't disturb a bereaved family.

CLEOSTRATOS: Oh, my poor uncle!

[Then Daos recognizes his master and embraces him; they go indoors together, and Act 4 ends.]

Act 5 consists of 29 mutilated lines. The following scraps throw a little light on what took place:

> glad women . . . there is a double wedding . . . his own daughter . . . his entire estate . . . he shall reach his goal . . . by Heracles, come to me . . . Cleostratos . . . just now I thought . . . welcoming my dear . . . feasting . . . in a way, he has saved my life . . . to have this pledge . . . before witnesses . . . to Chaireas what he wishes . . .

Probably about 90 lines following this are lost altogether; but from another source we have also these few lines which, since they point a moral, may well belong to the final scene:

> O wretched misers! What advantage have they over other people? What a pitiful existence they drag out, who guard castles or possess fortresses! If they so easily suspect every man who comes near them of having a dagger in his hand, what a penalty they pay!

THE HERO

The outline[1] of the plot is as follows:

A young unmarried woman, Myrrhine, having given birth to twins, a boy and a girl, exposed them. They were found by a farm-bailiff, Tibeios, who took them to his home and brought them up. Later Myrrhine married the man who had seduced her, Laches. In course of time Tibeios died, owing money to Laches; to pay off the debt, the boy, Gorgias, went with his sister, Plangon, to work for Laches. Neither he nor Laches knew of their relationship. A slave of Laches, Daos, fell in love with Plangon, supposing her to be a fellow-slave. Plangon, however, had already been seduced by a neighbour, Pheidias. Daos wanted to take upon himself responsibility for Plangon's pregnancy; and the mother, Myrrhine, not knowing that Daos was innocent, was very angry. When everything became known, the old man Laches found his own children and recognized them by tokens left with them when they were exposed; and the seducer, Pheidias, willingly married Plangon.

The only surviving fragment of any size is a part of the Prologue, a conversation between Daos and another slave, Getas. There is some evidence to suggest that after this Prologue a god appeared to give an exposition of the plot, as in *The Unkindest Cut*; and that here the god was a 'Hero', the spirit of some famous ancestor who was worshipped as tutelary deity of the household of Laches and Myrrhine.

1. This outline is adapted from the metrical Argument prefixed to the text.

PROLOGUE

GETAS, DAOS.

GETAS: Daos, it seems to me you must have carried out
  Some frightful crime, and now you're sweating at the
      thought
  Of being chained to the treadmill. Something's wrong,
      that's clear.
  Why do you beat your head like that? and then stand still
  And tear your hair out? and then groan?
DAOS: Oh, gods above!
GETAS: I'm right, I knew it: you bad lot! Then wouldn't it
  Be wise to hand over to me, for a little while,
  Any small savings you may have, in case you bring
  More trouble on yourself? You won't? Then I'm fed up
  With you, and no wonder: always suspicious!
DAOS: What on earth,
  For God's sake, are you drooling about? I'm in a spot.
  It's got me down. I simply don't know what to do.
GETAS: Well, it's your own fault, damn you!
DAOS: Friend, for pity's sake,
  Don't damn a man when he's in love.
GETAS: What's that? In love?
DAOS: Yes, I'm in love.
GETAS: Your master gives you more than double
  The standard ration. A bad thing, Daos. It's probably
  Just overeating.
DAOS: It's not the stomach, it's the heart,
  Getas. She's a young, innocent girl who lives with us,
  A slave like me; and every time I look at her –
GETAS: A slave, is she?
DAOS: Well, in a way, yes. There was a man
  Tibeios, a shepherd, who lived here in Ptelea –

250

A slave, when he was young. He had two children,
   twins –
Or so he always said; one was this girl Plangon
That I'm in love with –

GETAS: Yes, I follow.

DAOS: – and a boy
Called Gorgias.

GETAS: That lad who works as a shepherd here?

DAOS: Yes. Well, Tibeios their father, getting on in years,
To help him feed the children, borrowed money from
My master Laches; and again, when times were hard
And prices high, borrowed some more; and then he died.

GETAS: Because your master wouldn't give him a third loan?

DAOS: Perhaps. Well, when Tibeios was dead, young
   Gorgias
Borrowed a little more, and with it gave the old man
A proper funeral and a grave; and then came here
To us, bringing his sister with him; and here he stays
While he works off the debt.

GETAS: And what does Plangon do?

DAOS: She's with my mistress; helps at spinning; serves at
   meals.

GETAS [mocking Daos' indignant tone]: A young girl serves at
   table?

DAOS: You're making fun of me.
I tell you, she's –

GETAS: No, not at all!

DAOS: You'd never tell
She wasn't free-born; she's so modest, so –

GETAS: Well, now,
What are you doing to help your cause?

DAOS: I've tried nothing
Underhand. I told my master all about it; and he's
Promised to let her live with me, once he's discussed
The matter with her brother.

GETAS: Well, then, why are you
So gloomy?

DAOS: Because my master's been away three months
On some business in Lemnos. Oh! If only he'd
Come safely home!

GETAS: I long for that as much as you.
Heaven bring him back to us!

DAOS: Why don't we offer sacrifice?
The gods might send a blessing.

GETAS: A most suitable
And excellent plan. If I were in love, I'd sacrifice
Regardless, however poor I was – you bet I would.
        [*He turns to an imaginary person in the audience.*]
Hey! Firewood-merchant! Bring us a load of firewood,
    quick,
For a sacrifice!

DAOS: Getas, have you never been in love?

GETAS: No; I never had a full stomach.

A number of small fragments, of two lines or less, can be assigned
to later scenes in this play; but the only one that seems worth adding
here is this, from a speech of Daos to Myrrhine:

DAOS: Mistress, there's nothing in this world stronger than
    love.
Why, even Zeus, who is king of all the gods in heaven,
Cannot resist, but yields to love in everything.

The course of events in the rest of the play seems to be as follows:
    In the later part of the Prologue Daos tells Getas that the real
reason for his distress is his knowledge that Plangon is pregnant, and
near her time. He does not know who was responsible; but is
prepared to assume responsibility himself. During the course of the
action Plangon's child is born; and Laches returns from Lemnos.
Myrrhine finds in Plangon's possession some tokens which she
recognizes as those which she left with her own children when she

exposed them. She has never told her husband Laches that she had these children before she married him; and she is terrified at the thought that he may discover it. In some way, however, it is found that these same tokens also identify Laches as the father of the twins. Thus they are proved free-born, and are accepted by their parents. The father of Plangon's child is Pheidias, a rich neighbour, who loves her and wants to marry her; now that she is known to be free-born this becomes possible, and the wedding is arranged. Daos is probably consoled for his disappointment by being given his freedom.

THE FARMER

On the stage are two houses. In one of them lives a poor widow called Myrrhine, with her daughter, whose name we do not know. In the other lives a rich citizen, who has a son by his first wife and a daughter, Hedeia, by his second. This son has just returned home from Corinth. Before he went away he had an affair with the poor widow's daughter, and she is now pregnant. The son is in love with her and wants to marry her; but his father, not wishing his son to marry a girl with no dowry, has during the boy's absence decided that he shall marry his half-sister Hedeia; and hearing that the youth would return home today, has made all arrangements for an immediate wedding.

The widow has also a son called Gorgias; he is at present in the country, working under a farmer called Cleainetos. Gorgias is the son of Myrrhine's late husband; but Myrrhine's daughter is older, and is the child of another man – in fact, of Cleainetos, who had an affair with Myrrhine before her marriage. Cleainetos has a bad conscience about his desertion of Myrrhine; he has never married; and though reasonably well off, still lives a life of rigorous labour on the farm.

In the first surviving scene the rich citizen's son comes out of his father's house in great agitation and addresses the audience. He tells of his entanglement with his poor neighbour's daughter; of his love for her, and his fear that the present situation may cause enmity between himself and her half-brother Gorgias.

. . . But what I'd done was not a crime; I didn't feel
Guilty. Well, Gorgias then was spending all his time
Away in the country; and I went off on certain business
To Corinth. While I was there, the disaster happened
    which
Has simply shattered me. When I came home last night I
    found
Another wedding being prepared for me; the gods
All wreathed in flowers, my father offering sacrifice.

And who was the bride's father? My father was that
   too!
You see, I've a half-sister who's the daughter of
My father's present wife. So I'm in a cleft stick;
How I can struggle out of it I just don't know.
I only know I'm in a spot. I've just walked out
Of the house without saying anything. Suppose I quit
This wedding: I'm very fond of my half-sister, and
To abandon her like that would be unkind, unfair,
A breach of family loyalty. And then again
I thought I'd knock at Myrrhine's door, and talk it over
With the girl I really love; but still I hesitate.
Her brother Gorgias may be home now from the farm –
I just don't know. I've got to think of everything.
Well, for the moment I'll clear off, and try to plan
One thing: how to escape this wedding.

> [*Exit.* MYRRHINE *enters from her house, with an old
> slave or nurse called Philinna.*]

MYRRHINE: Listen, dear:
   You're a friend I can trust. That's why I talk to you,
   Philinna, and tell you all my troubles. So now you know
   Just how things are.
PHILINNA: I do; and by the holy gods,
   After what I've heard, my dear, I've a good mind to go
   Straight to that door and call out the disgraceful scamp
   And tell him what I think of him.
MYRRHINE: Philinna, please!
   I'd rather let him go.
PHILINNA: What, that blackguard? Go where?
   To hell, that's where he ought to go! When he's behaved
   Like that to our poor girl, is he to marry now?
MYRRHINE: Now, do have done with all this talk. Look who
   comes here:
   It's Daos from the farm. Let's stand aside a while.
PHILINNA: Why, what concern of ours is Daos?

MYRRHINE: All the same

It's quite a good idea.

It is not clear whose slave Daos is, the rich citizen's or Cleainetos'.

[DAOS *comes in accompanied by another slave called*
SYROS, *and carrying a sheaf of flowers and sprays.*]

DAOS: I don't know any man that works a better farm.
Got a real sense of duty, that land has! Look there:
Myrtle-berries; fine ivy-sprays; a heap of flowers . . .[1]
And anything else you like to plant – it pays you back
Not more, nor less; just fair, good measure. – Here,
    Syros,
Take everything we've brought, the whole lot, straight
    indoors;
It's all for the wedding. – Why, good day to you,
    Myrrhine.
MYRRHINE: Good day to you too.
DAOS [*To Philinna*]: Noble and distinguished Madam,
I didn't see you. How are you getting on? Listen:
I'm going to feast you with good news – or rather, with
News of good things to come, God willing; and I want
To be the first to tell you. A few days ago
Cleainetos, whose farm your son is working on,
Was digging in his vineyard, when he cut his leg
Wide open – a grand gash!
MYRRHINE: Oh, no! How terrible!
DAOS: Courage! there's more yet. Three days later, from
    this wound
The old man had a swelling ulcer; fever then
Set in; and he was in a bad state.
PHILINNA: Is this what
You call good news? You rubbish, sweep yourself away!
MYRRHINE: Now keep quiet, Granny!

1. A line continuing the list is missing at this point.

DAOS: Then, just when he needs someone
To look after him, his house-slaves, like the barbarous lot
They are, all begin saying, This puts paid to him;
This is good-bye, they say. But your son Gorgias –
You'd think it was his own father, the way he tended him.
Rubbed him with oil, washed out the ulcer, brought him
      food,
And cheered him up – for a wound like that is dangerous.
In fact, his care has brought the old man back to life.

MYRRHINE: Oh, splendid lad!

DAOS: Yes – and, well done Cleainetos!
For, while he was recovering, lying quiet indoors,
Free from his spade and all his troubles – well, you know
The rough, hard life he lives – he questioned Gorgias
About himself and his affairs; no doubt he knew
Something already. So the lad got talking to him;
And when he put in a word about his sister and you,
And the trouble you've had here, the old man, deeply
      moved
In a way that's not uncommon, felt that on every score
He should make some return for services received.
So, being old and lonely, he made up his mind:
He's going to marry your daughter! Yes, he's given his
      word.
So that's the long and the short of it. He and Gorgias
Will be here any minute; and the old man will take
Your daughter back with him to the farm. So you'll be
      able
To stop your daily fight with that intractable
And sullen monster, Poverty; especially since
You live in the town here. Either one should have money,
Or live in a place where one's misfortunes aren't laid bare
For all the world to witness. In a case like yours
Some quiet country spot is a blessing. Well now, that's
My good news. – All the best!

MYRRHINE: And all the best to you!
　　[*Exit* DAOS.]
PHILINNA: Why, what's the matter, child? Why do you
　　walk about
　Wringing your hands like that?
MYRRHINE: How can I help it, though?
　I simply don't know what to do!
PHILINNA: Do about what?
MYRRHINE: About my daughter, Philinna. She's very near
　　her time.

There are five other fragments from this play; four being parts of
speeches by Cleainetos, the farmer, to Gorgias, and one spoken by
Daos to the young man who doesn't want to marry his half-sister.
None of them gives any real clue as to what happened in the rest
of the play. The reader can therefore have the pleasure of working
out for himself the various possible lines of development which this
opening offers.

CLEAINETOS: I'm a rough countryman, I don't say other-
　　wise.
　I don't know all the ins and outs of city ways.
　Still, I keep learning more and more as time goes on.

　This man, whoever he is, who has taken such unjust
　Advantage of your poverty, has in the same act
　Started a curse which may recoil on his own head.
　He may be well off; but his comfort's insecure;
　The stream of Fortune tends to change course overnight.

　A poor man, Gorgias, however sensibly
　He talks, always invites contempt; for people think
　His talk has one sole object: gain. The man who wears
　An old and shabby coat, even if he happens to be
　The injured party, is put down as a blackmailer.

Gorgias, the man of greatest strength is he who knows
How to endure the greatest wrongs with self-control.
This furious anger, this deep bitterness, betrays
At once to all the world mere pettiness of mind.

DÁOS: Well, have you been struck by lightning? When
    you've managed to fall in love
With a free-born girl, you've not a word to say?
    Ridiculous!
You'll stand by and let them fix your wedding – with the
    wrong sweetheart?

THE SICYONIAN

CHARACTERS

The Speaker of the Prologue
CICHESIAS, *an old Athenian*
PHILUMENE, *his daughter*
STRATOPHANES, *a young soldier*
DROMON, *a slave of Cichesias*
THERON, *Stratophanes' parasite*
PYRRHIAS, *Stratophanes' slave*
MOSCHION, *Stratophanes' brother*
SMICRINES (?) *and another man; an old man from Eleusis*

*

Scene: Athens

This fragment is the most recently discovered. It is written on pieces of papyrus which were used as wrapping for an Egyptian mummy kept in a Paris museum, and the first transcript of it was published in 1964. Whereas other fragments of comparable length give us a whole scene or two or more, this manuscript gives us no whole scenes, but fairly long passages from several parts of the play. There are several passages where a part – the beginning or end – of each line is missing, but enough is left to convey the general sense; and here it has seemed worth while, for the sake of continuity, to write conjectural lines, which are indicated by square brackets.

Another difference between this and the other fragments is that here, in what the MS gives us, there is no sign of any moral issue such as forms the main theme of *The Arbitration*, *The Unkindest Cut*, and *The Samian Woman*; nor are there any passages of reflection on ethical or social topics such as form a large proportion of the smaller fragments found as quotations in other writers. In fact, three-quarters of what is left of *The Sicyonian* consists of narrative; part of it apparently from a Prologue, but most of it from a very long Messenger's Speech which is spoken to two characters about whom we know almost nothing. This speech, however, tells us something about Menander and his attitude to other dramatic writers; for it seems to be written as a sort of echo of the Messenger's Speech in Euripides' *Orestes*. There the Messenger recounts a meeting of the Argive Assembly to try Orestes and Electra for the murder of Clytemnestra; here the Messenger tells how an informally constituted assembly of Athenian citizens discuss who is to be legal guardian of an apparently orphan girl. Menander's narrative parallels that of Euripides in several features, notably in the opening passage, which was well known.

The central character of the play is Stratophanes, a young soldier who has just returned to Athens from military service in Asia Minor. He thinks he is a native of Sicyon, a town on the Corinthian Gulf, a little to the west of Corinth; but his supposed mother is a resident of Athens. On his arrival he sends his slave Pyrrhias ahead to break to her the news of his safe return; and Pyrrhias comes back saying that the 'mother' has died, and bringing with him her will, and a letter and a parcel that she left for Stratophanes. The letter tells him something about his parentage, and the parcel contains tokens to establish his identity. Stratophanes meets and falls in love with Philumene, who as an infant had been captured by pirates and sold in Asia Minor. Eventually both discover that they are of Athenian parentage, so that they can be legally married.

The first fragment is from the Prologue.

... I say that she was this man's daughter. When the
   pirates
Had all three in their power, they thought it not worth
   while
To carry off the old woman; but they took the child
And the slave to Mylasa, a Carian town, and offered them
For sale in the market. So this slave was sitting there
Holding his little mistress on one arm; when soon
A man called Hegemon, seeing they were for sale,
Came up and asked how much they were. He was told the
   price,
Agreed, and bought them. Another man, who was near
   this slave,
Brought there by the pirates to be sold at the same time,
Said, 'Cheer up, friend; this Sicyonian who has bought you
Is Hegemon, an excellent man, and very well off.'

The next passage begins with twenty-four lines each of which has
the first three, four, or five syllables missing; the complete lines start
at 'She didn't want you to live on ...'

THERON: Stay here; don't presume to ... There will be a
   time for that later on.
STRATOPHANES: By Zeus, you're quite right.
THERON: If you ... him he will fly into a rage; and then ...
STRATOPHANES: Let us agree on that. Now, by Zeus, I am
   resolved to stay here ...
THERON: I want no one else but you to have the benefit of
   what is yours ...
STRATOPHANES: Look, here he comes.
THERON: Who? ...
STRATOPHANES: Pyrrhias, whom I sent to my house to ...

and to say that we have arrived safely ... I know [our return
will have been welcome] to my mother; then what can be the
reason that he is walking back slowly and looking downcast?
What news have you brought, Pyrrhias? Is my mother –?

PYRRHIAS: Your mother died last year.

STRATOPHANES: Died? Oh, Pyrrhias! I am sad to hear this.
    She was very old.

PYRRHIAS: She, in fact, though, wasn't your mother; and
    you're going to be involved,

Stratophanes, in tiresome business that you never reckoned
    for.

You were not her son, apparently.

STRATOPHANES: Whose son am I then?

PYRRHIAS: Listen.

On her death-bed she wrote down the truth about your
    birth. It's here.

        [He indicates a packet he is carrying.]

People dying, they say, do all they can for those who go
    on living.

She didn't want you to live on in ignorance of your family.

This was not the only thing, though. When your father
    was alive

He lost a lawsuit – so it now appears – to some Boeotian.

STRATOPHANES: Yes, I heard.

PYRRHIAS: The sum involved was many talents, Stratophanes.

STRATOPHANES: News of all this reached me straight away
    by letter, in Caria.

That same letter told me of my father's death.

PYRRHIAS: Your mother then

Learnt from legal experts that both you and all your
    inheritance

Could be seized to pay this debt; so took this step to safe-
    guard you,

And, since she was dying, restore you to your family, as
    was right.

STRATOPHANES: Give me the letter.

PYRRHIAS: There. Look now, besides
the letter, I've brought these.
See, they're tokens; they'll identify you to your family;
So your mother used to say when she was alive – the people
who
Gave me these things said she did!

THERON: Divine Athene, make him yours!
So that he can have Philumene, and I can have Malthace!

STRATOPHANES: Come on, Theron!

THERON: You don't tell me –?

STRATOPHANES: This way; and stop talking, do!

THERON: Oh, all right, then; coming!

STRATOPHANES: Pyrrhias, you come too; and presently,
When I've told them, you'll produce the evidence, and
show it there
Large as life, for anybody who wants to see with his own
eyes.

Here the Scene ends. A performance 'Of the Chorus' follows; then
the next Scene begins. The speakers in this dialogue are not named;
I have called the first two A and B (A may possibly be named
Smicrines), and the third, the Old Man, since he is thus addressed
by B.

The first five lines of this Scene are complete; the next twenty-nine
are fragmentary; then seven or eight are missing; next, thirty-four
are fragmentary or missing; then come twenty-two complete lines;
and the rest of the scene is fragmentary.

A: You're just a fraud, a tiresome bagful of hot air,
If you think that a man who weeps and begs like that
Is telling the truth. Listen: behaviour of that kind
Is pretty well proof, these days, that the man's up to no
good.
You can't find out the truth that way. It's better to get
A few people to talk things over.

B: There you go –
 Rule by committee! You'd get away with robbery.
A: I swear my way's the better; and I'll stand by that.
B: Oh, you authoritarians! By Heracles,
 You drive me mad.
A: But why bellow abuse at me?
B: I hate you – yes, and your whole supercilious tribe!
 You're a public pest – as one day you'll admit.
A: Never!
 [I (suspect) you of stealing from the rich man his . . . and his
 equipment . . . Perhaps you don't actually carry the cash out
 of his house (but you abet) those who take it away . . .
B: Go to hell; you're full of hot air yourself.
A: If I had made you my fellow– . . .
         [*An* OLD MAN *appears.*]
B: Old man, stay here with us . . .
OLD MAN: Here I am. What is the subject of your loud
    dispute?
B: Wait to . . . a small . . .
A: We want to hear about . . .
OLD MAN: I happened to be (on my way) neither (from the
    country) nor, by Zeus, . . . (Someone), thinking he was doing
    me a favour, (told me there was a dispute going on; so, since
    I enjoy hearing about) other people's troubles – I'm a terrible
    man on a jury – . . . – and the backbone of the country they
    are, too.]
 Well, I had just come back from the city to meet the man
 From our village who'd got the job of sharing out
 A skinny half-sized bullock, and being told by those
 Who got the shares exactly what they thought of him –
 Well, I was one of them – I'm an Eleusinian,
 You see, from the deme of the Great Goddess. So I came,
 When I saw the crowd – 'Excuse me,' I said, and I got a
    place
 Right by the door. And there I saw this girl sitting;

And straight away, out of the people standing round
A sort of jury was constituted. [A man stood up
And said he was] legal guardian of the young girl.

Here seven or eight lines are missing, and three defective. Probably
the Old Man at this point tells of one or more others who took part
in the dispute about the girl; one must have been Dromon.

Well, that was what he did. And we all shouted out,
'The girl's an Athenian citizen!' And even so
It was hard to quell the hubbub and make them quiet
   again.
When there was silence, we saw a young man – beardless,
   pale,
And smooth – go up to the slave and try to whisper to
   him.
We wouldn't let him. 'Speak up, louder!' There were
   shouts
Of 'What does he want?' 'Who is he?' 'What are you
   saying there?'
The youth replied, 'This slave knows well enough what
   I'm saying.'
Then a very manly-looking man ... came forward ... then
another man, and a third; and [when the first man] looked
closely [at the girl] he suddenly [poured forth] a stream [of
tears] and in a passion gripped [his hair] groaning. Those
who stood round were [astonished on seeing this].

When the MS resumes, the Old Man is telling what Stratophanes
(the 'manly-looking man') has said to the crowd.

'... [This man here, Dromon, was a slave] of the girl's
   father.
He's my slave now; therefore I give him back to her,
Renounce my claim to him, and want nothing in return.

Now let her find her father and her family;
I put no obstacle in her way.' 'Well said,' we cried.
'Now, gentlemen, hear my proposal. Since you yourselves
Are this girl's legal guardians – which she owes to me,
And now has nothing to fear – entrust her to the care
Of the priestess, and let *her* keep her on your behalf.'
These words won strong approval, as was fair. The crowd
All shouted, 'Quite right! Speak again!' So he went on,
'I used to think I too was a Sicyonian;
But now this man here, Pyrrhias, comes bringing me
My mother's will, and tokens establishing my birth.
And my belief is, if I can trust this document
And use it as proof, that I'm your fellow-citizen.
Don't rob me of this hope yet; but, if it is proved
That I too am a fellow-citizen of this girl
Whom I have brought back safe for her father, then let me
Ask him for her and marry her; and don't let any
Of my opponents get this girl into their power
Before her father appears.' 'Quite right!' 'Well said!'
    'Bravo!'
They shouted; 'Take her off to the priestess.' Suddenly
That pale-faced chap jumped up and said, 'Am I to believe
This man's got hold of a will from somewhere, just like
    that?
That he's your fellow-citizen? and that after this
Melodramatic abduction he'll just set her free?'
'Why don't you kill that smooth-face?' shouted everyone.
'It's you'll get killed, whoever you are,' the pale youth
    cries.
'You dangerous man,' says the soldier, 'crawl out of my
    reach.'
'All right, I'm going. Kindest regards to all!' – 'Come on,'
The soldier says to the girl, 'you can go.' The slave got up.
'She'll go, gentlemen,' says he, 'when *you* tell her to go.
So tell her.' – 'Very well; go!' Then she got up and went.

Well, that's as long as I stayed. What happened after that
I couldn't tell you; at that point I came away.

The next surviving passage gives only fragments of lines. From these
it is clear that it showed a recognition between a father, a mother,
and a son; and it seems likely that the son was Stratophanes. It
explains that his parents had sent him away in infancy to a foreign
woman. It seems too that the 'birth-tokens' which Pyrrhias brought
to Stratophanes figure in this scene; and just before the end of the
scene it transpires that Stratophanes is the brother of Moschion, the
beardless young man mentioned in the long narrative speech.

The final passage brings us nearly to the end of the play. The
opening situation here is puzzling; E. W. Handley convincingly
explains it by the suggestion that Theron has been trying to bribe
Cichesias to claim Philumene as his daughter, and so establish her as
an Athenian by birth; he refers to a clearly parallel situation in
Plautus' play *Poenulus*, which may well have owed some features
to Menander.

The name Scambonides means a member of the 'deme' of the
Scambonidae; this was one of the divisions of the Athenian citizen
body. The tradition said that Theseus had brought together the
various demes of Attica and united them in the single city of Athens.
The adjective *scambos* means 'bow-legged'; so Theron in adding the
description 'snub-nosed' is making what must have been a very
well-worn joke.

CICHESIAS: Go and hang yourself, you're a perfect pest!
    Get away from me!
  Do you imagine Cichesias would do such a thing?
  Or take money from anyone? What a monstrous trick!
  What, I? Cichesias? And a Scambonides?
THERON: That's just the point. So, take your pay – not now
    for what
  I said at first, but for this very thing.
CICHESIAS: What thing?
THERON: You are Cichesias.
CICHESIAS: Yes, and a Scambonides.

THERON: So much the better; you seem to have the hang of
  the thing.

  Be him! As it happens, you're snub-nosed, and short as
    well,

As that slave said at the time.

CICHESIAS [*depressed*]:   I am the old man I am.
  And add to that – at Halae I lost my little daughter
  Of four years old; Dromon my slave too.

THERON: True enough,
  You lost them.

CICHESIAS: Taken by pirates. You have reminded me
  Of all that has gone wrong – all my sorrow and suffering.

THERON: Good! Now continue weeping for her – just like
  that!

  [*To Dromon*]: What a good-hearted man he is!

DROMON: Cichesias,
  Your daughter, my young mistress, is in safe keeping . . .

[CICHESIAS: What do you say?

DROMON: I tell you again, your daughter's safe;
  And I am Dromon your slave. I have looked after her
  For all these years.

CICHESIAS: Can I believe you? Is this true?]

DROMON: She is alive, and she is here.

            [*Cichesias faints.*]

                              Cichesias!

  Don't faint! Get up! – Theron, some water, water, quick!

THERON: By Zeus, I'll run in and get some. – Why, Stratophanes

  Is indoors; I'll send him out to you.

DROMON: Don't bother now
  About the water.

THERON: All the same I'll call him here.

DROMON: He's coming round. Hello, Cichesias!

CICHESIAS: What's all this?
  Where am I? And what was it I heard someone say?

DROMON: You have your daughter, she's alive and safe.

CICHESIAS: Dromon,
Do you mean really safe, or just – alive?

DROMON: She's still
A virgin. No man has touched her.

CICHESIAS: Good.

DROMON: But you, master –
How are you?

CICHESIAS: I am alive, I can say that much, Dromon.
Beyond that – when you see an old, poor, lonely man,
Why, naturally, then everything must be all right.

> [*Enter* STRATOPHANES *from the house; as he enters he
> speaks to his mother who is indoors.*]

STRATOPHANES: I'll come back soon, mother, when I've
looked into this.

DROMON: Stratophanes, here's Philumene's father.

STRATOPHANES: Who is he?

DROMON: This man here.

STRATOPHANES: Greeting, father!

DROMON [*to Cichesias*]:   This is the man who has saved
Your daughter.

CICHESIAS: May the gods make him a happy man!

STRATOPHANES: With your consent, father, I shall be happy
indeed
And richly blest.

[DROMON: Stratophanes, let's go at once
To the priestess and find Philumene.

STRATOPHANES: First I must go
Indoors and tell them . . .

DROMON: Come, Cichesias.

STRATOPHANES: Hey, Donax!
Donax, where are you? Go indoors and tell Malthace
To have my cases, bags and baskets – everything,
Brought to our neighbour's house. Tell Malthace herself
To go there, too; and bring the Carian slaves with you,

And Theron, and the donkeys. And I'll go myself
To see Philumene's father and arrange everything.
   [*They all move off. Enter* MOSCHION *alone.*]
MOSCHION: Moschion, as things are now, you'd better not
  so much
As glance at her. Just grin and bear it, Moschion.
What pure white skin she has! What lovely eyes! Ah, well!
My brother's a lucky bridegroom . . .
        . . . And I shall be best man!

And may the noble, smiling maiden, Victory,
Bless all our ways, and stay our friend for evermore!]

SHORTER FRAGMENTS

The fragments which follow are selected from the Loeb text edited by F. G. Allinson and are given the same numbering, which is taken from Kock's *Fragments of Attic Comedy-Writers*. The first thirty-three are from plays whose titles are known; the rest from unidentified plays.

From *The Robe-Bearer* or *The Flute-Girl*

65. If you've got sense, you won't give up your present life
    For matrimony. I'm married myself; and for that reason
    My advice to you is, Don't get married.

    Go on, then, marry; I wish you luck. You're setting sail
    On a real sea of trouble; not the Libyan Sea,
    Nor the Aegean, nor the Sicilian sandbanks, where
    Three ships perhaps in thirty may avoid shipwreck:
    In marriage no survivor has ever yet been known.

66. This Myrtile – you've only got to look at her,
    Or call out, 'Nurse!' – she'll rattle on and never stop.
    I tell you, it's easier to silence the bronze bell
    Of Dodona, which rings the whole day long, they say,
    If a passer-by just touches it, than to stop the tongue
    Of Myrtile; *she*'ll talk through the whole night as well.

From *The Superstitious Man*

109. A: Now send me a blessing, honoured gods! – Look: I
        was just
        Getting my shoes on, when my right-hand shoe-lace
        broke.

B: Of course it did, you nit-wit – it was rotten; and you
   Were too damned mean to buy yourself a decent pair.

Now, for example, take the Syrians.
Those people, every time they eat fish, by a kind
Of personal incontinence, begin to swell
In the feet and belly; then they dress themselves in
      sacking
And go and sit down in the road on a heap of dung,
And thus by extreme self-abasement they attempt
To propitiate the goddess.

From *The Bridesmaid*

114. Blessed is he that hath both money and common-sense;
     For such a man will use his money sensibly.

From *The Girl Twins*

118. He married off his daughter – he told me so himself –
     On thirty days' approval.

From *The Double Deceiver*

125. He whom the gods love dies young.

From *The Woman Set on Fire*

156. You think you're somebody, and you're proud of think-
     ing so.
     That's ruined a thousand others, and it'll ruin you.

From *The Promiser*

160. If you hold your own humble state in dignity,
    My friend, then others will respect it; but if you
    By holding it in contempt make it look humble, then
    In the world's eyes you'll be a self-made laughing-stock.

From *The Charioteer*

201. Look here: no god brings money and pours it in your
        lap;
    But a god, if well-disposed, will find a way for you,
    Show you some opening that may lead to fortune.
        Then,
    If you let that go, don't blame the god; it's time you
        picked
    A quarrel with your yoke-mate – your own feebleness.

From *Thais*

217. This is the sort of girl I'd have you sing about,
    O Muse! – bold, ripe and lovely, hard to contradict;
    Who'll jilt you, lock you out, never stop wheedling
        you,
    Never love anyone, never stop pretending to.

218. The thing that spoils good character is bad company.

From *The Possessed Woman*

223. If some god were to come to me and say, 'Craton,
    After your death you shall have your life over again;

You shall be whatever you choose – dog, sheep, goat,
    man, or horse;
You're to have a second life; that is decreed by
    Fate,
So make your choice – ' I think I'd answer straight
    away,
'Anything but a man. Man's the sole living creature
Whose good fortune and bad are allotted him unfairly.
A first-rate horse, for example, 's much more carefully
Looked after than another; if you're a good dog
You're valued much more than a bad one. A thorough-
    bred cock
Lives on a special diet; an inferior one
Is even afraid of a better cock. But a good man,
A man of birth and breeding – in this age of ours
Gets no advantage whatsoever. Bum-suckers –
They come off best of any; blackmailers come next;
Slanderers a good third. Better be born a donkey
Than see your inferiors living in better style than you.'

From *The Treasure*

235. Then is not Eros the most mighty of all gods,
    And the most honoured? Why, there's not a living
        man
    So sunk in meanness, so cut-and-dried in all his ways,
    As not to give up some share of his livelihood
    To Eros. Now, if Eros treats you kindly, then
    He makes you act like this while you're still young; but
        if
    You're one of those who put it off till they've grown
        old,
    You'll pay your dues with interest for the time you've
        lost.

From *Thrasyleon*

240. This 'Know Yourself' is a silly proverb in some ways;
     To know the man next door's a much more useful rule.

From *The Doorkeeper*

923. It's no joke, to plunge into a family dinner-party, where
     First papa leads off the speeches, cup in hand, and gives
        them all
     Pointed good advice; mama comes second; then a
        grandmother
     Rambles on a little; then great-uncle, in a growling
        bass;
     Then comes some old lady who alludes to you as 'dear-
        est boy'.
     All the time you nod your head and beam at them . . .

From *The Priestess*

245. Madam, no god helps one man at another's prayer.
     If man, by clashing cymbals, can deflect a god
     To his own will, this makes him greater than the god.
     Such theories are invented by unscrupulous men
     To brazen out a living; fabrications which
     Make human life a mockery.

From *The Carthaginian*

261. No man knows who his own father is; but all of us
     Make some assumption about it, or hold some belief.

It is no easy matter in a single day
To change a habit of folly deep ingrained by time.

From *The Guitar-Player*

A father speaks:
And now what can this mean? It's not at all like *him*!
Moschion sends and asks me to come up to town.
In the past, if ever I happened to be in town
He'd shoot off to the country; and if I went there
He'd come back here again – and drink. Well, fair
   enough;
No father here to tell him how to behave. Mind you,
I never get angry with him; I myself was one
Of those who have a gift for running short of
   money.
That's one thing I can't blame my wife for; it's a gift
He got from me. Anyway, the boy's doing no good.
Better go in and see if he's here; and if he's not
I'll go straight to the market-place. I'll find him there,
I know, somewhere in Hermes Street.

I used to think once, Phanias, that wealthy men,
Having no need to borrow money, never lie
Awake at night, groaning and tossing up and down,
Saying, What shall I do? but fall into a sweet
And gentle sleep, leaving such tortures to the poor.
But now I see that you who are called the lucky ones
Have troubles just like ours. In fact, trouble itself
Is twin brother to life. When life holds luxury,
Trouble's there too; when life brings fame, there's still
   trouble;
And if you're poor, trouble grows old along with
   you.

From *The Pilots*

301. Take money, now: do you, young man, regard it as
    Useful for buying just the daily necessities –
    Bread, flour, vinegar, oil – or more important things?
    Money can't buy you immortality, not if
    You gathered in one heap all the gold of Tantalus.
    You'll die and leave all that to others. See what I mean?
    However rich you are, don't pin your faith to wealth;
    And what's more, don't look down on us because we're
      poor.
    Prove to the world, each day, that you deserve your
      luck.

302. A bachelor speaks:
    What chatterers we are, we wretched suffering men,
    All of us so blown up about ourselves! Why, men
    Don't know the nature of their own kind. Now, there's
      a man –
    You look at him in the street, and call him fortunate;
    But once he opens his front door – poor wretch! His
      wife
    Rules the whole roost, gives orders, quarrels day and
      night.
    He suffers a thousand agonies; I suffer none!

From *Drunkenness*

319. Like offering, like fortune, that's the truth of it.
    Suppose I bring to the gods a wretched sheep that cost
    A bare ten drachmas, and then spend nearly a talent on
    Flute-girls, guitar-girls, scented oil, expensive wine
    From Mende or Thasos, eels, and honey, and cheese;
      so that

I can claim in honesty to receive ten drachmas'
    worth
Of blessing, if the sacrifice proves acceptable,
And if it doesn't, on top of all there's a fine to pay–
Doesn't sacrificing let me in for a double loss?
If I were a god I'd forbid them ever to lay the rump
On the altar unless they dedicated the eel as well –
As a fee for the death of their rich uncle Callimedon.

From *The Necklace*

402. From today on my heiress-wife will sleep at ease,
    Whichever side she lies on. A great deed's been done,
    A notable deed. She's bundled out of the house – the
        way
    She wanted to – that woman who got under her skin,
    So that everyone may gaze on the face of Crobyle,
    And she be known as my wife, mistress of the house.
    As for that face which she's the proud possessor of –
    You know the saying about 'a donkey among apes'? –
    Well, there you are. What I could say about that night
    When this disaster started! – but I won't. Oh, gods!
    To think I married Crobyle – ten thousand pounds
    For dowry, and a nose just eighteen inches long.
    Am I to let her snort me off like that? By Zeus,
    Lord of Olympus, and by Athene, I will not.
    A nice, obedient little girl – and Crobyle
    Must whip her off like that before you could say knife!

From *The Soldiers*

447.   When you're in any difficulty,
    Go off alone and think about it. Good ideas

Don't come with shouting; but they show up clear
    enough
When a man sits down and reasons things out by him-
    self.

From *Trophonius*

462. This dinner is for entertaining a visitor.
    What visitor? Where's he from? That makes a difference
    To a Cook, you know. Now, take these fancy visitors
    From the islands, reared on fresh-caught fish from far
        and near –
    They don't find sea-food all that wonderful; to them
    It's just a side-dish. Seasoned stuffing, savoury sauce –
    That's what those gentry go for. Now, an Arcadian –
    He's different; doesn't live by the sea; what fetches
        him
    Is limpets. Then there's your Ionian: rich and coarse.
    Thick soup I give him; Lydian hot-pot; tasty stews
    Flavoured with Aphrodisiac herbs.

From *The Changeling*, or *The Rustic*

481.   I'll tell you, Parmenon,
    Who seems to me to have the happiest life: the man
    Who takes a steady look at the majestic sights
    Our world offers – the common sun, stars, water, clouds,
    Fire; and having seen them, and lived free from pain, at
        once
    Goes back to where he came from. These same sights
        will be,
    If you live to a hundred, always there, always the same;
    And equally if you die young; but you will never

See more majestic sights than these. Think of this time
I speak of, as a people's festival, or as
A visit to some city, where you stand and watch
The crowds, the streets, the thieves, the gamblers, and
   the way
People amuse themselves. If you go back early
To your lodging, you'll have money in your pocket, and
No enemies. The man who stays too long grows tired,
Loses what he once had, gets old, wretched, and poor,
Wanders about, makes enemies, or falls a prey
To plotters; till at last an ignominious death
Sends him off home.

482. Stop talking about 'mind'; the mind of man can do
    Nothing. It is Chance (has Chance a 'mind' or a 'holy
      spirit'?)
    – Whatever you call it, Chance steers, governs, and
      preserves
    Everything. Human forethought is all smoke, all bilge.
    It's true – you take my word; you'll never say I'm
      wrong.
    Each single thought, each word, each act of ours is just
    Chance. All you and I can do is sign on the dotted line.

483. Chance steers the world. You talk of 'brains', 'wisdom':
      you're wrong.
    'Chance', you should say – unless you love meaningless
      words.

From *The Ghost*

A summary[1] of the plot of this play has survived, and the substance
of it is as follows:

1. This summary is quoted from F. C. Allinson's edition of Menander in
the Loeb Library, page 448.

A young man has a stepmother who, before she married his father, has had by a neighbour a daughter. The maiden, whom she wishes to have continually with her, is brought up secretly in the adjoining house, and the party wall between the neighbour's and her husband's house is pierced by a passage with its entrance made to resemble a shrine which she covers with garlands and boughs. Under the pretext of ritual performances she is able to enjoy regular visits from her daughter. The young woman, however, is seen by the stepson, who at first is terrified, as he takes the maiden for a ghost. Further encounters change terror into love, and a happy marriage is arranged with the consent of all parties concerned.

In the first of these fragments a 'household divinity', probably the god worshipped at the make-believe shrine, is explaining the situation to the audience.

Now, she is no ghost, but a real girl of flesh and blood,
And daughter to this married woman, who long ago
Had this child by a neighbour, and disposed of her,
Before she came here, to a nurse to keep and rear.
The girl now lives with this nurse in the house next door.
Whenever the husband is at home, the girl is kept
Indoors and closely guarded; but at other times,
When he's away at sea and there's less need for care,
She leaves the house she lives in usually, and appears
Here. Now I'm sure you all want to know exactly how
This apparition comes. Her mother has made a hole
Right through the wall, so both of them can keep an eye
On everything; this doorway is completely hidden
With wreaths and branches, so that no one coming in
Would see it; there's an altar to the goddess too.

The young man in the story, the stepson Pheidias, has to be told a few home-truths by a family slave before he can qualify to win the girl.

SLAVE: What price does wheat fetch in the market nowadays?

PHEIDIAS: Why, what's that got to do with you?

SLAVE: Nothing. I just
Wanted to use the subject to point out a truth.
If wheat is dear, just worry a bit on *my* account –
I'm poor. Remember, Pheidias, not only you
Are human, but an unhappy man is human too.
Don't crave for things beyond your reach. You say you have
Insomnia. Why? Examine the sort of man you are,
And you'll learn why. You take a stroll to the market-place;
Soon you come back; and if your legs are tired you take
A comfortable bath; after your bath you bolt a meal
Ad lib. Your whole life's one long doze. To sum it up:
There's nothing wrong with you; your only illness is
The luxurious way you've spent your life. – A coarse expression,
Master, occurs to me – forgive me – as they say,
You're so packed round with blessings, you don't know where to shit;
And that's the truth.

PHEIDIAS: I hope you die before next year!

SLAVE: I swear it's the plain truth I've told you. Your disease
Is this and nothing else.

PHEIDIAS: But, damn it all, I'm ill!
I'm really ill!

SLAVE: Your folly is just feebleness
And self-indulgence.

PHEIDIAS: Say it is, then: what do you think
I ought to do? You seem to have this all worked out.

SLAVE: You want my advice? Then you shall have it, Pheidias.
If you had any real complaint you'd have to find
A real cure for it; but you haven't – it's a sham.

Well, then, find a sham remedy for it. Just pretend
That something's doing you good. Get all the women
  slaves
Round in a ring, and let them massage you all over
And fumigate you. Get some water from three springs,
Put in some salt and peas, and sprinkle it over you . . .

531. Young master, if when your mother brought you into
the world
You were born the only one on earth to do as you liked
All through your life, and still be always fortunate –
If some god made an arrangement with you on these
terms,
You're rightly indignant; he's deceived you; it's
outrageous.
But if you breathe this common air of heaven – to use
A phrase that smacks of Tragedy – on the self-same
terms
As all of us, then you must bear this trouble with
A better courage. Reason with yourself. The long
And short of the whole matter is, you are a man;
And there's no creature living that can suffer change –
Up to the top or down to the depth – more rapidly
Than a man. And very rightly; man himself is weak,
But handles mighty matters; when he falls, he brings
Much that is excellent down with him to the dust.
Now you, young master – what were those good things
you've lost?
Nothing extraordinary; and the troubles you have now
Are merely average; bear them, then, and keep your
balance.

532. The right way to go marrying, by Saviour Zeus,
Is the same way you go shopping. You shouldn't
haggle over
Irrelevant details – who was the girl's grandfather,
Or grandmother – while giving never a thought or look

To the character of the bride herself, the woman you
    mean
To live with; and what's the use of hurrying off to the
    Bank
With her dowry-money, to get the Banker to test the
    coin –
Which won't stay in the house five months – if you
    don't apply
A single test to the woman who's going to settle down
In your house for the rest of your life, but take
    haphazard
An inconsiderate, quarrelsome, difficult wife, who even
May be a talker.
                I shall take my own daughter round
The whole city: 'You who want to marry this girl,' I'll
    say,
'Just chat with her; find out beforehand the true
    measure
Of the pest that you're acquiring. A woman *is* a pest –
That can't be helped; the luckiest man's the one who
    gets
The least unbearable pest.'

533. A daughter speaks:
Family? I'm fed up with this talk of 'family'.
Mother, don't – if you love me – every time I mention
A man, start talking about his family. People who
Haven't a single good quality to call their own –
They are the ones who talk like that of family,
Or titles, or decorations; reel off grandfathers
One after the other, and that's all they've got. Can you
Tell me of a man who hasn't got grandfathers? or how
A man could be born without them? People who, for
    one
Reason or another – living abroad, or losing friends –

Can't name their grandfathers – are they any worse born
  than those
Who can? Mother, if a man has a noble character
Which prompts him to a good life, then he's of noble
  birth,
Even if he's a black African. And you 'don't like
Scythians'? To hell! Wasn't Anacharsis[1] a Scythian?

534. Animals enjoy a life that's full of blessings – and
They've much more sense than men have. Take this
  donkey here:
A donkey's an unfortunate beast, we all agree;
None of his troubles come to him by his own fault,
He has them all by Nature's gift. But we, apart
From troubles which are inevitable, must needs
  invent
Others ourselves. Schemes, reputations, rivalries,
Laws – all these curses men have added to Nature's ills.

535. So, now you see how just it is that pictures show
Prometheus always nailed up on a rock; and he has
A torch-race – that's his only honour; nothing else.
Why? He created, what all gods must surely loathe:
Women. You honoured gods, what a hateful race they
  are!
Is there any man here who's going to marry? I said
  'marry'.
From then on, evil concupiscence will be his life's
Secret story: an adulterer wallowing in his bed;
The poison-trade; and that worst of all sicknesses,
Which a woman lives with all her life long – jealousy.

1. A Scythian of royal rank, who early in the sixth century B.C. visited Athens and became a friend of Solon the Athenian law-giver, and was widely admired for his wisdom.

536. A young man addresses the audience:
   By Athene, gentlemen, I can't find a metaphor
   To illustrate what has happened – what's demolishing me
   All in a moment. I turn things over in my mind.
   A tornado, now: the time it takes to wind itself up,
   Get nearer, hit you, then tear off – why, it takes an age.
   Or a gale at sea; but there, you've breathing-space to
      shout
   'Zeus save us!' or 'Hang on to those ropes!' or to wait
   For the second monster wave, and then the third, or try
   To get hold of a bit of wreckage. But with me – oh, no!
   One touch, one single kiss – I'd had it, I was sunk.

537. Epicharmus[1] tells us that the gods are: water, wind,
   Earth, fire, the sun, the stars. But I've got an idea
   The useful gods for you and me are silver and gold.
   Put up a shrine at home for those two; pray to them.
   What do you long for? You shall have it all: estates,
   Houses and servants; silverware; friends; jurymen;
   Witnesses. Pay – that's all: you'll have the gods them-
      selves
   Your obedient servants.

540. Perhaps, young man, it's never struck you that every-
      thing
   Goes rotten by a corruption that's peculiar to it;
   Each thing's corruption originates within itself.
   For instance, look at rust – the way it eats up iron;
   Or moths eat woollen cloaks, or woodworms devour
      wood.
   Just so, the most evil of all evil things, envy,
   Causes consumption of the soul; it always has,
   And always will; envy, the impious tendency
   Of a wicked heart.

   1. A Pythagorean philosopher, and writer of comedies, 540–450 B.C.

541. This passion of love – have you ever wondered where it
     finds
     Its origin? What actual thing enslaves a man?
     A face? Nonsense, if that were so, all men would fall
     For the same girl. If merely looking makes the choice,
     All men have equal eyes. Or, is what draws men on
     As lovers, the pleasure a woman gives in intercourse?
     If so, then why does one man leave her bed heart-whole
     And go off laughing at her, while another's caught for
     life?
     This sickness of man's heart lies in the crux of time;
     And when you're wounded, the blow's dealt inside
     yourself.

542. If each of us would willingly take our part, and join
     In stout resistance, call each unjust act a blow
     Aimed at ourselves no less than at our neighbour, if
     We worked and fought in common, we wouldn't every
     time
     See crime succeed; we'd keep a watch on wicked men,
     Get them their just deserts; and soon they'd be reduced
     To a mere handful, easily kept under control.

545. 'Demonstration'[1] is my name; Truth and Outspoken-
     ness
     Are friends of mine, and Freedom is my first cousin.
     The only mortals I'm an enemy to are those
     Who fear my tongue. I know everything; and what I
     know
     About your secrets, I unfold in clear detail.
     To me, a fig's a fig; I call a spade a spade.

1. The Greek word translated 'demonstration' is one used in English as a
term in Logic – 'elenchus'. It means 'proof' provided by the demonstration
or uncovering of facts which constitute evidence.

549. Being mortal, never pray for an untroubled life;
     But ask the gods to give you an enduring heart.
     For if you want to live your whole life free from pain
     You must become either a god or else a corpse.
     Consider other men's troubles; that will comfort yours.

551. A man whose heart is sound finds Fortune his ally.
     Every man is attended from the hour of birth
     By a spirit to guide him through the mysteries of life –
     A good spirit. We should not believe that there exists
     Any evil spirit inflicting harm on human lives
     Or evil in its own nature; but that every god
     Is himself good. People of evil character
     Who have made a tangle of their own lives, or ruined
        those
     Of others by their folly – these are the people who
     Say it's God's doing, and blame God for their own
        fault.

552. Old age, our human body's enemy, you thief
     Of beauty's moulded treasures, who re-draw the clean
     Contour of manly limbs to make it ugliness,
     And change swiftness of foot to endless faltering!

554. We all from time to time – isn't this true, father? –
     Turn from our drinking, from our pleasures of every
        day,
     And seek someone to share the heart's core of our life.
     And every man is sure he has found a marvellous
     Treasure, if he gains even the semblance of a friend.

560. At family prayers there's always one thing I leave out:
     I never pray for harmony in domestic life.
     There are times in every household when a spontaneous
     Feud between servants can be a most useful thing.

572. When you engage in an honest undertaking, hold
    Good hope as a shield before you, and be sure that God
    Himself lends strength to boldness in a righteous cause.

594. It's clear Fortune can have no bodily existence; but
    Those who can't bear the natural course of life's events
    Call by the name of Fortune their own character.

595. It's always so: your saved man is a thankless thing.
    Offer help – and that moment all the gratitude
    Which he, when helpless, swore he'd feel for ever, dies.

620. It seems to me sheer folly, my Philumene,
    To have all the perception that one ought to have
    And then not guard against what one ought to guard
      against.

627. If you observe, it's not the number of cups that makes
    A man drunk, but the character of the man who drinks.

632. When a man bears a secret guilt, however bold
    He may be, conscience makes him very cowardly.

638. I'm rather young; but when I speak, don't think of
      that;
    Just notice if I'm speaking like a man of sense.

639. It's not white hair that makes a man intelligent;
    Some people have a mind that's naturally mature.

659. Don't cause your father any distress; the man who loves
    You most is angered too by the most trivial things.

690. I hate the poor man who brings presents to the rich.
    It just makes clear to everyone how starved he is.

698. Slave, if you're slave to one who was born a slave, look
     out:
    The freed ox never remembers what the yoke was like.

702. To teach a woman to write is not a good idea;
    You might as well feed poison to a deadly snake.

704. Don't offer your wife even the very best advice.
    She'll take her own, and for her pleasure do her worst.

745.   . . . But a woman who pays you compliments
    Is really something to be afraid of.

760. There's one slave of the whole household, and that's the
    master of it.

767. I hate a bad man when he speaks what's honourable.

PENGUINEWS *AND*
PENGUINS IN PRINT

Every month we issue an illustrated magazine,
Penguinews. It's a lively guide to all the latest
Penguins, Pelicans and Puffins, and always contains an article on a major Penguin author, plus
other features of contemporary interest.

Penguinews is supplemented by *Penguins in
Print*, a complete list of all the available Penguin
titles – there are now over four thousand!

The cost is no more than the postage; so
why not write for a free copy of this month's
Penguinews? And if you'd like both publications
sent for a year, just send us a cheque or a postal
order for 30p (if you live in the United Kingdom)
or 60p (if you live elsewhere), and we'll put you
on our mailing list.

Dept EP, Penguin Books Ltd,
Harmondsworth, Middlesex

Note: *Penguinews* and *Penguins in Print*
are not available in the U.S.A. or Canada.

a Pelican Original

GREEK LITERATURE IN TRANSLATION

EDITED BY MICHAEL GRANT

Greek literature provides powerful evidence in support of Sophocles' statement that language is what raises mankind above the animals. Not only did Greek provide the earliest literature in the western world, but it maintained a flow of masterpieces for a thousand years, well into Roman imperial times; and today (because of the Greek writer's faculty for reaching to the heart of his subject) this literature still possesses significance.

In this companion volume to his *Roman Readings* Michael Grant displays, as far as possible, the whole range of Greek poetry and prose, from Homer and Hesiod to the Hellenistic poets and the works of Ptolemy, Galen and Plotinus. His selection vividly demonstrates the extraordinary extent of Greek achievement in every literary field – in epics, lyrics and drama, in history, biography and oratory, in philosophy, criticism and satire, and in works of fundamental scientific thought.

Moreover Michael Grant's choice of English versions serves to show how the mounting wave of modern translations now challenges the splendid output of the Elizabethans.